TIME
We the People

Authentic Readings for Students of English

Selected by

Linda Schinke-Llano

National Textbook Company
a division of *NTC Publishing Group* • Lincolnwood, Illinois USA

Acknowledgments

With appreciation to Rebecca Rauff and Michael Ross of National Textbook Company, with whom it is always a pleasure to work, this book is a present for my daughter Melissa: May it serve as an album of your world.

Linda Schinke-Llano holds a Ph.D. in Linguistics and an M.A. in TESOL. Specializing in second-language acquisition, English as a second or foreign language, and bilingual education, she has taught at Northwestern University, the University of Puerto Rico, and the University of Seville.

Articles from TIME Magazine are republished by permission of Time Inc., the copyright proprietor.

Contents

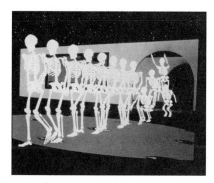

HEALTH & FITNESS 101

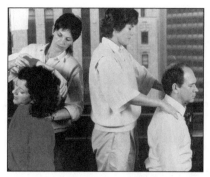

SPORTS & ENTERTAINMENT 123

FADS & FASHIONS 145

Introduction

TIME magazine, the world's leading English-language newsweekly, is read by millions of people and readily recognized by millions more. With its up-to-date, informative articles and accompanying photographs, charts and illustrations, each issue presents topics of current concern to Americans and to anyone interested in life in the United States.

Just as *TIME* offers a unique view of the United States and its people, *TIME: We the People* presents a special reading opportunity for students of English. Forty-six recently published articles from *TIME* have been selected to represent a wide range of topics and issues, from the fanciful to the serious and from the culture-specific to the universal. Divided into seven sections similar to those used in *TIME* (*Lifestyles, Education, Environment, Science & Technology, Health & Fitness, Sports & Entertainment*, and *Fads & Fashions*), the text presents a broad view of contemporary life in the United States—its problems and pitfalls, as well as its challenges and rewards.

Although the articles are grouped into subject categories, they are not sequenced by difficulty level and may be read in any order. Each reading is preceded by *Background Notes* (consisting of Preview, Culture, and Vocabulary) intended to prepare the reader for the article. The Preview section presents a brief summary of the article. The Culture section explains culture-specific references that may be problematic to nonnative readers, just as the Vocabulary section defines words that may be difficult for many readers. In both the Culture and Vocabulary sections, phonetic transcriptions are provided for those items whose pronunciation is particularly unusual or difficult. (See Guide on page vi.) In addition, Culture and Vocabulary entries that are regarded as slang (unconventional language) or colloquialisms (informal language) are marked as such.

Following the reading are *Questions and Activities* that consist of Comprehension Questions, Discussion Questions, Group Activities, and Individual Work. The Comprehension Questions aid the reader's understanding of the article. Both the Discussion Questions and the Group Activities encourage critical thinking about the issues presented. Finally, the Individual Work enables the reader to express opinions in both written and spoken English. Throughout the text, there is ample opportunity for cross-cultural comparisons, as well as for viewing topics in a global perspective.

With its combination of authentic contemporary articles and specially designed pre- and post-reading activities, *TIME: We the People* can serve as a bridge to the independent reading of other authentic writings. More specifically, the text has been developed with four goals for its readers:

1. to increase comprehension of written English through the use of authentic materials widely read by native speakers;
2. to improve oral skills in English through meaningful communicative activities, both within the classroom and outside of it;
3. to practice written skills in English through focused assignments; and
4. to develop a knowledge of the United States and its people through contemporary writings.

It is hoped that all readers will not only achieve these goals, but also enjoy the text in the process.

Linda Schinke-Llano

Guide to Pronunciation

Vowels & Diphthongs:

[i]	heed, bead, see
[ɪ]	hid, lid, tin
[e]	shade, played, trade
[ɛ]	head, sled, men
[æ]	had, glad, sad
[u]	shoot, glue, shoe
[ʊ]	put, foot, would
[o]	home, glow, so
[ɔ]	caught, raw, yawn
[ɑ]	odd, clock, wad
[ə]	hut, about, tuna, parade
[ɚ]	hurt, shirt, butter
[ɑɪ]	height, mine, sigh
[ɑʊ]	house, brown, shout
[ɔɪ]	coin, joy, hoist

Consonants

[p]	pipe, top, pie
[b]	boat, job, bone
[t]	town, coat, right
[d]	road, deer, down
	water, charity, waiter
[k]	duck, king, cone
[g]	girl, frog, ghost
[f]	friend, fix, phantom
[v]	have, vent, save
[θ]	with, thing, throw
[ð]	this, then, soothe
[s]	miss, soft, mouse
[z]	zoom, buzz, phase
[ʃ]	wish, shave, ship
[ʒ]	measure, azure, pleasure
[h]	house, who, help
[tʃ]	chew, catch, chart
[ʤ]	edge, job, Gene
[m]	room, mother, some
[n]	sun, nest, nurse
[ŋ]	sing, rang, swing
[w]	win, swing, twist
[j]	yellow, you, yes
[l]	will, lip, slick
[r]	red, wrist, tree
[']	precedes syllables with primary stress.
[ˌ]	precedes syllables with secondary stress.
( )	encloses sounds that are sometimes not pronounced.

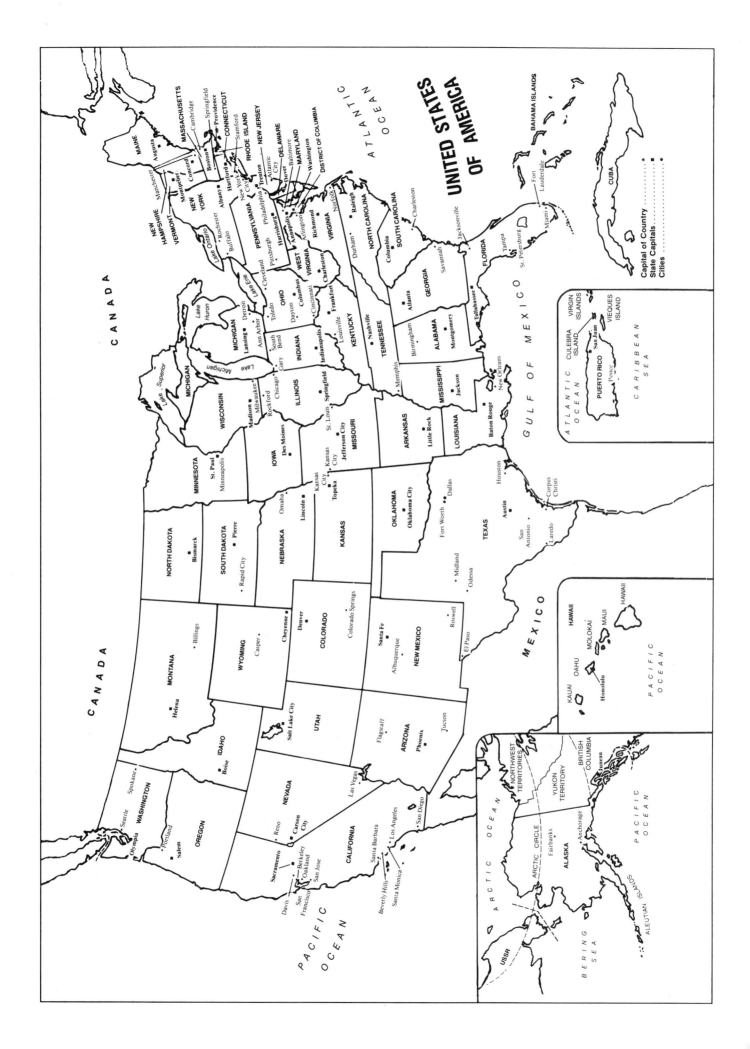

UNITED STATES
OF AMERICA

Capital of Country . . . . ★
State Capitals . . . . ■
Cities . . . . •

Lifestyles

BACKGROUND NOTES

for **Show Me the Way to Go Home**

Preview

*The 1970s trend for young adults to live independently from their parents is changing.
For a variety of reasons, many are returning home or are not leaving home at all.
Families are reacting in different ways to this societal change.*

Culture

condominium [ˌkɑndəˈmɪniəm]: an apartment that is owned, rather than rented. The owner pays a monthly fee to the condominium association for repairs and maintenance of the building and grounds. A condominium is often referred to as a **condo.**

equipment technician: a person who repairs equipment. The phrase is a complimentary way of saying "repair person."

ranch house: a one-story house. This architectural style is found throughout the United States.

U.S. Census Bureau: a division of the federal government that conducts a national census every 10 years. The Census Bureau also studies characteristics of the population.

welcome mat: a small rug placed in front of the door of a house or apartment. Often such a rug will have the word "welcome" printed on it.

Vocabulary

accommodation: adaptation; adjustment; changing one's behavior to suit another

amenity [əˈmɛnəˌdi]: a feature or an item that provides comfort and convenience. Fireplaces, garages, dishwashers, additional bathrooms, and air conditioning are often regarded as amenities in a home.

bogged down [ˌbɔg(d)ˈdaʊn]: stuck; slowed down; overcome; overwhelmed

compromise [ˈkɑmprəˌmaɪz]: an agreement in which all the participants concede something

detrimental: harmful; having negative results

exorbitant [ɛgˈzorbətənt]: excessively high or large

hassle [hæsəl]: a disagreement; an argument

inadequacy [ˌɪnˈædəkwəˌsi]: a state of feeling inadequate or insufficient

migraine [ˈmɑɪˌgren]: a severe headache often accompanied by nausea and vomiting

nest: one's original home; the place where one was born and raised. **Nest** usually refers to the place where birds lay their eggs and raise their young.

offspring: one's children

skyrocketing: rising or increasing rapidly

sociologist [ˌsosiˈɑlədʒəst]: a specialist in sociology. A sociologist studies society, its social institutions, and the relationships among its members.

spontaneously [ˌspɑnˈteniəsli]: naturally; in a manner that is not contrived or forced

stress: physical or emotional tension. Stress is often caused by the inability to cope with certain factors in the environment.

take a crack at: to try; to attempt

touched [tətʃt]: emotionally affected

Show Me the Way to Go Home

Unexpected numbers of young adults are living with their parents

In Denver, live-in Daughter Esther Rodriguez prepares dinner with her parents

"The good life is not spontaneously generated out there."

First Maggie, then 20, asked Stepmom and Dad if she could store a few boxes with them in Washington while she looked for another place to live. Then Maggie said she would like to move in to be with her boxes until her boyfriend Joe bought a condominium. Next Maggie asked whether Joe could move in "temporarily" until the condo deal was closed. When Lucy and Pablo Sanchez returned home from vacation last Christmas, they found their small living room crammed with his boxes and a second welcome mat next to their own on the front porch. Lucy Sanchez immediately did what any loving but put-upon parent would do: "I had a migraine," she says.

Such tales are becoming abundantly familiar as American parents are forced to make room for their adult children. "There is a naive notion that children grow up and leave home when they're 18, and the truth is far from that," says Sociologist Larry Bumpass of the University of Wisconsin in Madison. Today, according to the U.S. Census Bureau, 59% of men and 47% of women between 18 and 24 depend on their parents for housing, some living in college dorms but most at home. In 1970 the figures were 54% and 41%. Also, 14% of men and 8% of women ages 25 to 34 are dependent on their parents for housing, in contrast to 9.5% and 6.6% in 1970. "This is part of a major shift in the middle class," declares Sociologist Allan Schnaiberg of Northwestern University. He should know: Schnaiberg's stepson, 19, moved back in after an absence of eight months.

Analysts cite a variety of reasons for this return to the nest. The marriage age is rising, a condition that makes home and its amenities particularly attractive to young people, say experts. A high divorce rate and a declining remarriage rate are sending economically pressed and emotionally battered survivors back to parental shelters. For some, the expense of an away-from-home college education has become so exorbitant that many students now attend local schools. Even after graduation, young people find their wings clipped by skyrocketing housing costs. Notes Sociologist Carlfred Broderick of the University of Southern California in Los Angeles, who has a son, 31, and a daughter, 27, in residence: "They are finding that the good life is not spontaneously generated out there."

Sallie Knighton, 26, moved back to her parents' suburban Atlanta home to save enough money to buy a car. Her job as a teacher provided only enough money to cover car payments and an additional loan she had taken out. Once the loan was paid off, she decided to take a crack at a modeling career. Living at home, says Knighton, continues to give her security and moral support. "If I had lived away," she says, "I would be miserable still teaching." Her mother concurs, "It's ridiculous for the kids to pay all that money for rent. It makes sense for kids to stay at home." Bradley Kulat, 25, makes about $20,000 a year as an equipment technician in a hospital. That is enough to support a modest household, but he chooses to live at his parents' split-level ranch house outside Chicago, as does his sister Pamela, 20, who commutes to a nearby college. He admits to expensive tastes. He recently bought an $8,000 car and owns an $800 stereo system, a $300 ten-speed bike and an elegant wardrobe. Says his mother Evelyn: "It keeps you thinking younger, trying to keep up with them."

Sharing the family home requires adjustments for all. There are the hassles over bathrooms, telephones and privacy. Some families, however, manage the delicate balancing act. At 34, Esther Rodriguez dreaded returning to her parents' Denver home after three years of law school forced her $20,000 into debt. "I thought it was going to be a restriction on my independence," she recalls. Instead, she was touched when her father installed a desk and phone in the basement so she would have a private study. The Sanchez family too has made a success of the arrangement. Says Lucy Sanchez: "Family is family, and we believe and act on that." But for others, the setup proves too difficult. Michelle Del Turco, 24, of Englewood, Colo., a Denver suburb, has been home three times—and left three times. "What I considered a social drink, my dad considered an alcohol problem," she explains. "He never liked anyone I dated, so I either had to sneak around or meet them at friends' houses."

Just how long should adult children live with their parents before moving on? Lucille Carlini of Brooklyn returned home with her two daughters after a divorce. That was almost twelve years ago. She is now 37 and her daughters 18 and 16. They still live with Carlini's mother Edie, who has welcomed having three generations in the same house. Still, most psychologists feel lengthy homecomings are a mistake. Offspring, struggling to establish separate identities, can wind up with "a sense of inadequacy, defeat and failure," says Kristine Kratz, a counselor with the Personal Development Institute in Los Angeles. And aging parents, who should be enjoying some financial and personal freedom, find themselves bogged down with responsibilities. Says Debra Umberson, a researcher at the University of Michigan: "Living with children of any age involves compromise and obligation, factors that can be detrimental to some aspects of well-being. All children, even adult children, require accommodation and create stress."

Brief visits, however, can work beneficially. Five years ago Ellen Rancilio returned to the Detroit area to live with her father after her marriage broke up. She stayed only seven months, but "it made us much closer," she says. Indeed, the experience was so positive that she would not hesitate to put out the welcome mat when her own three sons are grown. Declares she: "If they needed help like I did, yes."

—By Anastasia Toufexis.
Reported by Barbara Cornell/Washington, with other bureaus

3

QUESTIONS AND ACTIVITIES

Comprehension Questions

1. What are some of the situations that have caused the young adults in the article to return to their parents' homes?

2. What have been the results—both positive and negative—of these changes in lifestyle?

3. Why do some psychologists believe that it is unhealthy for several generations of a family to live together for a long period of time?

Discussion Questions

1. In your home culture, do the majority of young single adults live with their parents or independently? If an individual does not conform to the behavior of the majority, are there problems?

2. In your home culture, do the majority of young married adults live with their parents or on their own? If with their parents, do they generally live with the wife's parents or the husband's parents? If on their own, under what circumstances is the majority behavior not followed?

3. In your opinion, what special adjustments, if any, are necessary when different generations of a family live together?

4. Given your experiences in your home culture, do you agree with the psychologists who say that it is difficult for a young adult to achieve a separate identity if he or she lives with parents?

Group Activities

1. In groups of three or four, discuss the advantages of several generations of a family living together.

2. Once again in groups or three or four, discuss the disadvantages of several generations of a family living together.

Individual Work

1. Look in the "apartments for rent" section of your local newspaper. Find a listing for an apartment appropriate for your needs. Write a monthly budget that includes rent, groceries, utilities, clothing, entertainment expenses, etc. What salary do you think would be necessary to finance this budget?

2. If you are currently living with your parents, interview a young adult who is living independently. (Or, if you are currently living independently, interview someone who is living with his or her parents.) Ask that person to identify the advantages and disadvantages of the living arrangement.

Article Two

BACKGROUND NOTES

for **Spiffing Up the Urban Heritage**

Preview

City planners in many locations were once anxious to replace old buildings with parking lots and high-rise buildings. Today many city officials and individuals are interested in preserving older architecture.

Culture

Aprica: a brand of stroller used for babies and young children. Apricas are attractive, durable, and relatively expensive.

art deco [ˌɑrt ˈdɛkˌo]: a style of architecture popular in the 1920s. Art deco buildings and home furnishings are enjoying a revival.

Babbitty [ˈbæbəˌdi]: characteristic of Babbitt, the main character in the novel *Babbitt* by Sinclair Lewis. Babbitt longed for change, but he was too self-conscious to pursue it.

Gemütlichkeit: good nature; kindliness; pleasantness. This German term is frequently used to describe the atmosphere in a restaurant or neighborhood.

gentrification [ˌʤɛntrəfəˈkeʃən]: the moving of middle-class homeowners into poor urban neighborhoods. These new homeowners ''gentrify'' the area by restoring older homes to their former state.

landmark: a building or other object that highlights or helps identify a locality. Owners of buildings that are given landmark status are usually eligible for financial assistance to help restore them.

National Register of Historic Places: a federal agency with the power to designate buildings and neighborhoods as landmarks. A house on the National Register cannot be altered without permission.

preservationist: a person who is interested in preserving the nation's heritage. Preservationists often save important buildings from demolition.

Ralph Laurenized [ˌrælf ˈlorənˌɑɪzd]: characteristic of products designed and produced by Ralph Lauren. Clothing and accessories designed by Ralph Lauren are classic in style and are meant to appeal to wealthy tastes.

urban renewal [ˈɚbən ˌriˈnuəl]: the movement to bring cities back to life by tearing down old structures and constructing parking lots and high-rise buildings. Urban renewal projects were prevalent in the 1950s and 1960s.

Whitmanesque [ˌwɪtmənˈɛsk]: characteristic of the writings of Walt Whitman, a 19th century poet and essayist. One of Whitman's favorite themes was the equality of all people.

Vocabulary

aesthetic [əs'θɛdək]: relating to beauty; appreciative of beauty

binge [bɪndʒ]: a spree; excessive behavior

blithely ['blɑɪð,li]: casually; lightheartedly; in a carefree manner

cliché [,kli'ʃe]: a phrase, idea, or situation that has become overfamiliar. Many trends eventually become clichés.

comatose ['komə,tos]: unconscious; characteristic of a coma; without movement or activity

confection: a concoction; a compound; something that has been made of other things

demographic: relating to demography, the study of a population, its size and distribution

eclectic [,ɛ'klɛktɪk]: containing the best of various styles; composed of parts of various approaches. Urban neighborhoods are often quite eclectic in architecture.

façade [fə'sɑd]: the front of a building. Façades often contain special architectural details.

fluke [fluk]: a chance happening; an occurrence that is not planned

freeway: a toll-free highway. Entire neighborhoods were often destroyed in order to build freeways.

funk: earthiness; rawness; unusualness in appearance (slang)

gargantuan [,gɑr'gæntʃuən]: extremely big; huge. Gargantua, a fictional character invented by the French writer Rabelais, was a giant.

giddy ['gɪdi]: silly; frivolous; dizzying

glib: superficial; characterized by ease in speaking or writing

grubby: dirty; run-down (colloquial)

momentum: impetus; forward motion; a driving force

nostalgia [,nɑ'stældʒə]: a sentimental affection for the past; a longing for the past and things associated with it

pandemic [,pæn'dɛmək]: affecting a large percentage of the population

penchant ['pɛntʃənt]: a tendency; a strong attraction to something

phenomenon [fə'nɑmə,nɑn]: an observable fact or event; an unusual occurrence

pizazz [pə'zæz]: attractiveness; liveliness

prescience ['pri,ʃiən(t)s]: a knowledge of future events

proliferation [prə,lɪfɚ'eʃən]: rapid and widespread development

quirky [kwɚki]: idiosyncratic; unusual; having peculiar traits

raffish ['ræfəʃ]: unconventional; suggestive of crudeness or vulgarity

renovation [,rɛnə'veʃən]: restoration to a former state

serendipity [,sɛrən'dɪpədi]: the gift of finding valuable and enjoyable things without looking for them

slum: a section of a city characterized by deteriorating buildings. Slums are usually overcrowded and inhabited by people with low incomes.

spiff up: to improve the appearance of (something); to make (something) look good

ticky-tack: anything characterized by poor taste. Not all old buildings are architecturally important; many are just ticky-tack.

trendiness: the state of being fashionable; the state of being in vogue

turret ['tɚət]: a small tower. Mansions built in the 1900s often had turrets.

Boston's revitalized Union Park

Spiffing Up The Urban Heritage

After years of neglect, Americans lavish love and sweat on old downtowns

Back when city planning was still a matter of deciding which neighborhood to carve up with the new freeway and how many grim apartment towers to insert in a newly leveled megalot, the Los Angeles Community Redevelopment Agency decided to move its offices. The agency was stuck in an unfashionable downtown building on grubby, declining Spring Street, so in 1955 the city's official redevelopers fled to new quarters.

Such prescience. Such vision.

During the 1980s Spring Street, like so many other neglected, down-and-dirty streets around the country, is shuddering back to life, becoming a gleaming circa-1920s boulevard. Many of its handsomely scaled old masonry buildings were renovated: derelict art moderne office buildings became cool art moderne apartment buildings, and the art deco stock exchange was reborn as an art deco disco. There were more than two dozen major restorations in all—including what had been the CRA's office building. The CRA, as it happened, had helped foster this revival. So in 1980 back came the urban-planning bureaucrats to their original building, back this time as historic preservationists, back to the very downtown district they had abandoned a generation earlier.

How did Americans manage to forget for so many years that downtowns are invigorating and old cities grand? That the dignity and *Gemütlichkeit* of 18th century buildings and 19th century streets are incomparable? That the physical past is worth preserving? Did a majority of Americans in 1970 actually prefer Century City to San Francisco? Were people fetched by the shiny new discord of Houston suburbs more than by shabby, genteel New Orleans, by the glass and steel of downtown Minneapolis more than by the brick and stone of downtown St. Paul?

If so, then the nation has had a great change of heart. The change has been so complete that it is difficult today to remember how recently people were blithely ripping out and throwing away the warp and woof of America's cities. In only 20 years, marvels James Marston Fitch, an internationally known preservationist, "the whole balance has radically changed in our favor. I'm astonished at what a complete turnabout there has been in the whole climate of public opinion."

The bad old days were just yesterday, after all. It was in 1978 that the Supreme Court upheld New York City's right to designate Grand Central Terminal a landmark, thus saving the beaux arts wonder from having a gargantuan 54-story modernist tower built over its waiting room. And it was a mere 20 years ago, give or take, that St. Louis razed 40 quaint blocks of riverfront warehouses; that Pasadena, Calif., tore up a fine commercial neighborhood to build a standard aluminum shopping mall; that Madison, Wis., let Burger King raze an 1850s stone house for its headquarters; that New York City tore down McKim, Mead and White's glorious Pennsylvania Station.

So the tide has turned. Today it is almost obligatory for a city to have a fine old theater or train station or office building that has been saved, spiffed up and put back to good, if not necessarily its original use—a building that 20 years ago would have been pulled down without a second thought. Buying paperbacks and chocolate-chip cookies in what used to be a warehouse and watching stand-up comedians in what used to be a stable and living in what used to be a factory are now, happily, coast-to-coast clichés, not novelties. As ever, there are trade-offs: such transformations, especially as they become pandemic, can seem overbearingly glib, clean and cute.

Yet Louis Sullivan's 1895 Guaranty Building in Buffalo and the Peabody hotel in Memphis, a grand 1920s confection, have been restored perfectly, and they are not flukes but two redemptions among dozens, among hundreds. Downtowns are being preserved, piece by piece, and have been rediscovered, city by city, as places to live as well as work. "Almost every city, down to the third tier—places like Dayton and Toledo—has done something," says Northwestern University Urbanologist Louis Masotti. "It's not a fad. It's a demographic phenomenon. The 1980s have been the decade of the cities' revival.''

The economic prosperity of the mid-'80s has of course helped stimulate both new construction and renovation, particularly in those cities blessed with high employment and booming industry. And some of the new downtown buildings are impressive. On the other hand, many cities have not revived. Detroit is still comatose, Gary, Ind., is not much healthier, and development in Oakland is lagging.

But the new urbanity has footholds all over the place, and preservationism has achieved extraordinary momentum. Cincinnati's city council made charming West 4th Street a historic district last year. Among the latest local projects: the conversion of a down-at-the-heels Renaissance Revival textile building into offices. The former Tivoli Union brewery in Denver, a pseudo-Bavarian fantasy, is a giddy complex of shops, offices, restaurants and movie theaters. The vast old Bullock's department store in downtown Los Angeles has been turned into the country's largest wholesale jewelry mart, and Houston's art deco Alabama Theater has merely exchanged one muse for another. The place is now a bookstore. Pioneer Square in Seattle, with its raffish characters, is proving that preservation and up-market transformation do not necessarily mean the death of funk.

The new attitude toward cities and old buildings seems altogether uncharacteristic of the U.S.—delightfully un-American, in fact. Americans are supposed to have a deep distrust of cities and a Babbitty, hard-charging faith in the new and improved. Indeed, preservation on today's scale was an unthinkable Luddite fantasy a scant generation ago.

With the proliferation of postwar suburbs, which sucked millions of families out of the cities, downtowns quickly lost their old pizazz. Then the redevelopment binge of the '50s and '60s came disastrously close to indulging the American antiurban instinct to the point of no return. Political pressure to build new housing for the inner-city poor was intense. Urban renewal, a well-intended and wrongheaded federal mission, in those days meant tearing down quirky, densely interwoven neighborhoods of 19th and early 20th century low-rise buildings and putting up expensive, charmless clots of high-rises. Or, even worse, leaving empty tracts. (The resistance of Charleston, S.C., and Savannah to Great Society efforts to clear their slums accounts for those cities' remarkably intact historic districts today.) In the mid-'60s, 1,600 federally supported urban-renewal projects were under way in nearly 800 American cities. Not only in Viet Nam was the U.S. Government proposing to destroy the town in order to save it.

But urban renewal had its rearguard critics, and vital downtowns had their influential advocates. The right laws were passed. Cases were won. In 1965 New York City passed the Landmarks Preservation Law, setting up a commission that could restrict any changes to designated historic buildings; a year later, Congress enacted its version, which established the National Register of Historic Places and provided preservation grants to states.

Meanwhile, a whole generation of middle-class travelers was discovering the civilized pleasures of European cities as well as domestic oases like Washington's cozy Georgetown and Santa Barbara's adobe Pueblo Viejo. In San Francisco, always the belovedly quaint U.S. city, there was the novel Ghirardelli Square, a shopping center created near the Bay from a group of old factory buildings.

At about the same time, Americans were realizing the need to protect the natural environment, and for some of the same quasi-spiritual reasons, they discovered that old buildings had a level of craftsmanship and stylistic integrity seldom achieved in modern buildings and a patina that could not be faked. The upper classes had always prized antiques and reveled in the old. For the first time, the upwardly ambitious American middle class acquired that aristocratic penchant.

The rediscovery, however, is not merely a matter of fashion and status seeking. It is more visceral than that. ''We feel better,'' an architecture critic and preservationist Brendan Gill has written, ''when we find ourselves in the presence of the past, with its evidence of the mingled aspirations and disappointments of our ancestors.'' Walking along an old street among old buildings, the implicit history and sense of continuity are both reassuring and invigorating. The graceful proportions of façades are not arbitrary but the result of craft wisdom worked out over generations of trial and error. The scale of buildings and streets, based on human size and pedestrian stride, makes intuitive sense. Indeed, old sections of cities embody all sorts of folk and classical principles concerning residential density and building size and materials and zoning. In the very arrangements of alleys and building setbacks is a time-tested plan, a kind of urban genetic code.

Is it too Whitmanesque to suggest that it is the hurly-burly pleasures of democracy—pluralism incarnate—that pulled Americans back downtown? Old cities are architecturally eclectic places, where Queen Anne turrets bump up against an International Style library. On a single block, even in a single building, people work as well as live as well as shop. In good cities, infants in Apricas share sidewalks with octogenarians, Salvadoran immigrants with manicured executives. In good cities, eras and generations and races and pursuits are a jumble. Serendipity and surprise are the point.

What has come to be known as gentrification—the migration of (mainly white) middle-class homesteaders into poor (mainly black and Hispanic) urban neighborhoods—is neither the cause nor an effect, exactly, of the historic renovation boom. But the two trends have abetted each other. The original '60s militants of the preservation movement were the shock troops of the upper middle class, and it was a broader swath of the same class who in the '70s made living amid urban antiquity seem both virtuous and stylish. Restored carriage houses and pressed-tin ceilings have seduced more children of the suburbs back to the city than mean, shiny apartment towers.

Trendiness goes only so far. Money talks. The mania for preservation has been propelled for the past decade by federal tax laws. Developers who rehabilitate historic buildings can get back 20% of their renovation costs in the form of income tax credits, as long as they put the buildings to commercial use. Under the program, which began in earnest in 1981, an estimated $11 billion has been spent to renovate some 17,000 historic buildings in 1,800 cities and towns.

Preservation has its indirect costs as well. The owners of protected landmark structures, prohibited from tearing down their buildings, are deprived of the potential profit of building something bigger or more commercially successful. Thus Preservationist Fitch suggests that governments subsidize owners ''who are unfortunate enough to own properties of significance.'' According to Fitch, ''If the state demands that they preserve the buildings, then they should be aided in that activity.''

Preservation can set up a self-destructive cycle. When a historic neighborhood is restored, it becomes desirable and prices go up, and when prices go up sufficiently, developers think dollars per square foot, high-rise, wrecking ball. They wind up selling the view of a historic district from a condominium tower that has supplanted a piece of that history.

Not every old building can be saved. Not every old building should be saved. Except for set pieces like fussy little Colonial Williamsburg or the elegant Upper East Side of Manhattan, cities should not remain stuck in time. Even preservationists, most of them, agree in principle. Says Gene Norman, chairman of New York City's Landmarks Preservation Commission: ''We are not trying to create a museum city.''

Yet the reflexive impulse to preserve everything, even the relatively new and banal, occasionally shows signs of getting out of hand. ''People are just beginning to talk about ''50s classics' now, which is a term that embraces some really appalling ticky-tack,'' says the British-born architectural historian Reyner Banham, who lives in California. ''There is a tendency to overlook the aesthetic quality of a building and just keep it because it is old,'' says Robert Winter, a cultural historian at Occidental College in Los Angeles. ''Too often the reason for declaring something [a historic landmark] is sentimental.'' Sentiment is inadmissible? Isn't the new feeling for preservation and for cities inherently romantic, clear-headedness clouded by a large dose of nostalgia?

The '60s, a generous, hopeful time, produced terrible urban policy and dispiriting

New York City
A Mix of Technology and Art

Modernizing the New York Public Library, the apogee of the city's beaux arts architecture, required the soul of an artist and the mind of a systems engineer. The problem, explains Architect Lewis Davis, who has overseen much of the project, "was how to bring 20th century technology into a 19th century building without being too obvious." The $75.5 million publicly and privately funded restoration, begun in 1981, has produced some artful solutions. In the Periodical Room, Architect Giorgio Cavaglieri has not only spruced up the old marble and wood but has also discreetly added modern lighting to supplement old brass chandeliers. The once gloomy card-catalog room now offers computer terminals for high-speed searches of the literature. Throughout the building, air-conditioning ducts and wiring have been concealed behind existing structures, and two new levels of subterranean stack space will allow the library to nearly double its collection. Among the most striking restored rooms are Astor Hall, the formal entranceway, and the Celeste Bartos Forum, a glorious glass and cast-iron domed chamber, clad with Sienese marble. Now used as a lecture hall, it had been a storage space.

architecture, while in the '80s, a gilded, ungenerous age, the nation is saving buildings and repairing cities. An uncomfortable irony, but preservation is a conservative movement. Thus it carries with it a whiff of complacency and rue.

Alas, another irony: while gentrifiers as they first venture into an old neighborhood may be democratically inspired—The diversity! The grit!—they attract mobs of merely stylish followers who diminish the diversity and sweep away every last speck of grit. The oldline residents and the anchors of their communities—the hardware stores, the cobblers, the taverns—are driven out by suddenly high rents. Gentrification is not fun for everyone.

Hearteningly, the fate of reviving districts is not always black and white. Preservationists are not all chèvre eaters and squash players. Among the thousands of tax-delinquent houses New York City has sold off during the past five years, more than half have been bought by black and Hispanic homesteaders. The Longwood section of the South Bronx has had itself declared a historic district, and the predominantly black and Hispanic residents are restoring scores of neo-Renaissance houses. In Savannah, the National Trust has provided seed money so that 300 apartments in the Victorian historic district can be set aside for low-income residents. In a rough-and-tumble north Toledo neighborhood 165 Victorian buildings recently rehabilitated for $20 million are now occupied by more than a thousand federally subsidized tenants. And in Boston's South End, not far from Union Park, the Villa Victoria neighborhood stands as a monument to several unlikely successes. In the late '60s the row houses of Villa Victoria were to be razed and the mainly Hispanic residents moved. The houses were fixed up by the residents. The neighborhood stayed a neighborhood. The place is gorgeous.

The new popularity of the old has taught some fine lessons and a few dubious habits. The Ralph Laurenized marketing of snobby antiquity is a side effect the country could probably do without. Postmodernism has become popular along with the antique buildings that inspired it, which was fine until every second shopping-center architect became a second-rate postmodernist. Now, with historicism broadly popular, modernist architectural style is on the verge of a comeback—but a modernism that has learned from old buildings about small scale, simplicity of construction and the pleasure of materials.

Indeed, the act of preservation—poking around an old building, studying half-forgotten design principles up close, figuring out how to put the structure right, buttressing, straightening, sanding, replastering, painting—is profoundly instructive. Restoring a 19th century house makes thoughtful architects and planners think differently about how they design new buildings and new neighborhoods. "The great value of doing preservation in our office," says Architect James Stewart Polshek, whose firm restored Carnegie Hall, "is that it helps reinforce in young architects an attitude about the way buildings still could be built."

Planners are discovering that regenerating the city is much harder and slower than the last generation believed, that to work, it must be a building-by-building, street-by-street evolution. The planning for New York's new Battery Park City development, for instance, quite nicely incorporates many of the old ways; visual surprise was designed in, gradual changes of scale were carefully planned, stylistic variety and overall cohesion were both encouraged. "What we've learned," Fitch says, "is that if you want to rejuvenate a city, you have got to be very careful not to throw any kind of tissue away."

Precisely. These days, who would not agree?

In fact, quite a few people don't, some with the clout to act on their preferences.

Take Donald Trump. Trump, who in 1980 pulled down and smashed a set of art deco bas reliefs from an old Fifth Avenue building ("They were stones with some engravings on them"), says today that "a lot of times preservation is used as an excuse to stop progress" and "as a method of stopping anybody from progressing a city." Trump's current idea of "progressing a city" is to put up a set of nine gigantic high-rise towers, among them the tallest building in the world, on Manhattan's old Upper West Side.

No, preservation has not been carried too far. The passion for good old downtowns has not yet got out of hand. The lessons of the past two decades have not been learned too well.

—By Kurt Anderson.
Reported by Daniel S. Levy/New York and Edwin M. Reingold/Los Angeles, with other bureaus

QUESTIONS AND ACTIVITIES

Comprehension Questions

1. What factors contributed to the decay of the downtown sections and neighborhoods of many cities?

2. Why were many architecturally interesting and important buildings torn down during the 1950s and 1960s?

3. What factors contributed to the interest in renewing and preserving urban areas?

4. It is now possible to have a building designated as a landmark. What are the advantages and disadvantages of this designation?

5. In the urban preservation process, many buildings are now being used for purposes other than their original ones. What are some examples of buildings and their new uses?

6. What is a possible negative result of the restoration of an urban neighborhood?

Discussion Questions

1. In your opinion, should all old buildings be preserved, or only certain ones? Explain your answer.

2. In your home culture, when is a building considered old?

3. Where you are currently living, is there any restoration of old buildings going on? If not, why do you think not? If so, what are the restored buildings being used for?

4. Do you think you would like to restore a house? Why or why not?

5. Would you prefer to live in a restored 100-year-old building or a brand-new one? Explain your answer.

Group Activities

Suppose that in your city there is a railroad station that is no longer being used. The city officials want to tear the station down to build a high-rise parking garage so that more shoppers can come to the downtown section. A group of preservationists, however, wants to save the station because it was designed by a famous architect. Imagine that half the class are city planners; the other half are preservationists. In groups of five or six, develop arguments in support of your position. Present your arguments to the opposing group.

Individual Work

Take a walk in your neighborhood or in the neighborhood around your school. Notice whether any building has been restored or whether there is a building that could be restored. Be prepared to tell the class about the building. You might include the following information:
    a. when you think it was built
    b. why you find it interesting or unusual
    c. what needs to be done to restore it

Article Three

BACKGROUND NOTES

for **Here Come the DINKs**

Preview

The number of married couples in the United States with two incomes and no children has risen dramatically in recent years. At issue is whether their fast-paced lifestyles allow time for children.

Culture

akita: a breed of dog. Akitas are expensive and currently quite popular in some social circles.

BMW: An automobile made by the Bavarian Motor Works in West Germany. Relatively expensive, BMWs are valued for their performance and their "snob appeal."

Burberry: the brand name of a British clothing manufacturer. Rather costly, Burberry clothes are noted for their classic styling.

cellular phone ['sɛljələ 'fon]: a type of portable telephone often found in automobiles. Many business people rely on cellular phones to stay in contact with their offices and homes.

Cheers: a television comedy series popular among yuppies. "Cheers" is the name of a bar where the characters gather.

deep freezer: an appliance used for freezing and storing large quantities of food. People with large families often have deep freezers.

DINKerbells ['dɪŋkə,bɛlz]: children of DINKs. The term refers to Tinkerbell, the fairy in James Barrie's play *Peter Pan*.

exurb ['ɛksəb]: a region outside the suburbs of a city. The exurbs are usually inhabited by relatively wealthy people.

head-hunting firm: a company that specializes in identifying and recruiting talented professionals for employment at firms in competition with the firms for which they are working.

hippie ['hɪpi]: a "flower child"; a member of the anti-establishment movement of the 1960s and 1970s. Hippies protested against the Viet Nam War and were proponents of peace and free love.

L.A. Law: a television drama series focusing on the lives of several young lawyers in Los Angeles

Le Menu™: the trademark of a relatively expensive brand of frozen dinners. Le Menu™ offers gourmet fast food.

M.B.A.: a master's degree in business administration. M.B.A. degrees are considered prestigious because they are thought to be the prerequisite for well-paying jobs.

Samoyed ['sæmə,jɛd]: a breed of dog. Samoyeds are expensive and currently quite popular in some social circles.

station wagon: a car whose interior is larger than a sedan's, providing space for many people or items. Stereotypically, suburban couples drive station wagons to transport children, groceries, dogs, etc.

yuppie ['jəpi]: a "young urban professional"; a person whose career and salary allow a comfortable lifestyle in a large city. Many yuppies of the 1980s were once hippies in the 1960s and 1970s.

Vocabulary

acronym ['ækrə,nɪm]: a word formed by the first letter or letters of the words of a phrase. For example, DINK is an acronym that represents "Double Income, No Kids."

cocoon [kə'kun]: a protective covering made by insect larvae; any protective covering or surroundings. Some people view their homes as a kind of cocoon that protects them from the outside world.

discretionary [dɪs'krɛʃə,nɛri]: relating to free choice; relating to independent decisions. Discretionary income is income left over after living expenses are paid.

frenzy: intense activity; agitation

high roller: a person who lives well and spends a great deal of money. High-rollers are not necessarily wealthy.

hip: aware of and interested in the latest trends in society (colloquial)

paralegal ['pɛrə'ligəl]: one who assists an attorney. Paralegals do not have law degrees.

pomegranate ['pɑmə,grænət]: a red fruit with many seeds. Pomegranates are relatively expensive in the United States and are considered exotic.

pooch [putʃ]: a playful and affectionate word for *dog*

pundit ['pəndət]: an authority; a critic; a person who offers opinions in an authoritative way

techie ['tɛki]: a person who uses and enjoys high-technology equipment. Techies are often upscale individuals.

upper-crust: belonging to the top levels of society

upscale: associated with higher socioeconomic levels. Upscale purchasers often buy expensive high-technology equipment for themselves.

The Eagles cuddle with pooch Earthquake and contemplate a takeout pizza snack

Here Come the DINKs

Double-income, no-kids couples are the latest subset

The members of this newly defined species can best be spotted after 9 p.m. in gourmet groceries, their Burberry-clothed arms reaching for the arugula or a Le Menu frozen flounder dinner. In the parking lot, they slide into their BMWs and lift cellular phones to their ears before zooming off to their architect-designed houses in the exurbs. After warmly greeting Rover (often an akita or golden retriever), they check to be sure the pooch service has delivered his nutritionally correct dog food. Then they consult the phone-answering machine, pop dinner into the microwave and finally sink into their Italian leather sofa to watch a videocassette of, say, last week's *L.A. Law* or *Cheers* on their high-definition, large-screen stereo television.

These speedy high rollers are upper-crust DINKs, double-income, no-kids couples. They flourish in the pricier suburbs as well as in gentrified urban neighborhoods. There is no time for deep freezers or station wagons in their voracious, nonstop schedules. Many enterprising DINK couples slave for a combined 100-hour-plus workweek, a pace relieved by exotic vacations and expensive health clubs. Their

hectic "time poor" life-style often forces them to schedule dinners with each other, and in some supercharged cases, even sex.

Consider the pace of Michele Ward, 26, and Kenneth Hoffman, 31, top executives at different Connecticut management-consulting firms. "The prime purpose of our answering machine at home is so we can keep in touch with each other," says Ken of their jammed schedules. For pleasure, they sail and "cook seriously together," whipping up veal Normandy or Persian duck in pomegranate sauce. They subscribe to four gourmet magazines and have a collection of 150 cookbooks. Most recent vacation: three weeks in Tahiti and Bora Bora. "Part of me would like children, but, practically speaking, I don't see how," says Michele, who estimates the earliest date for childbearing is 1993. Their ranch-style house has three bedrooms: one for them, one for the computer and one for their Samoyed, Dillon.

David Eagle, 33, a Hollywood television producer, and Nancy Weingrow Eagle, 31, an entertainment lawyer, also fill out the DINK profile. In order to earn their hefty incomes, each one works 50 to 60 hours a week. They

have two dogs and care for them the way they decorate their home—which is to say, lavishly. "Earthquake, our Labrador-husky mix, has beautiful blue eyes. I have blue eyes, so people think I'm his father," jokes David. "We're going skiing tomorrow and taking both dogs with us." In the late 1960s he supported Eugene McCarthy and was labeled a hippie. In the late 1970s he became a yuppie, and accepts DINK as a natural evolution. Little DINKerbells, however, are not yet part of the progression. "We have big responsibilities just being double income-ites," explains David. "We aren't ready to give up the quality time that is necessary to devote to our careers and transfer that to children."

The origin of the acronym is not known, but it is often attributed to glib real estate agents or clever marketing M.B.A.s bored with the term yuppie. What separates DINKs from most other Americans is a much greater percentage of discretionary income. "DINKs are one of the few groups that are doing much better than the previous generation," says Frank Levy, an economist at the University of Maryland.

Social pundits warn that DINKdom is often just a transitory state. "It is the moment before tradition sets in," says Faith Popcorn, chairman of New York City's BrainReserve, a hip consulting firm. "There is a desire for security, privacy, a nest. Anything you can make that is easy and secure, warm and available, you can market to their cocoon." Philip Kotler, professor of marketing at Northwestern, divides DINKs into upper and lower classes: U-DINKs and L-DINKs. No doubt, while the L-DINKs are rushing to graduate from K mart to Marshall Field, the U-DINKs will be deserting the Banana Republic for Abercrombie & Fitch. Because busy U-DINKs tend to miss mass-media advertising, upscale magazines and direct mail are the most effective way to target them. Kotler cites the *Sharper Image,* a top-of-the-line techie catalog, as defining U-DINK style.

The big DINK dilemma is when or whether to have children. In 1986 the cost of raising a child to age 18 averaged almost $100,000; of course, that figure does not include future college expenses. Like many DINKs, William Cohen, 33, an Atlanta lawyer, and Susan Penny-Cohen, 28, founder of a head-hunting firm for lawyers and paralegals, have not yet planned to reproduce. "As our income grew, we found that we had less time," says William. Northwestern's Kotler suspects that the double-incomers' frenzy of consumption will exhaust itself, and more couples will see children as desirable: "Children may be the next pleasure source after the DINKs have tried everything else."

Therefore, DINKs will not be the last of the snappy acronyms. Get ready for TIPS (tiny income, parents supporting) and, finally, NINKs (no income, no kids).

—By Martha Smilgis.
Reported by Christine Gorman/New York and Bill Johnson/ Los Angeles

QUESTIONS AND ACTIVITIES

Comprehension Questions

1. What does the acronym DINKs stand for? What are U-DINKs and L-DINKs?

2. What kinds of jobs do DINKs generally have? How many hours per week is it usual for them to work?

3. What do DINKs do with their relatively small amount of free time?

4. What kinds of possessions are DINKs likely to have?

5. What is the major dilemma for DINK couples?

Discussion Questions

1. Are there DINKs in your home culture? If not, why do you think not? If so, how are they regarded by the majority of people?

2. What is your opinion of the DINK lifestyle described in the article?

3. Do you think that many DINK couples will choose to have children? If so, do you think they will be good parents? Why or why not?

Group Activities

1. In groups of five or six, outline what you think would be a typical week's schedule for a DINK couple. Use your imagination. Be sure to include time spent at work, as well as leisure activities and household tasks.

2. In the same group of five or six, estimate the cost of the week's activities you outlined in Group Activity 1.

Individual Work

1. Look through several upscale magazines and cut out at least three advertisements that you believe are aimed at DINKs. Be prepared to explain why you think that the products advertised would appeal to DINKs.

2. Calculate the cost of raising a child in your home culture to age 18. Be sure to include estimates for food, clothing, medical services, and education. Be prepared to present this budget to the class and to compare it with those of the other students.

BACKGROUND NOTES

for **Trapped Behind the Wheel**

Preview

As metropolitan areas continue to grow, and as public transportation fails to expand, more workers find themselves in daily traffic jams. Many have found unusual ways to cope with this urban reality.

Culture

bald eagle: the national bird of the United States, now near extinction. On the list of endangered species, the bald eagle is rarely seen in the wild.

car pool: a group of people who ride to and from work in the same car. In some locations, car pools can use special express lanes on the highway.

Egg McMuffin℗ [ˌɛg məkˈməfən]: a product of the McDonald's fast food chain. Eaten for breakfast, an Egg McMuffin℗ is a sandwich filled with a fried egg, cheese, and meat (either sausage, ham, or bacon).

rush hour: a period of time (not necessarily an hour) when people are going to or returning from work. During rush hour, streets are filled with cars, buses, and pedestrians.

singles club: an organization of unmarried individuals interested in meeting others who are not married. Singles clubs are found in most large cities.

VFW: an abbreviation for Veterans of Foreign Wars. VFW is a national organization of former military people who meet for civic and social purposes.

Vocabulary

adrenaline [əˈdrɛnələn]: epinephrine; a hormone produced by the adrenal gland. Adrenaline stimulates the heart and constricts the blood vessels.

broker: a financial agent who negotiates purchases and sales. Brokers work in brokerage houses.

buzz: a topic of conversation (slang)

commuter [kəˈmjudɚ]: a person who travels (commutes) back and forth to work from home. Some commuters drive; others take public transportation.

daydream: to have dreams or pleasant thoughts while awake

dummy: a copy or imitation of someone or something

entrée [ˈɑntre]: the main course of a meal. An entrée is served after soup or salad.

fetus [ˈfidəs]: an unborn child. The issue of legal rights of fetuses is controversial.

free-lance: working independently and contracting with a number of people for work. Some writers and photographers prefer free-lance work to working with only one employer.

Lifestyles

gridlock: a condition in which traffic cannot move. Gridlock is becoming a frequent occurrence in places such as New York City.

laid back: relaxed; not worried. Some people believe that being laid back fights stress.

nest-building: preparing one's surroundings to be homelike (or ''nestlike'')

paralysis [pə'ræləsəs]: a state of immobility; the inability to move

real estate: property; land and the buildings on it

rear-view mirror: the mirror attached to the inside center of the windshield of a car. It enables the driver to see what is behind the car.

saga ['sɑgə]: a long narrative about a person's adventures. The oldest written sagas date from the 12th and 13th centuries in Iceland.

slurp: to drink noisily

speed demon: a person who drives too fast

stasis ['stesəs]: a state of inactivity; a condition of stopping

traffic: the movement of vehicles or pedestrians through an area

turnoff: something, such as a sight or topic, that makes people react negatively or be uninterested

worked over: over-used; exploited

Going nowhere on the Long Island Expressway:
"Your body releases more adrenaline, your blood vessels constrict, your pressure rises . . .
You are still wound up three or four hours later."

Trapped Behind The Wheel

Clever commuters learn to live in the slow lane

There are trends, all too easily discernible, in dinner conversations. The saga of domestic help is a persistent one—pretty worked over by now. Real estate is an ongoing turnoff, but the new buzz is even more boring and more inescapable. It is traffic.

In a scene replayed thousands of times each evening in Los Angeles, New York, Chicago and burgeoning suburbs nationwide, the last guests for a 7:30 dinner straggle in 40 minutes late, muttering their astonishment—but not, significantly, their apologies—that it took them 90 minutes to drive ten miles. Their woes inevitably inspire the other guests to a round of competitive traffic horror stories that continue well into the entrée.

There is the one about the drivers who sneak into the lane reserved for car pools by planting inflated dummies in the passenger seats. And the pregnant woman who successfully argued in court that she and her fetus were entitled to use the carpool lane because they were separate persons. Then there are the days that live in legend—like Oct. 29, 1986, when a single midafternoon accident on the San Diego Freeway spread gridlock along connecting freeways and surface streets from

downtown Los Angeles to the San Fernando Valley, trapping tens of thousands of motorists for eight full hours. (Survivors of such mythic urban struggles brag about them like good ole boys at the VFW bar.)

There are reasons for the quickening national paralysis: more and more people live and work in locations that are not linked to adequate public transport, millions of women have entered the work force and are new rush-hour drivers, ingenious alternatives seem to get stymied by lack of imagination or money or both, and, above all, gas is cheap. In places where gas is still below a dollar, many drivers have reverted to old habits, and in some parts of the U.S. a two-occupant car is about as common as a bald eagle.

In California the state government estimates that each day 300,000 work hours are lost to traffic jams at a cost of $2 million. On the Capital Beltway near Washington, gridlock costs employers as much as $120 million a year in lost time. But the toll on the individual commuter, usually lone but hardly a ranger, is heavier still. Without hope of release, he sits in his little cell inhaling exhaust fumes and staring blankly at the zinc sky.

Some drivers try to fight the sentence. Take Jeff Seibert, an associate professor of pediatrics at the University of Miami School of Medicine, who finds that his 25-minute ride to work, which includes the unpredictable Dolphin Expressway, can stretch into an hour and 15 minutes. "When the radio traffic announcer advises to stay clear of a certain area, I drive right to that point," he says, figuring that the warning has cleared the congestion by dispersing most commuters onto different routes. Others, like Kathi Douglas, a recent graduate of Spelman College in Atlanta, undergo an attitude change. "I'm laid back and talkative, yet once I get on the road, I have no respect for rules and regulations," says Douglas. "You get to be really aggressive because you think it's the only way to get out of this madness."

Extreme frustration can lead to violence. Four freeway shootings have been reported in the Los Angeles area in the past eleven months. On the Santa Ana Freeway, a speed demon angered by a car that did not move from the fast lane pulled up alongside the offending vehicle and fatally shot a passenger in the front seat.

There are saner approaches to highway stasis. Ken Jenson, 28, a Los Angeles salesman, used to spend much of his hour-long commute singing with the radio. Last year he stopped the music and began studying to become a stockbroker. "I made tapes of the texts and took notes while I listened on the drive to and from work," explains Jenson, who is now a broker in the Westwood office of Merrill Lynch. "It's amazing that I didn't hit anyone." Using the rear-view mirror, many men shave with electric razors and women often apply their makeup. Some people even dress behind the wheel. Janice Conover, a Hampton Jitney Co. bus driver who regularly plies the Long Island Expressway (popularly known as the Long Island Parking Lot), has seen motorists so engrossed in the morning newspaper that they drift from one lane toward another, luckily at minimal speed.

Hungry drivers gobble breakfast, often an Egg McMuffin, from Styrofoam cartons and slurp coffee from no-slosh mugs. Others balance checkbooks, do crossword puzzles and dictate letters and grocery lists into pocket-size tape recorders. Hot summer weekends offer an opportunity for passengers to take partial charge of the car. Inching along to the approach to the George Washington Bridge between New Jersey and Manhattan, occupants of cars without air conditioning who face delays of more than an hour hold the doors open for a little circulation.

It is possible to transform an auto into a slow-rolling "home away from home." Larry Schreiner, a free-lance reporter for a Chicago radio station and several local TV stations, often lives and works in his Mercedes 560 SEL. "I have everything I need," says Schreiner, whose longest continuous stretch on wheels was 36 hours. His office supplies include five two-way radios, two cellular phones, one headset (so he can talk on radio shows while working on videotapes), two video cameras and three video recorders. That's not all. In the trunk Schreiner keeps batteries, lighting equipment, three still cameras, telephone books, road maps and a change of clothes.

For nest-building commuters, the place to go is Chicago's Warshawsky & Co., which bills itself as the largest auto parts and accessory store in the world. It offers in-dash televisions ($300), compact-disc adapters, orthopedic seat cushions, heated seats for winter, and computers with cruise control and estimated time of arrival (up to $149). Upscale

Patiently waiting to get onto the Bay Bridge, a San Francisco commuter eats breakfast.

drivers install $2,000 car phones (although in Los Angeles, where there are 65,000 subscribers, airwaves are jammed in rush hours). Ordinary folk can ape "techie" drivers by ordering an imitation antenna from Warshawsky for a mere $12.

Traffic is thick enough to defeat just about anything except perhaps the mating instinct. In fact, some have found that choked freeways can enhance the possibilities of finding a mate. Ruth Guillou, an enterprising Huntington Beach, Calif., widow, was idling along when she saw a "charming-looking man in a yellow Cadillac. I couldn't get him out of my mind. There should have been a way for me to make contact with him." Thus was born the Freeway Singles Club, a mail-forwarding service whose participants pay $35 for a numbered decal that identifies them as members. The group has a roster of 2,000 in Southern California and has expanded to 16 states.

According to Manhattan Psychiatrist T.B. Karasu, motorists can be divided into two categories: adaptives, those who accept things as they are and understand that they cannot be in control of all situations, and nonadaptives. The nonadaptives, says Karasu, "blow their horns and irritate everybody else as well as themselves. Noise is an external and excessive stimulus that increases rather than decreases tension. When you yell or are yelled at, your body releases more adrenaline, your blood vessels constrict, your pressure rises, and you get headaches. You are still wound up three or four hours later." Karasu points out that nonadaptive behavior, or the inability to cope with freeway stress, could lead to heart attacks or strokes for some. He advises motorists to relax by thinking they are passengers in an airplane with a captain running things. "Listen to music, daydream, focus on things you normally don't find time to think about," says Karasu. "Above all else, accept that you are where you are, and there is nothing that you can do about it."

—*By Martha Smilgis.*
Reported by Dan Goodgame/Los Angeles, with other bureaus

QUESTIONS AND ACTIVITIES

Comprehension Questions

1. What are the causes of the current traffic problems?
2. What are some of the negative results of such heavy traffic?
3. What kinds of things do drivers do to cope with their daily commute?

Discussion Questions

1. What are the different ways that people commute to work in your home culture? What do the majority of people do?
2. Is traffic a problem in your hometown or city? If so, what are its causes?
3. What solutions have people used in your hometown or country to deal with traffic problems?
4. Do you think that traffic problems are an inevitable part of the growth of cities, or can they be prevented?

Group Activities

1. In groups of three or four, imagine that you are transportation commissioners for a major U.S. city. Identify as many solutions as you can to the traffic problems described in the article. What one solution would you recommend if the city had unlimited financial resources?
2. In groups of three or four, again imagine that you are transportation commissioners for a major U.S. city. This time assume that the city has no money to improve existing conditions. What recommendations would you make to the general population? Would you want laws passed to change people's behavior?

Individual Work

1. Keep a one-day record of your commuting to classes and/or work. What modes of transportation do you use? How much time do you spend in total? What is the total distance you travel? Multiply your figures for time and distance to get a figure for the week, the month, and the year. Do the figures surprise you? Why or why not?
2. Interview one other person, finding out the same information as in Individual Work 1 above. Does that person's commuting differ from yours? If so, how?

Article Five

BACKGROUND NOTES

for **The Child-Care Dilemma**

Preview

As more women enter the workforce, families are faced with the problem of who will care for the children. Unfortunately, the options are rarely ideal.

Culture

apple pie: a supposed symbol of American life. Motherhood is usually mentioned along with the American flag and apple pie as being "sacred" to Americans.

au pair [oˈpɛr]: a young woman who lives with a family and takes care of the children. Au pairs often come to the United States from western European countries.

Beaver [ˈbivɚ]: a character on a popular 1960s television show. Beaver was the younger son of the Cleaver family, an idealized American family in which the father worked and the mother stayed home.

day care: care provided to children whose parents work. Such care is available in day-care homes (in which an individual takes care of a few children at home) or day-care centers (a business with a staff of child-care workers).

extended family: the family, including parents, children, grandparents, uncles, aunts, etc. Often the extended family is relied upon for child care.

fringe benefit [frɪndʒ ˈbɛnəˌfɪt]: a payment or service received in addition to the salary earned at a job. Fringe benefits usually include health and life insurance.

Montessori [ˌmɑn(t)əˈsori]: pertaining to the educational approach developed by Maria Montessori, an Italian physician and educator. The Montessori system stresses individual guidance of children, not strict control.

nuclear family: the immediate family; the family consisting of parents and children. Households in the United States usually contain nuclear families, rather than extended families.

nursery school: a school, usually privately run, for two- and three-year-old children. Classes are generally held two mornings per week; day care is sometimes available at the same center for the rest of the time.

preschool: a school, usually privately run, for three- and four-year-old children. Classes are generally held three mornings per week; day care is sometimes available at the same center for the rest of the time.

Donna Reed: an actress who starred in "The Donna Reed Show," a popular 1960s television show about the Stone family. Donna Stone was the idealized American mother who stayed at home to care for her family.

soap: short for **soap opera**, a continuing television melodrama. Soaps were originally designed for daytime viewing by housewives; today some soaps are broadcast in the evening and appeal to a wider audience.

Benjamin Spock: a famous pediatrician. His book, *Baby and Child Care*, has been a primary source of information on children for more than 40 years.

waiting list: a list of names of people who have requested a service and are waiting for it. Waiting lists are very typical at day-care centers.

Vocabulary

affluent [ˈæˌfluənt]: wealthy; materially comfortable

bristle [ˈbrɪsəl]: to behave in an agitated manner; to act angrily or aggressively

catalyst [kædələst]: something that causes or enables something else to occur

cope: to overcome problems; to manage difficulties (colloquial)

dilemma: a problem with two equally unsatisfactory solutions; a difficult situation with no apparent solution

fret: to worry; to be troubled

guru: an expert; a guide for one's behavior

incredulous [ˌɪnˈkrɛdʒələs]: skeptical; expressing disbelief

maneuver [məˈnuvɚ]: to scheme; to manipulate; to perform certain actions to achieve a goal

mortify: to humiliate; to shame; to make someone feel guilty

pantheon [ˈpænθiˌɑn]: the gods of a people; the collection of ideals of a people

pothole [ˈpɑtˌhol]: a hole in a road. Potholes are caused by wear, weather, and poor construction.

premature [ˌpriməˈtʃɚ]: happening before the usual time; occurring before someone or something is ready

preoccupation: a worry; a concern

quandary [ˈkwɑnˌdri]: a state of doubt; a dilemma

siblings: brothers and sisters

toddler: a child who has just begun to walk. A one-year-old is generally thought of as a toddler.

waft [wæft]: to float, as if on air or water

wastrel [ˈwestrəl]: a homeless child

wrenching [ˈrɛntʃɪŋ]: causing emotional stress; causing anguish

zombie [ˈzɑmbi]: literally, a dead body capable of walking and moving; metaphorically, a human who appears lifeless and speechless

The most anguished moment of the morning: Adam Kieczowski, 4½, is about to be dropped off by his mother at a Rahway, N.J., day-care center funded by Merck & Co.

The Child-Care Dilemma

Millions of U.S. families face a wrenching question: Who's minding the kids?

The smell of wet paint wafts through the house on a tree-lined street on Chicago's North Side. Marena Mcpherson, 37, chose a peach tint for the nursery: a gender-neutral color. But the paint had a will of its own and dried a blushing shade of pink. Ah well, no time to worry about that. With the baby due in less than a month, there are too many other concerns. Like choosing a name, furnishing the baby's room, reading up on infant care and attending childbirth classes. Above all, McPherson must tackle the overriding problem that now confronts most expectant American mothers: Who will care for this precious baby when she returns to work?

An attorney who helps run a Chicago social-service agency, McPherson has accumulated two months of paid sick leave and vacation time. She plans to spend an additional four months working part time, but then she must return to her usual full schedule. So for several months she has been exhaustively researching the local child-care scene. The choices, she has learned, are disappointingly few. Only two day-care centers in Chicago accept infants; both are expensive, and neither appeals. "With 20 or 30 babies, it's probably all they can do to get each child's needs met,"

says McPherson. She would prefer having a baby-sitter come to her home. "That way there's a sense of security and family." But she worries about the cost and reliability: "People will quit, go away for the summer, get sick." In an ideal world, she says, she would choose someone who reflects her own values and does not spend the day watching soaps. "I suspect I will have to settle for things not being perfect."

That anxiety has become a standard rite of passage for American parents. Beaver's family, with Ward Cleaver off to work in his suit and June in her apron in the kitchen, is a vanishing breed. Less than a fifth of American families now fit that model, down from a third 15 years ago. Today more than 60% of mothers with children under 14 are in the labor force. Even more striking: about half of American women are making the same painful decision as McPherson and returning to work before their child's first birthday. Most do so because they have to: seven out of ten working mothers say they need their salaries to make ends meet.

With both Mom and Dad away at the office or store or factory, the child-care crunch has become the most wrenching personal problem facing millions of American families. In 1986,

9 million preschoolers spent their days in the hands of someone other than their mother. Millions of older children participate in programs providing after-school supervision. As American women continue to pour into the work force, the trend will accelerate. "We are in the midst of an explosion," says Elinor Guggenheimer, president of the Manhattan-based Child Care Action Campaign. In ten years, she predicts, the number of children under six who will need daytime supervision will grow more than 50%. Says Jay Belsky, a professor of human development at Pennsylvania State University: "We are as much a society dependent on female labor, and thus in need of a child-care system, as we are a society dependent on the automobile, and thus in need of roads."

At the moment, though, the American child-care system—to the extent that there is one—is riddled with potholes. Throughout the country, working parents are faced with a triple quandary: day care is hard to find, difficult to afford and often of distressingly poor quality. Waiting lists at good facilities are so long that parents apply for a spot months before their children are born. Or even earlier. The Empire State center in Farmingdale, N.Y., received an application from a woman attorney a week after she became engaged to marry. Apparently she hoped to time her pregnancy for an anticipated opening. The Jeanne Simon center in Burlington, Vt., has a folder of applications labeled "preconception."

Finding an acceptable day-care arrangement is just the beginning of the struggle. Parents must then maneuver to maintain it. Michele Theriot of Santa Monica, Calif., a 37-year-old theatrical producer, has been scrambling ever since her daughter Zoe was born 2½ years ago. In that short period she has employed a Danish au pair, who quit after eight months; a French girl, who stayed 2½ months; and an Iranian, who lasted a week. "If you get a good person, it's great," says Theriot, "but they have a tendency to move on." Last September, Theriot decided to switch Zoe into a "family-care" arrangement, in which she spends seven hours a day in the home of another mother. Theriot toured a dozen such facilities before selecting one. "I can't even tell you what I found out there," she bristles. In one home the "kids were all lined up in front of the TV like a bunch of zombies." At another she was appalled by the filth. "I sat my girl down on the cleanest spot I could find and started interviewing the care giver. And you know what she did?" asks the incredulous mother. "She began throwing empty yogurt cups at my child's head. As though that was playful!"

Theriot is none too sure that the center she finally chose is much better. Zoe's diapers aren't always changed, instructions about giving medicine are sometimes ignored, and worse, "she's started having nightmares." En route to day care on a recent day, Zoe cried out, "No school! No school!" and became distraught. It is time, Theriot concludes, to start the child-care search again.

Fretting about the effects of day care on children has become a national preoccupation. What troubles lie ahead for a generation reared by strangers? What kind of adults will they become? "It is scaring everybody that a whole generation of children is being raised in a way that has never happened before," says Edward Zigler, professor of psychology at Yale and an authority on child care. At least one major survey of current research, by Penn State's Belsky, suggests that extensive day care in the first year of life raises the risk of emotional problems, a conclusion that has mortified already guilty working parents. With high-quality supervision costing upwards of $100 a week, many families are placing their children in the hands of untrained, overworked personnel. "In some places, that means one woman taking care of nine babies," says Zigler. "Nobody doing that can give them the stimulation they need. We encounter some real horror stories out there, with babies being tied into cribs."

The U.S. is the only Western industrialized nation that does not guarantee a working mother the right to a leave of absence after she has a child. Although the Supreme Court ruled last January that states may require businesses to provide maternity leaves with job security, only 40% of working women receive such protection through their companies. Even for these, the leaves are generally brief and unpaid. This forces many women to return to work sooner than they would like and creates a huge demand for infant care, the most expensive and difficult child-care service to supply. The premature separation takes a personal toll as well, observes Harvard Pediatrician T. Berry Brazelton, heir apparent to Benjamin Spock as the country's preeminent guru on child rearing. "Many parents return to the workplace grieving."

New York City Police Officer Janis Curtin resumed her assignment in south Queens just eight weeks after the birth of Peter. The screaming sirens and shrill threats of street thugs were just background noise to a relentless refrain in her head: "Who can I trust to care for my child?" She tried everything, from leaving Peter at the homes of other mothers to handing him over to her police-officer husband at the station-house door when they worked alternating shifts. With their schedules in constant flux, there were snags every step of the way. Curtin was more fortunate than most workers: police-department policy allows a year of unpaid "hardship" leave for child care. She decided to invoke that provision.

The absence of national policies to help working mothers reflects traditional American attitudes: old-fashioned motherhood has stood right up there with the flag and apple pie in the pantheon of American ideals. To some people day-care centers, particularly government-sponsored ones, threaten family values; they seem a step on the slippery slope toward an Orwellian socialist nightmare. But such abstract concerns have largely receded as the very concrete need for child care is confronted by people from all walks of life.

Without much federal help, the poorest mothers are caught in a vise. Working is the only way out of poverty, but it means putting children into day care, which is unaffordable. "The typical cost of full-time care is about $3,000 a year for one child, or one-third of the poverty-level income for a family of three," says Helen Blank of the Children's Defense Fund in Washington. As a result, many poor mothers leave their young children alone for long periods or entrust them to siblings only slightly older. Others simply give up on working.

Child care has always been an issue for the working poor. Traditionally, they have relied on neighbors or extended family and, in the worst of times, have left their children to wander in the streets or tied to the bedpost. In the mid-19th century the number of wastrels in the streets was so alarming that charity-minded society ladies established day nurseries in cities around the country. A few were sponsored by employers. Gradually, local regulatory boards began to discourage infant care, restrict nursery hours and place emphasis on a kindergarten or Montessori-style instructional approach. The nurseries became nursery schools, no longer suited to the needs of working mothers. During World War II, when women were mobilized to join wartime industry, day nurseries returned, with federal and local government sponsorship. Most of the centers vanished in the postwar years, and the Donna Reed era of the idealized nuclear family began.

Two historic forces brought an end to that era, sweeping women out of the home and into the workplace and creating a new demand for child care. First came the feminist movement of the '60s, which encouraged housewives to seek fulfillment in a career. Then economic recessions and inflation struck in the 1970s. Between 1973 and 1983, the median income for young families fell by more than 16%. Suddenly the middle-class dream of a house, a car and three square meals for the kids carried a dual-income price tag. "What was once a problem only of poor families has now become a part of daily life and a basic concern of typical American families," says Sheila B. Kamerman, a professor of social policy and planning at Columbia University and co-author of *Child Care: Facing the Hard Choices*. Some women are angry that the feminist movement failed to foresee the conflict that would arise between work and family life. "Safe, licensed child care should have been as prominent a feminist rallying cry as safe, legal abortions," observes Joan Walsh, a legislative consultant and essayist in Sacramento.

In the early 1970s, there was a flurry of congressional activity to provide child-care funds for the working poor and regulate standards. But under pressure from conservative groups, Richard Nixon vetoed a comprehensive child-development program in 1971, refusing, he said, to put the Government's "vast moral authority" on the side of "communal" approaches to child rearing. The Reagan Administration has further reduced the federal role in child care. In inflation-adjusted dollars, funding for direct day-care subsidies for low- and middle-income families has dropped by 28%.

California, Minnesota, Massachusetts, New York and Connecticut are among the few

WORKING MOTHERS OF CHILDREN UNDER SIX

55%
47%
39%
32%
23%
19%

'60 '65 '70 '75 '80 '86

A Woman's Place

In a poll for TIME by the firm Yankelovich Clancy Shulman*, 80% agreed with the statement that "many women today are having a hard time balancing the demands of raising children, marriage and work." Here are some of the findings:

Illustration for TIME by Joe Lertola

More women are working outside the home these days. Do you think this is good or bad for:

	Total Good	Total Bad	Women Good	Women Bad	Men Good	Men Bad
Marriages	45%	36%	46%	34%	44%	39%
Children	24%	57%	26%	53%	22%	61%
The workplace	66%	12%	69%	10%	62%	15%
Women in general	72%	14%	70%	14%	73%	13%

In your view, most married women who work do so primarily:

	Total	Women	Men
Because they want to	19%	16%	23%
For economic reasons	66%	68%	64%

*The findings are based on a telephone survey of 1,014 adult Americans. The potential sampling error is plus or minus 3%.

If one of you had to give up your job for some reason, whose job would it be?

	Total	Women	Men
Husband's	10%	11%	9%
Wife's	84%	84%	83%

Should business provide day care?

	Total	Women	Men
Yes	51%	56%	46%
No	39%	34%	46%

Should government do more to provide day care?

	Total	Women	Men
Yes	54%	56%	51%
No	43%	39%	48%

states that have devoted considerable resources to improving child-care programs. Most states have done virtually nothing. Thirty-three have lowered their standards and reduced enforcement for licensed day-care centers. As of last year, 23 states were providing fewer children with day care than in 1981.

Nor have American businesses stepped in to fill the void. "They acknowledge that child care is an important need, but they don't see it as their problem," says Kamerman. Of the nation's 6 million employers, only about 3,000 provide some sort of child-care assistance. That is up from about 100 in 1978, but most merely provide advice or referrals. Only about 150 employers provide on-site or near-site day-care centers. "Today's corporate personnel policies remain stuck in a 1950s time warp," charges David Blankenhorn, director of the Manhattan-based Institute for American Values. "They are rooted in the quaint assumption that employees have 'someone at home' to attend to family matters."

There are basically three kinds of day care in the U.S. For children under five, the most common arrangement is "family" or "home-based" care, in which toddlers are minded in the homes of other mothers. According to a Census Bureau report called *Who's Minding the Kids,* 37% of preschool children of working mothers spend their days in such facilities. An additional 23% are in organized day-care centers or preschools. The third type of arrangement, which prevails for older children and for 31% of those under five, is supervision in the child's own home by a nanny, sitter, relative or friend.

Experts worry that a two-tier system is

emerging, with quality care available to the affluent, and everyone else settling for less. "We are at about the same place with child care as we were when we started universal education," says Zigler of Yale. "Then some kids were getting Latin and Greek and being prepared for Harvard, Yale and Princeton. Other kids were lucky if they could learn to write their own name."

In an era of towering federal deficits, much of the future initiative will have to come from the private sector. By the year 2000, women will make up half the work force. Says Labor Secretary Bill Brock: "We still act as though workers have no families. Labor and management haven't faced that adequately, or at all."

A few companies are in the forefront. Merck & Co., a large pharmaceutical concern based in Rahway, N.J., invested $100,000 seven years ago to establish a day-care center in a church less than two miles from its headquarters. Parents pay $550 a month for infants and $385 for toddlers. Many spend lunch hours with their children. "I can be there in four minutes," says Steven Klimczak, a Merck corporate-finance executive whose three-year-old daughter attends the center. "It's very reliable, and that's important in terms of getting your job done."

Elsewhere in the country, companies have banded together to share the costs of providing day-care services to employees. A space in Rich's department store in downtown Atlanta serves the children of not only its own employees but also of workers at the Federal Reserve Bank of Atlanta, the First National Bank of Atlanta, Georgia-Pacific and the Atlanta *Journal* and *Constitution* newspapers.

Businesses that have made the investment in child care say it pays off handsomely by reducing turnover and absenteeism. A large survey has shown that parents lose on average eight days a year from work because of child-care problems and nearly 40% consider quitting. Studies at Merck suggest that the company also saves on sick leave due to stress-related illness. "We have got an awful lot of comments from managers about lessened stress and less unexpected leave time," says Spokesman Art Strohmer. At Stride Rite Corp., a 16-year-old, on-site day-care center in Boston and a newer one at the Cambridge headquarters have engendered unusual company loyalty and low turnover. "People want to work here, and child care seems to be a catalyst," says Stride Rite Chairman Arnold Hiatt. "To me it is as natural as having a clean-air policy or a medical benefit."

The generation of workers graduating from college today may find themselves in a better position. They belong to the "baby-bust" generation, and their small numbers, says Harvard Economist David Bloom, will force employers to be creative in searching for labor. Child-care arrangements, he says, will be the "fringe benefits of the 1990s." The economics of the situation, if nothing else, will provoke a change in the attitude of business, just as the politics of the situation is changing the attitude of government. In order to attract the necessary women—and men—employers are going to have to help them find ways to cope more easily with their duties as parents.

—*By Claudia Wallis.*
Reported by Jon D. Hull/Los Angeles, Melissa Ludtke/Boston and Elizabeth Taylor/Chicago

QUESTIONS AND ACTIVITIES

Comprehension Questions

1. What are the triple problems facing working parents?
2. What two factors brought women back to the workplace in the 1960s and 1970s?
3. What three kinds of day care are currently available?

Discussion Questions

1. Why do you think the government has not encouraged or financially supported the development of day-care centers?
2. Why do you think business and industry have been slow to provide day-care facilities for their workers?
3. In your home culture, do mothers usually work outside the home? If not, why not? If so, what options exist for child care?

Group Activities

Have the class divide into three groups. Each group should choose one of the following positions:

   a. Mothers of young children should stay at home and not work.
   b. Federal, state, and local governments should provide child-care facilities for working parents.
   c. Business and industry should provide child-care facilities for working parents.

In your group, develop as many arguments as you can in support of your position statement. Be prepared to present your arguments to the entire class.

Individual Work

Interview a working mother. Find out about her child-care situation. You might wish to learn the following:

   a. the number of children and their ages
   b. who cares for them
   c. whether child-care was difficult to arrange
   d. whether she is satisfied with the arrangement

Be prepared to report the information to the class.

Article Six

BACKGROUND NOTES

for **The Boom Towns**

Preview

Areas around many large cities have grown more rapidly than the cities themselves. Numerous problems have come with this rapid growth, however.

Culture

bedroom community: a suburb whose residents commute to the city to work. The name comes from the fact that the suburb or town is used for sleeping, not working.

The Man in the Gray Flannel Suit: a popular novel written by Sloan Wilson in 1955. The man in the title was a middle-aged, upper-middle-class suburbanite who felt life was passing him by.

megacounty: a county next to a large city that is characterized by rapid growth in population and new businesses

multiplex movie theater: a movie theater, often located in a suburban shopping center, that contains a number of smaller theaters. A multiplex may show as many as 12 movies at the same time.

pump jockey: a gas station attendant; a person who fills cars with gasoline at a gas station (slang)

senior citizen center: a place where older residents of a town or city can gather for activities and conversation. Older people are often called "senior citizens."

shopping mall [. . . mɔl]: a large area, usually under one roof, that contains many stores and services, such as travel agencies and hairdressers. Suburban shopping malls quickened the decay of urban downtowns.

Vocabulary

attaché case [ˌædəˈʃe ˌkes]: a briefcase; a case in which to carry business papers. An attaché case is often regarded as the sign of a professional.

barony [ˈbɛrəˌni]: the land or territory of a baron; a large private landholding

burgeoning [ˈbɚdʒənɪŋ]: expanding; developing rapidly

camaraderie [ˌkɑm(ə)ˈrɑdɚi]: friendship; fellowship. Neighborhood camaraderie is often lacking in rapidly growing areas.

chic [ʃik]: fashionable; trendy

feudalism [ˈfjudəlɪzəm]: the system of political organization prevalent in Europe during the Middle Ages; a political system similar to the medieval one

glitzy [ˈglɪtsi]: flashy; showy (slang)

hammock [ˈhæmək]: a kind of swinging couch made of net or canvas. Some suburbanites like to relax in a hammock in their backyards.

nerve-jangling: annoying; disturbing

obliterate [əˈblɪdɚˌet]: to destroy; to remove all traces of something

polarization: a division into two opposing groups

stifling [ˈstɑɪflɪŋ]: smothering; airless

swank [swæŋk]: elegant; fashionable

The Boom Towns

No longer suburbs, not quite cities: welcome to megacounties

Insurance Underwriter Joann Murphy moved to Oak Brook, Ill., 25 years ago "for the quiet and the country." But now her home in Du Page County is bracketed by office buildings and a huge shopping mall. A 31-story tower obliterates the view of trees and grass from her windows; its construction, still in progress, has sent clouds of dust and bursts of noise into her home. Laments Murphy: "This is like living in downtown Chicago."

Well, not exactly. If Du Page and dozens of other fast-growing counties all over the U.S. are beginning to look like spreadout cities, most of their residents can still loll in a hammock in a spacious backyard on a late-spring evening. But these counties are hardly suburbs anymore, at least in the traditional sense of being bedroom communities for nearby cities. Not only jobs but also gourmet restaurants and chic stores are close at hand. As a result, people like Engineer Daniel Nee, a resident of Gwinnett County, Ga., 18 miles from Atlanta, commonly go six months or more without feeling any necessity to take their families downtown.

What are these places then? They are a form of urban organization—or, sometimes, disorganization—so new that demographers have not yet coined an accepted name for them. But outside almost every major American city, one or more counties are developing the characteristics of Du Page or Gwinnett or Fairfax County, Va., across the Potomac from Washington, or Orange County, between Los Angeles and San Diego, or Johnson County, Kans., next to Kansas City. These sprawling, increasingly dense suburbs might be called megacounties.

Nowadays they are where the growth is— in population, construction, jobs, incomes. Gwinnett County's population has almost quadrupled, from 72,300 in 1970 to 250,000 today; since 1984 it has been the fastest-growing county in the nation. Oakland County, near Detroit, has got 40% of all jobs created in Michigan since the 1982 recession. Tysons Corner, an unincorporated area of Fairfax County 13 miles from Washington, was once a sleepy crossroads with little more than a gas station; today it contains more office space than either Baltimore or downtown Miami. The Corporate Woods office complex in Overland Park, Kans., boasts 275 businesses and 5,000 jobs; built on 300 acres, it has room for more. "Corporate Woods is the fastest-growing commercial area in either state, Kansas or Missouri," says Planning Consultant Myles Schachter.

It is less sheer growth than the type of growth, however, that has given the megacounties their distinguishing mark of self-sufficiency. The first great wave of American suburbanization that began right after World War II was a migration of the middle class from the cities to newly created bedroom communities. But for the past dozen years or so, that movement has been immensely reinforced by a flight of jobs following the people. It is being powered by some of the mightiest currents in modern life: the communications revolution and the switch from a manufacturing to a service economy. Says George Sternlieb, professor of city planning at Rutgers University: "Changes in technology and in our economy are making possible a lifestyle that could only be dreamt about a few years ago."

Thanks to computers and low-cost telephone hookups, a company no longer needs to cluster its headquarters, billing operations, advertising, accounting and legal departments near the mill or factory; they can be plumped down in cubist buildings scattered around a suburban "campus." Even warehouses do not have to sit near city railroad yards; open land from which trucks can swing onto the interstate highways is often a more efficient as well as a much cheaper location. Offices can be moved near the plush, tree-shaded communities where a firm's top executives often live, and companies can tap into a well-educated work force of middle managers and skilled technicians who have grown tired of the grinding commute into the central city.

In 1975 the nation passed a little-noticed landmark: for the first time suburban office construction slightly exceeded office construction in the central cities. Now the ratio is about 60% suburban, 40% city. The Corporetum, a 130-acre development along the East-West Tollway in Du Page County, will eventually include 16 buildings—a commercial space "about the size of the Standard Oil Building in downtown Chicago," says Developer John Colnon, "only we're building it horizontally rather than vertically."

The long-distance commuter, meanwhile, is becoming as passé as the 1955 novel, *The Man in the Gray Flannel Suit,* that memorialized him. As early as 1980, almost twice as many Americans were commuting from one suburb to another (27 million) as were still making a daily trek into a central city (14 million). Since then the proportions have undoubtedly grown even more lopsided.

Along with the offices, warehouses and electronics plants have come many of the other conveniences of city life. Orange County residents eager to dress for success have no need to journey to Rodeo Drive in Beverly Hills. They can load up on fashionable gowns and designer attaché cases at any number of swank shops in the giant South Coast Plaza retail center. Sports fans can get their fill of split-finger fastballs and blindside blocks at Anaheim Stadium, home to both the California Angels and the team that still calls itself the Los Angeles Rams. Expensive restaurants are mushrooming in the counties around Washington. "You don't have to go downtown to get a nice piece of veal anymore," says Mike Gorsage, a real estate executive in Tysons Corner. "That was something the suburbs really lacked, but it's changing." Salesmen calling on the many new or expanding businesses in those suburbs can bypass Washington and put up overnight in any of 6,760 Fairfax County hotel rooms; 1,452 have been added just in the past two years, and another 1,532 are scheduled to open in 1987.

Some other amenities are still sadly lacking. Multiplex movie theaters are shooting up almost as rapidly as offices, banks and stores, but many megacounty residents still have to drive into the city for a play or ballet or symphony. Indeed, social life often revolves around the shopping mall. "The mall is the center of the county," says Sara Strelitz, a Gwinnett housewife. "People go there to meet and shop." Growth and corporate transfers mean new neighbors almost every year, and some megacounty residents complain that they lack the camaraderie found in the old bedroom suburbs.

Still, many people flocking into the megacounties consider them a close-to-ideal blend of city and suburb. "There are few things you can't do here within an hour," says Orange County Teacher Greg Hickman. "You can head to the mountains, the desert, the water or a shopping center." Agrees Gemma Turi, a public relations consultant who switched from commuting into Los Angeles to a new job in Irvine, near her home in Newport: "It's like being on vacation except you get to live here."

But other aspects of suburban life are not in the least like being on vacation, and some burgeoning problems could even put a stop to the phenomenal growth. Among the worst:

CONGESTION. Traffic snarls are the No. 1 gripe everywhere. Offices and beaches may be close by, but getting to them can be as time consuming and nerve jangling as making the haul between suburb and city. During a stifling spring heat wave two weeks ago, one couple in Long Island's fast-growing Suffolk County took 1 hr. 15 min. to sweat through 15 miles of bumper-to-bumper traffic between their home and the ocean beachfront of Robert

Moses State Park. Du Page County's Morton Arboretum, a popular spot for local outings, is becoming a walled fortress. Managers are erecting a series of 40-ft.-high earth berms to protect the trees and shrubs from the lethal effect of de-icing salt splashed up by heavy traffic on the neighboring tollway. Mark Baldassare, a sociologist at the University of California at Irvine, predicts that by the 21st century Orange County traffic will become so hopelessly jammed that "the people in Irvine, for example, will rarely decide to go to another village. They will stay in their own small areas."

LABOR SHORTAGES. Unemployment rates in the megacounties are phenomenally low: less than 3% in Fairfield County, Conn., for instance. Middle managers and computer programmers can be enticed by high salaries, but where to find the laborers to build the new offices, the clerks to staff the stores, the pump jockeys to keep the cars running? Not from the local working class; in many communities there is none. Manual and low-paid clerical workers cannot afford the housing prices (Orange County median price for a new home: $125,000); indeed, many of the children who grow up in those houses must move elsewhere when they start their own families. And residents fearing still greater congestion fight bitterly and usually successfully against construction of low-cost, high-density apartments.

Labor shortages are so acute in Fairfax County that the new hotels are recruiting at local senior citizen centers. The American Automobile Association has announced that it will move its national headquarters from Fairfax County to Orlando in 1989. The reasons, said the AAA, were the difficulty of finding enough clerical workers in Fairfax and, of all things, traffic congestion.

Some employers are attempting to import workers from the central cities, where unemployment rates can be triple those of the suburban counties. AT&T uses a fleet of buses to pick up mostly black manual workers at a subway station on the edge of Atlanta and ferry them to its plants and offices in Gwinnett County. But not many city workers can afford to drive to low-paying suburban jobs, and public transportation in most of the megacounties ranges from poor to nonexistent. In Fairfield County, traveling the 20 miles from Shelton to Norwalk means taking seven different buses and paying 75¢ on each; besides that, the schedules rarely mesh.

MIXED-UP GOVERNMENT. The power structure of megacounties is a kind of elective feudalism: a series of petty neighboring baronies lacking the authority and, frequently, the will to police development. "Essentially, we're a city without municipal governance," complains Jack Knuepfer, chairman of the Du Page County board. "We're a city with 35 municipalities, nine townships and only the Lord knows how many special districts: fire districts, sanitary districts, school districts." The county government has been unable to prevent its component communities from fol-lowing what Knuepfer describes as a "beggar thy neighbor" policy.

Standout example: the village of Oak Brook does not like the glitzy 31-story office tower designed by Architect Helmut Jahn any more than Joann Murphy does. But neighboring Oakbrook Terrace gladly let a developer put it up—right on the border between the two communities. Then Oak Brook refused to widen a road running to one side of the building, even though the developer offered to pay for the work. Its argument: Oakbrook Terrace would get all the tax advantages of the new building, so let Oakbrook Terrace widen one of its own roads and choke on the ensuing traffic. Says Oak Brook Village President Wence Cerne: "By turning residential streets into arterials, you're denigrating the quality of life. Some of these communities keep approving and approving and approving, and by the time the traffic effects are seen, it's too late."

In Orange County, Community Activist Russ Burkett grouses about inadequate funding for such basic services as police protection and sewage systems in addition to transportation. Says he: "The landholders have such powerful control that they dictate policy for the entire county. They got rich by developing the land, but now they don't want to pay for all the services we need." Burkett has formed a group, Orange County Tomorrow, that plans to initiate a ballot proposal to stop growth in areas where traffic does not move freely.

The most disturbing trend in the rise of the megacounties, however, may be the increasing racial polarization it brings to American society. Says Gary Orfield, a political scientist

Modern suburbia: housing fields in Orange County, Calif.

at the University of Chicago: ''We've got these enormously affluent outer suburban areas that are almost 100% white growing at a tremendous rate. They are drawing not only the upper-income jobs but other jobs—in construction, for example—that might be available to people without high levels of education. These jobs are becoming completely inaccessible to the black and Hispanic people in our metropolitan areas; they are in another world.'' In their own way, Orfield adds, the megacounty whites are isolated too: ''A great many people who will be leaders will have grown up in these suburbs. They are going to have no skills in relating to or communicating with minorities.''

Unhealthy or not, the trend to suburbanization appears unstoppable. Pierre deVise, professor of public administration at Roosevelt University in Chicago, has this message for megacounty residents: You are already living in ''the future white community of the U.S.'' Twenty years after the Kerner Commission report predicted that the U.S. was resegregating itself into two separate and unequal societies, megacounties are threatening to confirm that disturbing thesis.

—By George J. Church.
Reported by Steven Holmes/Fairfax County and
J. Madeleine Nash/Du Page County

Du Page County, Illinois

When the East-West Tollway linking Du Page County to Chicago was completed in 1958, recalls County Resident Charlie Thurston, motorists on the highway could still see horsemen riding to the hounds through what is now the booming business center of Oak Brook. The tollway, which set the stage for the county's explosive growth, has become the main artery for the recently christened Illinois Research and Development Corridor. In addition to the high-tech facilities of AT&T, Amoco, ITT and Miles Scientific, Du Page is home to the federally funded Argonne National Laboratory and the Fermi National Accelerator Laboratory.

Situated just 15 miles west of Chicago's Loop and adjacent to Chicago-O'Hare International Airport, Du Page is dotted with well-manicured office complexes, including the national headquarters of McDonald's Corp. The county's population, 300,000 in 1960, has climbed to 700,000, and modern developments have come to outnumber villages of Victorian homes. Although residents are fighting to maintain the small-town character of communities like Wheaton and Glen Ellyn, the task is not easy: Naperville (pop. 70,000) features a river walk complete with covered bridge that harks back to its more bucolic past, but the corporate executives who live there are so prone to transfers that the average stay in town is just under three years.

QUESTIONS AND ACTIVITIES

Comprehension Questions

1. When did suburbanization in the United States begin? What was its main characteristic?

2. What factors have contributed to the growth of megacounties?

3. Why was 1975 an important year for construction?

4. How many people commute to central cities from the suburbs? How many people commute from one suburb to another?

5. What amenities are missing from life in the megacounties?

6. What are the three major problems facing residents of megacounties?

Discussion Questions

1. In the place where you currently live, is there anything similar to the megacounties described? If so, what problems exist? If not, do you expect megacounties to develop in the next 20 years? Why or why not?

2. Do you see the trend toward megacounties as a positive, negative, or neutral one in U.S. society? Explain your answer.

3. Would you like to live in a megacounty such as the ones described in the article? Why or why not?

Group Activities

Have the class divide into three groups. Each group should select one of the three problems of megacounties identified in the article. With your group, discuss solutions to the problem. Be prepared to present them to the class.

Individual Work

Write several paragraphs (one page maximum) describing what you think is the ideal place to live. You may wish to include such information as

    a. number of residents
    b. distance from a large city
    c. amenities

Article Seven

BACKGROUND NOTES

for **When Women Vie with Women**

Preview

Women in management and professional positions often find that their chief competition is from other women. The sisterhood of the 1970s may have been replaced by the rivalry of the 1980s.

Culture

feminist: a person who believes in the social, political, and economic equality of the sexes. Feminists were very active in the 1960s and 1970s.

Giorgio ['dʒɔrˌdʒio]**:** a brand of very expensive perfume. Giorgio is often associated with wealth and snobbishness.

Ms.: a term of address for women used instead of Miss or Mrs. (e.g., Ms. Smith). **Ms.** is considered by feminists to be the equivalent of **Mr.** since it does not indicate whether the person is married or single.

sister: another woman (not one's real sister). Feminists often refer to other women as sisters in order to create a feeling of unity.

women's movement: feminism; a movement to improve the social, political, and economic status of women. This movement was particularly strong in the 1960s and 1970s.

Vocabulary

affront [ə'frənt]**:** an insult; an offending remark or act

allegiance [ə'lidʒəns]**:** loyalty; obligation. Today's professional women may have less allegiance to their female colleagues than they used to.

assertiveness: extremely confident actions; aggressiveness. Now that more women are climbing the corporate ladder, they are showing the same assertiveness as their male colleagues.

barracuda [ˌbɛrə'kudə]**:** a type of saltwater fish. Barracuda are vicious predators.

competitive: characterized by rivalry; appearing as if one were in a contest with another person. People working together may be cooperative or competitive.

pamphleteering [ˌpæm(p)flə'tɪrɪŋ]**:** distributing pamphlets or small booklets of information about a particular topic. Supporters of a cause often use pamphleteering to publicize their message.

rapier ['reˌpiəʳ]**:** a light, two-edged sword associated with dueling

reprimand ['rɛprəˌmænd]**:** to scold; to blame someone strongly for his or her actions

sabotage ['sæbəˌtɑʒ]**:** to obstruct another's work; to do something deliberately so that another person's efforts will fail

scoff [skɔf]**:** to ridicule; to belittle

scurry ['skɚi]**:** to move quickly; to move in an agitated manner

spite: ill will; malicious treatment of someone believed to have wronged one

testimonial: evidence; information in support of a person or an idea

venom ['vɛnəm]**:** literally, a poison produced by certain animals, such as snakes; here, serious ill will directed at others

vie [vaɪ]**:** to compete; to contend

When Women Vie with Women

The sisterhood finds rivalry and envy can be the price of success

Laurie Bernstein well remembers starting at a small Southern law firm and getting distinctly icy treatment from the only other woman lawyer on the staff. When Bernstein was given one of her female colleague's cases to handle, resentment turned to spite: Bernstein discovered that she was not getting the court documents, letters and other important papers she needed to handle the case. Late one evening she and a senior partner found the missing material hidden in the woman's mailbox. Ms. Sabotage was severely reprimanded. "I felt terrible," recalls Bernstein, 30. "I had expected a camaraderie to emerge between the two of us as the only female lawyers at the firm. But quite the opposite occurred."

Now, hold on a minute. This is not the way it was supposed to be. All of that demonstrating and pamphleteering in the early '70s was supposed to have helped women move into professional and managerial jobs without resorting to destructive behavior. But as more women rise in the corporate power structure, they are discovering, much to their dismay, that they are not always sisters under the skin after all. In fact, many of them are acting suspiciously like . . . well . . . *men.* "Now women are encouraged to be as aggressive as men on the job," write Psychotherapists Luise Eichenbaum and Susie Orbach, co-authors of the just published book *Between Women: Love, Envy, and Competition in Women's Friendships* (Viking; $17.95).

The authors, who like many feminists have spent years trying to open corporate doors, are trying to comprehend the world they have entered. Female bonds are being broken, they say, as women discover that "the feelings of competition and envy, the scurry for approval, the wish to be acknowledged and noticed by other women are now a part of their daily work lives." Nor do some younger women seem to care much about feminist ideals. "I see a lot less concern among younger women about sticking together," declares Nancy Ferree-Clark, associate minister at Duke University. "They don't feel the allegiance to the women's movement that older women do. They say, 'Gee, that's passé. I can make it on my own.'"

Things can get pretty nasty behind the Escada suits and the hint of Giorgio perfume, if Author Judith Briles is to be believed. In her recently published book, *Woman to Woman: From Sabotage to Support* (New Horizon Press; $18.95), she sets down nearly 300 pages of testimonials supporting the hypothesis that

women are attacking women in the workplace with carefully veiled venom and viciousness. "If women are going to sabotage someone, it's more likely to be another woman than a man," declares Briles, 42, a former Palo Alto, Calif., stockbroker.

Many women scoff at this portrait of the female barracuda maneuvering her way around corporate reefs. "I have found a tremendous amount of helping and generosity among the women in my industry," says Mary McCarthy, 42, a senior vice president at MGM/UA Communications in Beverly Hills. Lawyers Renée Berliner Rush, 31, and Julie Anne Banon, 32, say they became best friends while working for

a Manhattan executive-search firm. "From the day we began working together, we believed that the way to succeed was to work with and help each other, not to work against each other," says Rush. The two women now run their own headhunting firm for lawyers.

Perhaps reality lies somewhere between the rapier thrust and the sympathetic ear. There may be a tendency for women to be more jealous of one another than men are of their colleagues, says Niles Newton, a behavioral scientist at Northwestern Medical School. That stems, she thinks, "from insecurities because they haven't been in the workplace as long as

men." Assertiveness and rivalry also make many women feel uncomfortable, "and it becomes much more a problem in the workplace, where they are a natural occurrence," says Anne Frenkel, a social worker with the Chicago Women's Therapy Collective. "Women have to understand that being competitive with someone doesn't mean you don't like them. Men can be competitive and still be friends."

Still, friendships between women—what Simone de Beauvoir called that "warm and frivolous intimacy"—are too often the casualties of success these days. Eichenbaum, 35, and Orbach, 41, are concerned that "in the world of every-woman-for-herself, the old support systems can be tragically undermined." That sometimes happens when women win promotions and find themselves supervising women who were once close friends. "I tend not to have relationships with women I supervise," says Kathy Schrier, 40, a union administrator in Manhattan. "Some women can't make that break, though, and it hurts them as managers."

Other women have problems relating to their female bosses. Even though MGM/UA's McCarthy has high praise for her female colleagues, she admits that in the past she has "felt sabotaged" by executive secretaries. "It was jealousy of my position from someone on a lower level," she says. Corporate Lawyer Deborah Dugan, 29, recalls that when she joined a Los Angeles law firm, her assigned female secretary "refused to work for me. She said she would have trouble taking orders from another female."

How can women cope with these conflicts? Chicago's Frenkel believes professional women must stop taking another woman's success as a personal affront. "They have to separate out business from personal issues," she says. For some women, that's impossible, as Laura Srebnik, 33, a Manhattan computer educator, discovered when she suddenly found herself supervising a "dear friend" at a political lobbying group. The friend, she says, became hostile, talked about her behind her back and then quit. The parting explanation, says Srebnik, was "that I had become one of 'them'"—the power structure. For some women in the workplace, that is still the ultimate insult.

By David Brand.
Reported by Andrea Sachs/New York, with other bureaus

QUESTIONS AND ACTIVITIES

Comprehension Questions

1. How does the article characterize the relationship between women in professional and managerial jobs?

2. Are there exceptions to the pattern of behavior described in the article? Give a specific example.

3. What sometimes happens when one woman in a friendship is promoted and becomes the supervisor of the other?

Discussion Questions

1. In your home culture, is it common for women to hold high professional and managerial jobs? If so, do you believe there is any rivalry between the women, or are they supportive of one another?

2. Why do you think that younger women today do not support the ideals of the women's movement?

Group Activities

Have the class divide into two groups. Each group should choose one of the following positions:

a. Rivalry among women in the workplace is an inevitable result of their climbing the corporate ladder.

b. The rivalry described in the article is typical of women who work together, but not of men.

Discuss the position in your group and then present evidence for the position to the opposing group.

Individual Work

1. Interview a women who holds a professional or managerial position. Ask if she has found her female colleagues to be supportive or competitive. If possible, have her give a specific example to support her answer.

2. Interview a man who holds a professional or managerial position. Ask if he has found his male colleagues to be supportive or competitive. If possible, have him give a specific example to support his answer.

Education

Article One

BACKGROUND NOTES

for **"Great Human Power or Magic"**

Preview

Children across the country are learning to write more effectively. They owe their success to their teachers who were trained at the Bread Loaf School of English.

Culture

Cheyenne [ˌʃaɪ'æn]: a group of people native to the western plains of North America

Eskimo: a group of people native to northern Canada and the state of Alaska; an individual member of this group. Eskimos often live in remote villages.

Fourth of July: Independence Day; the date that marks the independence of the United States from Great Britain in 1776. Fourth of July picnics and parades are held in towns throughout the country.

prep school: a private secondary school, often a boarding school. Prep, short for preparatory, schools "prepare" a student for university studies.

reservation: an area of land reserved by the federal government for use by the various Indian nations.

Sioux [su]: a group of people native to the central parts of North America. Major groups of the Sioux are the Lakota, Dakota, and Nakota.

Vocabulary

brainstorming: developing creative and useful ideas in a group. When members of a group brainstorm, they often produce more ideas than people do working independently.

cobbler: a kind of fruit pie with a thick top crust. "Selling like hot cobblers" is based on the phrase "selling like hotcakes," an expression used for anything that sells very well.

courtship: the period of time spent by a couple before their engagement and marriage

defray [də'fre]: to assist in the payment of something; to lessen the cost of something by contributing to the payment

devise [də'vaɪz]: to invent; to develop

elite [ə'lit]: a socially superior group; the best part of something

grist: interesting or valuable ideas that can be used as the basis of a story. Grist originally referred to grain for grinding at a mill.

hookup: a connection, often electrical, between various parts of something

legend ['lɛdʒənd]: a story from the past, often passed from generation to generation by storytellers. Many legends of the tribal groups in the United States have never been written down.

lore: a body of knowledge of a people; traditional beliefs of a group of people

skill and drill: a method of teaching writing that focuses on technical skills, not content

tribe: a group of people who share a common heritage and function as a social unit. Major tribes still in existence in the United States are the Cherokee, the Navajo, the Sioux, and the Ojibwa.

word processor: a computer program used mainly for writing letters, articles, and other texts. Many U.S. schools now use word processors in the classroom.

Teachers from around the country in class at Bread Loaf

"Great Human Power or Magic"

An innovative program sparks the writing of America's children

As school starts this fall in Tununak, a tiny Eskimo community on the windswept coast of Alaska, Teacher Ben Orr is planning to invite elderly storytellers into the classroom so his young students can learn and then write down traditional legends and lore of their vanishing culture. For Donna Maxim's third-graders in Boothbay, Me., writing will become a tool in science and social studies as students record observations, questions and reactions about what they discover each day. In Eagle Butte, S.D., Geri Gutwein has designed a writing project in which her ninth-grade students exchange letters with third-graders about stories they have read together. This year a few of her students will sit with Cheyenne women who tell tales as they knit together, their heritage becoming grist for today's young writers.

Although these teachers are separated by thousands of miles, their methods of trying to encourage children to write spring from a common source: the Bread Loaf School of English. There, near Vermont's Middlebury College, grade school and high school teachers give up part of their vacations each summer to spend six weeks brainstorming, studying and trading experiences as they try to devise new methods of getting their pupils to write. Says Dixie Goswami, a Clemson University English professor who heads Bread Loaf's program in writing: "We have nothing against 'skill-and-drill' writing curricula, except they don't work." Instead, Bread Loaf graduates have quietly created one of the nation's most inventive programs to encourage student writers.

The Bread Loaf literature and writing program began in 1920 as a summer retreat where English teachers studied for advanced degrees. Until the late 1970s most were teachers from élite Eastern prep schools. Bread Loaf "was failing in its social responsibility," says Paul Cubeta, a Middlebury humanities professor who has directed the program since 1965. "So we went looking in rural America for potential educational leaders." Foundation funds were raised to help defray the $2,500 cost for tuition and board. Over the past ten years nearly 500 rural instructors have studied in the shadow of the distinctly flattened mountain that gives the school its name. This summer 73 came to Bread Loaf from small towns in 32 states.

Bread Loafers are convinced that children are inspired to write well when they have information to communicate. In Gilbert, S.C., for instance, students interviewed old-timers to discover what life in their small towns was like many decades ago. The students' narrative accounts, vividly describing everything from butter making to courtship and marriage, were published in a magazine they named *Sparkleberry*. This summer at Gilbert's Fourth of July Peach Festival, the homemade magazines sold like hot cobblers.

Many of the new ideas that teachers took away from Bread Loaf seemed in danger of withering back home, remembers Cubeta. "We needed to devise a way for them to go back with support for their projects and for each other." One result was an idea called BreadNet: by setting up a network of word

processors, Bread Loaf-trained teachers could instantaneously connect their classrooms. Last year the project lifted off when a charitable trust donated $1.5 million for that and other programs.

The new national hookup provided evidence for another Bread Loaf belief: children will write freshly when given a new audience. Students in the tiny ranching community of Wilsall, Mont., began writing to children in Pittsburgh about farm life in winter. "Cows aren't smart enough to paw through the snow like horses, so you have to feed them," one child explained. A Sioux student on a reservation in South Dakota wrote candidly about what is happening to one branch of the tribe: "Life for the Lakota people is going in a downward direction . . . To control it would take great human power or magic."

This fall 68 teachers in 33 states will be able to send their students' writing electronically into distant classrooms. Later in the year, the fourth edition of *Voices Across the Wires*, a student-edited collection of BreadNet writing, will be published. "Having real situations to write about has really changed their attitude," says Joanne Tulonen, whose Wilsall students were among the first to use BreadNet. "Before, their writing was artificial. Now they see themselves as people with information worth sharing."

By Melissa Ludtke/Bread Loaf

QUESTIONS AND ACTIVITIES

Comprehension Questions

1. What was the original purpose of the Bread Loaf literature and writing program?

2. Who now attends the six-week summer sessions?

3. What kinds of writing projects are the students in the article involved in?

Discussion Questions

1. The article states that children write well when they have information to communicate. What does this statement mean? Do you agree with it? Why or why not?

2. The article also states that children write freshly when they have a new audience. Do you agree with this position? Why or why not?

Group Activities

1. In groups of five or six, imagine that you are writing teachers participating in the summer training program at Bread Loaf. Brainstorm a list of at least five writing projects or topics appropriate for secondary school or college students.

2. With the whole class, compile a master list of the 10 most interesting projects or topics the small groups have produced in their brainstorming sessions.

Individual Work

1. Choose one of the 10 topics identified in Group Activity 2. Make an outline of the procedures you would follow to complete the project.

2. Using the topic you just selected, complete the project from the outline.

BACKGROUND NOTES

for **The New Whiz Kids**

Preview

Asian-American students are outperforming all other groups in the nation's high schools and colleges. Their success, however, is sometimes accompanied by problems.

Culture

Charlie Chan: the main character in a series of novels written by Earl Derr Biggers in the 1920s and 1930s and in several movies based on the novels. Chan was a Chinese detective who solved his cases by understanding people's characters.

freshman: a student in his or her first year of secondary school or college. After freshman year, the student becomes a sophomore, then a junior, and finally a senior.

grade-point average: the numerical average of one's grades. Grade-point averages are an important measure of students' achievements in U.S. high schools, colleges, and universities.

liberal arts: studies in a college or university designed to provide general knowledge and to develop the intellect. Philosophy, history, languages, and literature belong to the liberal arts curriculum.

SAT ['ɛs'e'ti]: the Scholastic Aptitude Test; an examination given to secondary school seniors who wish to enroll in a college or university. Scores on this test range from 200 to 800.

"yellow peril": the irrational belief that Asians represent a danger to U.S. society. The now repealed Chinese Exclusion Act of 1882, which limited the immigration of Chinese, is an example of this fear.

Vocabulary

aspiration: a strong desire to achieve something

assimilation: the process of becoming a part of another cultural group. Assimilation is often a long and difficult procedure.

astonishing [ə'stɑnəʃɪŋ]: surprising; amazing

discrimination: the act of treating a group differently than other groups; the act of treating an individual differently than other individuals because he or she is a member of a particular group. Discrimination may be overt or very subtle.

gauge [geʤ]: an estimation; a measurement according to some standard

harassment ['hɛrəsmənt]: a continual annoyance; a persistent bothering

homework: academic work assigned to students to be done outside the classroom. Students sometimes complain that they have too much homework to do.

Education

immigrant [ˈɪməgrənt]: a person who enters a country for the purpose of living there. Immigrants sometimes enter a country illegally.

I.Q.: intelligence quotient; the measure of one's intelligence as indicated by a score on a particular type of test. The validity of I.Q. scores is somewhat controversial.

mainstream: belonging to the majority group

maniacal [məˈnaɪəkəl]: characterized by excessive enthusiasm

mired: bogged down; stuck; overcome; overwhelmed

ostracism [ˈɑstrəˌsɪzəm]: the act of excluding individuals socially

pace: rate of movement; rate of progress

peer [pɪr]: a person of equal standing with another

prestigious [prəˈstidʒəs]: having prestige; having high standing; honored

quota [ˈkwodə]: a number or amount of something, thought to represent an appropriate share. Quotas are sometimes used in making employment decisions.

refugee [ˈrɛfjuˌdʒi]: a person who flees his or her country to find safety elsewhere. Refugees may leave their countries for political, religious, or economic reasons.

rejection: the act of denying or refusing

resentment [ˌriˈzɛntmənt]: displeasure resulting from a perceived wrong or injury

sacrifice [ˈsækrəˌfaɪs]: something given up in order to achieve a goal; something lost in order to maintain a belief. Parents often make sacrifices for their children.

stereotype [ˈstɛrioˌtaɪp]: something conforming to a pattern; an overly simplified view of a person or a group of people. The stereotype of American tourists is that they chew gum, carry cameras, wear gaudy clothing, and talk loudly.

submerged: hidden; buried, as if by water

tantamount [ˈtæn(t)əˌmaʊnt]: equivalent; the same as

vandalism: destruction of property. Vandalism is sometimes directed against particular groups of people.

vexing: puzzling; distressing

whiz kid: an extremely intelligent young person

willpower: determination; strong intentions

zealous [ˈzɛləs]: extremely eager; fervent

The New Whiz Kids

Why Asian Americans are doing so well, and what it costs them

Some are refugees from sad countries torn apart by war. Others are children of the stable middle class whose parents came to the U.S. in search of a better life. Some came with nothing, not even the rudiments of English. Others came with skills and affluence. Many were born in the U.S. to immigrant parents.

No matter what their route, young Asian Americans, largely those with Chinese, Korean and Indochinese backgrounds, are setting the educational pace for the rest of America and cutting a dazzling figure at the country's finest schools. Consider some of this fall's freshman classes: at Brown it will be 9% Asian American, at Harvard nearly 14%, the Massachusetts Institute of Technology 20%, the California Institute of Technology 21% and the University of California, Berkeley an astonishing 25%.

By almost every educational gauge, young Asian Americans are soaring. They are finishing way above the mean on the math section of the Scholastic Aptitude Test and, according to one comprehensive study of San Diego-area students, outscoring their peers of other races in high school grade-point averages. They spend more time on their homework, a researcher at the U.S. Department of Education found, take more advanced high school courses and graduate with more credits than other American students. A higher percentage of these young people complete high school and finish college than do white American students. Trying to explain why so many Asian-American students are superachievers, Harvard Psychology Professor Jerome Kagan comes up with this simple answer: "To put it plainly, they work harder."

All this would appear to be another success story for the American dream, an example of the continuing immigrant urge to succeed and of the nation's ability to thrive on the dynamism of its new citizens. But there is also a troubling side to the story. Asian Americans consider the "model minority" image a misleading stereotype that masks individuality and conceals real problems. Many immigrant families, especially the Indochinese refugees who arrived in the years following the fall of Saigon in 1975, remain mired in poverty. Their war-scarred children, struggling with a new language and culture, often drop out of school. Further, the majority of Asian-American students do not reach the starry heights of the celebrated few, and an alarming number are pushing themselves to the emotional brink in their quest for excellence. Many also detect signs of resentment among non-Asians, an updated "yellow peril" fear. In particular, the country's best universities are accused of setting admissions quotas to restrict the numbers of Asian Americans on campus.

Even with these problems, many Asian-American students are making the U.S. education system work better for them than it has for any other immigrant group since the arrival of East European Jews began in the 1880s. Like the Asians, the Jews viewed education as the ticket to success. Both groups "feel an obligation to excel intellectually," says New York University Mathematician Sylvain Cappell, who as a Jewish immigrant feels a kinship with his Asian-American students. The two groups share a powerful belief in the value of hard work and a zealous regard for the role of the family.

The term Asian American covers a variety of national, cultural and religious heritages. In only two decades Asian Americans have become the fastest-growing U.S. minority, numbering more than 5 million, or about 2% of the population; in 1960 the figures were 891,000 and 0.5%. Then in 1965 a new immigration law did away with exclusionary quotas. That brought a surge of largely middle-class Asian professionals—doctors, engineers and academics from Hong Kong, Taiwan, South Korea, India and the Philippines—seeking economic opportunity. In 1975, after the end of the Viet Nam War, 130,000 refugees, mostly from the educated middle class, began arriving. Three years later a second wave of 650,000 Indochinese started their journey from rural and poor areas to refugee camps to the towns and cities of America.

As the children of these immigrants began moving up through the nation's schools, it became clear that a new class of academic

achievers was emerging. One dramatic indication: since 1981, 20 Asian-American students have been among the 70 scholarship winners in the Westinghouse Science Talent Search, the nation's oldest and most prestigious high school science competition. One of this year's 40 finalists—out of 1,295 entrants—was Taiwan-born David Kuo, 17, of New York City. The name is a familiar one to the competition's organizers: David's brothers John and Mark were finalists in 1985 and 1986. "My parents always equated a good education with doing well in life, so we picked up on that," says David.

Such achievements are reflected in the nation's best universities, where math, science and engineering departments have taken on a decidedly Asian character. At the University of Washington, 20% of all engineering students are of Asian descent; at Berkeley the figure is 40%. To win these places, Asian-American students make the SAT seem as easy as taking a driving test. Indeed, 70% of Asian-American 18-year-olds took the SAT in 1985, in contrast to only 28% of all 18-year-olds. The average math score of Asian-American high school seniors that year was 518 (of a possible 800), 43 points higher than the general average.

This inclination for math and science is partly explained by the fact that Asian-American students who began their educations abroad arrived in the U.S. with a solid grounding in math but little or no knowledge of English. They are also influenced by the promise of a good job after college. "Asians feel there will be less discrimination in areas like math and science because they will be judged more objectively," says Shirley Hune, an education professor at Hunter College. And, she notes, the return on the investment in education "is more immediate in something like engineering than with a liberal arts degree."

The stereotype of Asian Americans as narrow mathematical paragons is unfair, however, and inaccurate. Many are far from being liberal arts illiterates, according to a study that will be published this fall by Sociologists Ruben G. Rumbaut and Kenji Ima of San Diego State University. They found that in overall grade-point averages, virtually every Asian-American group outscored the city's white high school juniors and seniors. Many Asian-American students excel in the arts, from photography to music. New York City's famed Juilliard School has a student body estimated to be 25% Asian and Asian American. Juilliard President Joseph Polisi rejects the view that Asian students are uniquely talented. "It's not just being Asian that makes them good musicians," he says. "It's a matter of dedication, family support and discipline."

Successful Asian-American students commonly credit the influence of parents who are determined that their children take full advantage of what the American educational system has to offer. For many parents, personal sacrifice is involved. Daniel Pak, an 18-year-old from Dallas entering Harvard next month,

shines in everything he does, from math to violin. His brother Tony, 20, is studying physics at M.I.T. Their parents had such colleges in mind when they moved to the U.S. in 1970. The boys' father gave up his career as a professor of German literature in South Korea. Unable to get an academic position in the U.S., he eventually found work as a house painter.

A telling measure of parental attention is homework. A 1984 study of San Francisco-area schools by Stanford Sociologist Sanford Dornbusch found that Asian-American students put in an average of eleven hours a week, compared with seven hours by other students. Westinghouse Prizewinner John Kuo recalls that in Taiwan he was accustomed to studying two or three hours a night. "Here we had half an hour at the most." To make up the difference, John and his two brothers were often given extra assignments at home. "Asian parents spend much more time with their children than American parents do, and it helps," says his brother David.

Some Asian Americans may be pushing their children too hard. Says a Chinese-American high schooler in New York City: "When you get an 80, they say, 'Why not an 85?' If you get an 85, it's 'Why not a 90?'" Many Asian-American parents even dictate their children's college courses, with an eye to a desirable future. New York City Youth Counselor Amy Lee, 26, remembers that when she changed her field from premed to psychology, her parents were upset, but pressed her at least to get a Ph.D. "They wanted a doctor in the family, and they didn't care what kind it was."

Many Asian Americans come from an educated élite in their native countries. Their children seem to do especially well. Julian Stanley, a Johns Hopkins psychology professor, studied 292 preteen high scorers on the math portion of the SAT, nearly a quarter of them Asian Americans. He found that 71% of the Asian-Americans' fathers and 21% of their mothers had a doctorate or a medical degree, vs. 39% of the fathers and 10% of the mothers of the non-Asians.

How then to explain the accomplishment of children whose refugee parents were less well educated? One claim is that Asians are simply smarter than other groups. A subscriber to this theory is Arthur Jensen, a controversial Berkeley educational psychologist. Jensen tested Asian children—500 in San Francisco and 8,000 in Hong Kong—then compared the results with tests of 1,000 white American children in Bakersfield, Calif. He contends that the children with Asian backgrounds averaged ten I.Q. points higher than the whites, and believes there are "genetic differences" in the rate at which Asians and whites mature mentally.

Most researchers are unconvinced by the natural-superiority argument. But many do believe there is something in Asian culture that breeds success, perhaps Confucian ideals that stress family values and emphasize education. Sociologist William Liu, of the University of Illinois at Chicago, argues that immigrants from Asian countries with the strongest Con-

fucian influence—Japan, Korea, China and Viet Nam—perform best. "The Confucian ethic," he says, "drives people to work, excel and repay the debt they owe their parents." By comparison, San Diego's Rumbaut points out, Laotians and Cambodians, who do somewhat less well, have a gentler, Buddhist approach to life.

Both the genetic and the cultural explanations for academic success worry Asian Americans because of fears that they feed racial stereotyping. Many can remember when Chinese, Japanese and Filipino immigrants were the victims of undisguised public ostracism and discriminatory laws. Indeed, it was not until 1952 that legislation giving all Asian immigrants the right to citizenship was enacted. "Years ago," complains Virginia Kee, a high school teacher in New York's Chinatown, "they used to think you were Fu Manchu or Charlie Chan. Then they thought you must own a laundry or restaurant. Now they think all we know how to do is sit in front of a computer." Says Thomas Law, a student at Brooklyn Law School: "We're sick and tired of being seen as the exotic Orientals."

The performance of Asian Americans also triggers resentment and tension. "Anti-Asian activity in the form of violence, vandalism, harassment and intimidation continues to occur across the nation," the U.S. Civil Rights Commission declared last year. The situation can be particularly rough in inner-city schools. Young immigrant Asians complain that they are called "Chink" or "Chop Suey" and are constantly threatened. At New York City's Washington Irving High School, for example, there were reports last year of some 40 incidents of harassment and violence against Asian-American students.

To Asian-American activists, one of the most serious signs of discrimination is the admissions quotas they believe leading universities have established. "If you are an Asian-American student applying to Harvard, you have the lowest chance of getting in," says Peter Kiang, who teaches Asian-American studies at the University of Massachusetts, Boston. John Bunzel, a senior research fellow at the Hoover Institution, a conservative think tank at Stanford, says he has found indications that Stanford, Harvard, Princeton and Brown discriminate against Asian Americans in their admissions policy.

The recent case of Yat-Pang Au has intensified the debate. A straight-A student, Yat-Pang, 18, lettered in cross-country, was elected a justice on the school supreme court and last June graduated first in his class at San Jose's Gunderson High School. Berkeley turned him down. Watson M. Laetsch, Berkeley's vice chancellor for undergraduate affairs, insists that Yat-Pang was rejected only for a "highly competitive" engineering program. Had he applied to other colleges at Berkeley, "very likely he would have been accepted." Instead, Yat-Pang will study electrical engineering at DeAnza College near his home, and hopes to reapply to Berkeley for his junior year.

Satia Tor

A trauma of our times

As he talks about entering Stanford University next month as a freshman, Satia, 19, beams with optimism. But behind the smiles is the haunting memory of the horrors he witnessed during the ravaging of Cambodia by the Khmer Rouge in the 1970s. Today, when he recalls the killing fields, his eyes turn away in pain. "I wake up some mornings," he says, "and wonder if it was a dream or reality."

Satia was only seven when the Khmer Rouge took him away from his parents and twelve brothers and sisters. For the next $3\frac{1}{2}$ years he was part of a migrant child-labor force. The children were starved and beaten; some were forced to shoot their own parents or were murdered themselves. After the Vietnamese invaded Cambodia in late 1978, Satia made his way through minefields to a refugee camp in Thailand, where he was reunited with Sahieng, one of his sisters. When Sahieng and her husband immigrated to the U.S., Satia joined them. He went to Hawaii, where in 1984, he won a scholarship to the prestigious Iolani School; two years later he received another scholarship, to Phillips Academy, the prep school in Andover, Mass.

Until three years ago, he had assumed that his parents were dead. Then he received a letter from them, saying that the couple had reached the camp in Thailand. After exhaustive efforts, including letters to Senators, Satia managed to bring his parents to the U.S. This June the three were reunited at Satia's graduation in Andover.

His teachers say that bright, articulate Satia is marked for success. But the chilling memories of childhood cannot be erased. Once, in Hawaii, he won a contest with an essay about his experiences. Its title: "Cambodian Boys Can't Cry."

One vexing dilemma of the Yat-Pang case is not in dispute. Young Asian Americans tend to target the best schools, which have limited places even for students submitting top marks. While choosing this fall's freshman class, for example, Berkeley turned away 2,200 students from all backgrounds who had perfect grades.

To be that good and face rejection is tough for anyone, but seems more difficult for many Asian Americans. "They have almost a maniacal attitude that if they just work hard enough, they can do it," says Counselor Ilse Junod of New York's Baruch College. To some Asian Americans (and their parents), being only "very good" is tantamount to failure. In 1982, Leakhena Chan, a Cambodian student at South Boston High School, overwhelmed by the pressure of school and adjustment to a new country, tried to take her own life. She was one of eight Cambodians at South Boston who attempted suicide that year. Now a student at Lesley College in Cambridge, Mass., Leakhena can talk openly about the desperation that overcomes many Asian Americans who feel they cannot attain the academic success they expect of themselves. "I go to bed at 1 or 2 and get up early to study. You study so hard and still you don't have enough time to complete all the work. For me, whatever I do, I want to be perfect."

For Cambodians, in particular, stress also results from terrible memories of killing, torture and starvation as the Khmer Rouge savaged their country. The nightmare of those years, says Psychologist Jeanne Nidorf of the University of California at San Diego, produces a "posttraumatic stress disorder that just doesn't go away."

Asking for help is not easy for Asian Americans. "They are likely to say that willpower can resolve problems," explains Psychologist Stanley Sue, who has specialized in their emotional difficulties. He has found that the problems of these young people "are highly submerged" because they have been "taught not to exhibit emotions in public." Nidorf notes that youthful Indochinese are so conditioned to polite behavior that they hesitate to complain. She recalls the case of a Cambodian girl who was given the wrong textbook but said nothing. Because she was afraid to tell the teacher about the error, she suffered for months as she tried to keep up with the class. Indeed, the view of Asian Americans as passive and obedient is a stereotype that teachers tend to reinforce by not urging students to express themselves, says Hunter College's Hune.

To these problems must be added the strain of being poor. In California, at least 50% of Indochinese immigrants are on welfare, and according to the 1980 U.S. census, more than 35% of Vietnamese families in the U.S. are living below the poverty line. One of the toughest jobs facing educators is keeping many of these young people in school. "For every success story," says Hune, "there are also a lot of average students and an increasing number of dropouts." The Boston school system knows that only too well: with an increased number of Southeast Asian teenagers, the dropout rate went up from 14.4% in 1982 to 26.5% in 1985.

Ultimately, assimilation may diminish achievement. The Rumbaut-Ima data from San Diego show lower grade-point averages for Chinese-, Korean- and Japanese-American students whose families speak primarily English at home compared with those whose families do not. The New York *Times* has reported that a Chicago study of Asian Americans found third-generation students had blended more into the mainstream, had a lower academic performance and were less interested in school.

If assimilation and other trends mean that the dramatic concentration of super-students has peaked, talented young Asian Americans have already shown that U.S. education can still produce excellence. The largely successful Asian-American experience is a challenging counterpoint to the charges that U.S. schools are now producing less-educated mainstream students and failing to help underclass blacks and Hispanics. One old lesson apparently still holds. "It really doesn't matter where you come from or what your language is," observes Educational Historian Diane Ravitch. "If you arrive with high aspirations and self-discipline, schools are a path to upward mobility." Particularly when there is a close working relationship between the school and the family. "Schools cannot do the job alone," says Ernest Boyer, president of the Carnegie Foundation. "But schools must work much harder for all parents to be partners in the process."

As for those who fear or resent Asian-American academic accomplishment, their anxieties may be understandable but are unmerited. "It seems to me that having people like this renews our own striving for excellence," observes Emmy Werner, professor of human development at the University of California at Davis. "We shouldn't be threatened, but challenged." Mathematician Cappell, part of a Jewish immigrant success story, is thrilled by the new inheritors. "Their presence," he says, "is going to be a great blessing for society."

By David Brand.
Reported by Jennifer Hull and Jeannie Park/New York and James Willwerth/Los Angeles

QUESTIONS AND ACTIVITIES

Comprehension Questions

1. What evidence is there that Asian-American students do better than other groups of students?

2. On the average, how many hours of homework do Asian-American students do each week? Compare this to the amount of time other students generally spend on their homework.

3. What cultural explanation is often given for the success of students of Asian background?

4. What are some of the negative results of the pressures in Asian families to succeed academically?

5. What are some negative results of the academic success of Asian-American students?

Discussion Questions

1. Do you think that colleges and universities should use admission quotas for different groups of students? Why or why not?

2. As a result of their academic successes, do you believe that Asian-American students are being unfairly stereotyped as "brains," especially in math and science? Explain your answer.

Group Activities

The educational psychologist Jensen believes that there are genetic differences in the intellectual capacities of different groups of people. In groups of five or six, discuss this concept to determine whether people support his position or not.

Individual Work

Write your reaction (one page maximum) to the statement given below. You may agree or disagree with it.

Academic achievement is the most important goal in my life at this time.

BACKGROUND NOTES

for **Facing Up to Sticker Shock**

Preview

Students are facing high charges for tuition and room and board at colleges and universities throughout the country. At the same time, the institutions are struggling to control expenses.

Culture

acceptance letters: letters granting admission to students who have applied to a college or university. Those students who are not accepted receive rejection letters.

college: a four-year undergraduate institution of higher education. Colleges award B.A. and B.S. degrees.

name-brand: having the brand or mark of a prestigious maker. Some people will wear only name-brand clothing and desire to be associated with the best names in clothes, cars, universities, etc.

private college: a college that is not financially supported by a state's educational system

public college: a college that belongs to and is at least partly funded by a state's educational system. Public colleges and universities are less expensive to attend than private ones.

room and board: the charge for living expenses at a college or university. The costs of housing (''room'') and food (''board'') are included.

sheepskin: a diploma; a certificate indicating that one has graduated from a college or university. Such certificates were once made from parchment or sheepskin.

sticker shock: surprise at seeing the price of something. Buyers often experience sticker shock when they learn the cost of a new automobile. (Car dealers put the price of a car on a sticker attached to the window, thus leading to the term **sticker shock**.)

student aid: financial assistance given to students by the institution or by the federal government. Student aid can take the form of scholarships or jobs at the institution.

tenured ['tɛnjəd]: having a permanent position on the faculty of a college or university. Instructors must undergo several years of evaluation before being granted tenure.

university: an institution of higher education that offers undergraduate, graduate, and professional degrees. The graduate degrees are M.A., M.S., and Ph.D.; the professional degrees are often M.D. (for medicine) and J.D. (for law).

Vocabulary

allotment: an amount of money or goods set aside for a particular purpose

analogy [əˈnælədʒi]: a likening of one thing to another

budget [ˈbədʒət]: a financial plan for a business or an individual; an amount of money that is available for a particular purpose

endowment [ˌɛnˈdɑʊmənt]: a sizable donation made to a college or university. Endowments are sometimes made for specific purposes, such as the purchase of library materials or the provision of scholarships.

enrollment: the number of students attending an institution

expenditure [əkˈspɛndətʃɚ]: an expense; an amount of money paid out for a specific purpose

fat: an excessive amount of money in a budget; the amount of money in a budget beyond what is actually needed

greed: an excessive desire to acquire money or material possessions

hardware: computer equipment. The operating programs for computers are referred to as **software.**

incentive: a motive; a reason to act

inflation: a rise in the cost of goods and services in a country's economy

mismanagement: poor control of a business; bad direction of a situation

peculiarity: an unusual trait; an uncommon characteristic

tuition [ˌtuˈɪʃən]: the fees paid to a college or university in order to take courses. Tuition is separate from room and board.

utilities [ˌjuˈtɪləˌdiz]: public services, such as gas, electricity, and water, for which fees are charged

Facing Up to Sticker Shock

As tuitions soar ahead of inflation, colleges try to explain why

These days, acceptance letters from colleges are appearing in mailboxes all across the country. No sooner are the envelopes opened than many parents turn their attention from their child's good fortune to another kind of fortune: the small one the next four years will cost them. The price of a degree has been climbing throughout the '80s at a rate double that of inflation. The figures at elite universities, particularly, are enough to cause sticker shock, even though the current increases at many schools are the lowest in a decade. Dartmouth's tuition (not counting room and board) will be $12,474 next year, up from $8,190 five years ago; Stanford's will be $11,880, up from $8,220. Secretary of Education William Bennett charges that such increases result from mismanagement and greed. "Higher education is underaccountable and underproductive," he claims. "No one doubts that there is a lot of fat in some areas."

Perhaps no budget is without some fat, but university officials argue that their unique function requires special standards of evaluation. "One of the peculiarities of education is that our customer is also our product," says University of Pennsylvania President Sheldon Hackney. "That confuses most analogies between universities and profit-making enterprises." In universities, notes Northwestern President Arnold Weber, all the money is ploughed into the operation: "We don't declare dividends; we don't give stock options to our administrators." Tuition increases, say officials, are driven by the universities' costs, and even at that, tuition income typically covers less than 50% of college budgets. (Endowments and gifts make up the rest.)

Academic salaries are the largest budget item, generally accounting for around 60% of total expenses. During the '70s, professors' salaries grew at an overall rate of 73%, lagging far behind inflation at 112%. Universities have been playing catch-up in the '80s. This year's raises average 5.9%, which is 4% above inflation and the largest since 1972. Yet the typical tenured professor's salary of $43,500 still represents 10% less buying power than the equivalent salary in 1970.

The boom in technology has been an added burden, especially for research universities that have to keep up with the latest computer and scientific hardware, regardless of price. At the University of Chicago, the $225,000 allotment that covered equipment for physiology and biology research ten years ago has grown to $1.4 million. Moreover, universities must scramble to replace outdated facilities. Says

Northwestern's Weber: "We have buildings here that cost $1 million to build 80 years ago, and cost $5 million just to repair." And books are not any cheaper. To maintain its library, Northwestern orders 29,000 periodicals a year at a cost approaching $2 million. Other uncontrollable costs include insurance and utilities. Emory University in Atlanta expects next year's electric bill to rise 30%.

The third major cost cited by universities is the higher proportion of student aid they have undertaken to provide, partly to offset their own tuition increases but especially to cover declining federal assistance. At Princeton, the

Government's contribution to student aid has dropped from 26.7% of the total to 12.6% in six years. The additional expense to Princeton: $2.2 million. Secretary Bennett, however, maintains that more federal aid would only encourage universities to count on the Government to meet any increases they might impose.

Some observers note that relatively few students are affected by high price-tag tuitions. Only about 80 institutions charge more than $10,000. The average private-college tuition, by contrast, is $6,150. Public colleges, which account for 80% of the nation's enrollment, average out at $1,100. Terry Hartle of the

Drawing by W. Miller; © 1986 *The New Yorker Magazine*, Inc.

American Enterprise Institute questions whether elite colleges even have any incentive to control their prices. These schools, he points out, consistently have ''more qualified applicants than places for them.''

Nonetheless, some colleges are making efforts to trim budgets and pass along the savings. Penn hopes to save $12 million next year by closer management of employee benefits. Cornell is reducing operating expenditures across the board by 2%, allowing it to post a 7% tuition increase, its smallest in 14 years. A few institutions are dropping secondary programs. Georgetown, for example, has eliminated one-third of its graduate programs in the past five years and recently decided to close its dental school. ''We can't be all things to all students,'' says Treasurer George Houston.

Ultimately, colleges may be able to do only so much to rein in rising tuitions. With their commitment to speculative scientific research, large faculties and out-of-favor subjects like classics, they may be what University of Rochester President Dennis O'Brien calls ''inefficient in principle.'' For students intent on a name-brand sheepskin, that principle is likely to remain an expensive one, at least for the foreseeable future.

By John E. Gallagher.
Reported by Mary Cronin/Princeton and David E. Thigpen/New York.

QUESTIONS AND ACTIVITIES

Comprehension Questions

1. What item accounts for the largest percentage of total expenses at a college or university?

2. What causes expenses to be so high at research institutions?

3. What is the average tuition at public colleges? at private colleges? at the elite research universities?

4. What are some colleges and universities doing in an effort to cut expenses?

Discussion Questions

1. Do you think that an education at an elite research institution is worth the additional cost? Why or why not?

2. Do you think that the federal government should provide more or less financial assistance to students? Explain your answer.

Group Activities

1. The university systems in many countries charge little if anything for students to attend. In groups of four or five, discuss the advantages and disadvantages of such a system, as opposed to one that charges substantial tuitions.

2. The university systems in many countries allow admission to anyone with a secondary school diploma regardless of academic performance. In groups of four or five, discuss the advantages and disadvantages of such a system, as opposed to one with selective admission.

Individual Work

Interview a college or university student. Find out about his or her educational budget for room and board, tuition, books, and other expenses. You may wish to learn the following:

   a. the percentage of expenses paid by the student's family
   b. the percentage paid by the student as a result of employment or loans
   c. the percentage paid by the institution in the form of scholarships or work programs
   d. the percentage paid by the government

Be prepared to report your findings to the class. Do not use the name of the student you interviewed.

Article Four

BACKGROUND NOTES

for **Why Can't a Woman Be More?**

Preview

During the 1960s and 1970s, the enrollment at many women's colleges declined greatly. Today, however, women's colleges are once again being viewed as desirable.

Culture

coed ['ko͵ɛd]: coeducational; attended by students of both sexes. The majority of colleges in the United States are coed.

old-girl network: an informal system of contacts and associations among women who have studied or worked together. Modeled on the "old-boy network," this system aids many working women.

semester [sə'mɛstɚ]: a division of the academic year. U.S. colleges and universities operate either on a semester system (two semesters per academic year) or on a quarter system (three quarters per academic year).

senior: a student in his or her fourth year of a secondary school or college. Seniors graduate at the end of the academic year.

service academy: an institution of higher education associated with a particular branch of the military. The U.S. Naval Academy at Annapolis, Maryland, is one of the service academies, as is the U.S. Air Force Academy in Colorado Springs, Colorado.

***Who's Who in America*:** an annual publication that gives biographical information about certain outstanding people in the country

Vocabulary

alumnae [ə'ləmni]: the female graduates of an academic institution. Male and female graduates together are called *alumni.*

anachronism [ə'nækrə͵nɪzəm]: something that is chronologically wrong; something that is out of its proper time. Writing a letter by hand is sometimes viewed as an anachronism in the age of telecommunications.

bastion ['bæstʃən]: a stronghold; a secure position

bellwether: a leader; someone or something that helps establish a trend

cloistered ['klɔɪstɚd]: sheltered; protected from external influences

constituency [kən'stɪtʃuən͵si]: a portion of the population being served or represented

convent ['kɑn͵vɛnt]: a religious community of nuns; a cloister

conversion: a change; an alteration

counterpart: an equivalent; a person or object similar to another

crack: first-rate; of the highest rank

Education

edge: an advantage; a favorable position

ego: self-esteem; self-concept

enclave ['ɑnklev]: a group of people functioning as a unit within a larger group. Enclaves operate independently from the larger group.

exult [ˌɛg'zəlt]: to rejoice; to be extremely joyful

head count: an exact number of people

intimacy ['ɪntəməˌsi]: familiarity; close association; personal contact

intimidating [ˌɪn'tɪməˌdedɪŋ]: frightening; causing fear

median ['midiən]: the middle number of an ordered set of numbers

mentor: a friend and teacher; a trusted counselor. The mentor system is more prevalent in British universities than in U.S. ones.

niche [nɪtʃ]: a special place or position for which something or someone is well suited

nurturing ['nɚtʃɚɪŋ]: providing mental or physical nourishment; training; educating

pluralistic: having multiple approaches; providing more than one perspective. Because of its many nationalities, the United States is viewed as a pluralistic society.

prejudice ['prɛdʒədəs]: a preconceived opinion; an attitude of hostility directed against a group or an individual member of a group. Rarely based on experience, prejudices are generally learned from others.

resurgent [ˌri'sɚdʒənt]: coming to life again; regaining vitality

sexist: discriminatory for reasons of a person's sex; prejudicial due to another's gender. The women's movement of the 1960s and 1970s protested sexist behavior.

stagnant: not moving; inactive

tamper: to change something for the worse; to alter something for a purpose

tradition: an inherited pattern of thought or action. Traditions usually change very slowly in a society.

Macroeconomics class at Wellesley: not just equal opportunity, but every opportunity

Why Can't a Woman Be More?

She can—at women's colleges, which are flourishing once again

Last month Freshman Shannon Welcome, 18, of Woodstock, Ill., started classes at St. Mary's, a small women's college across the street from Notre Dame in South Bend, Ind. "I guess you could say it's my dream school," she exclaims. "I can take classes at Notre Dame but still have the intimacy and nurturing atmosphere of St. Mary's." Welcome is considering a law career, and, she says, "I think the competitive benefits of being in a women's college will give me an edge."

Mary Wadland, 20, feels much the same about her education at Hollins College in Virginia. "I've come out much stronger, I think, than I would have if I had attended a coed school," says Wadland, who graduated in June after serving as student-body president. "We knew we were going to have to compete with men all our lives," she observes, "and it was nice to be in that cocoon for four years and then come out charging."

These votes for women's colleges are just two in a newly resurgent constituency. The 1960s and '70s were lean years for women's education. The opening of such male bastions as Yale, Dartmouth and the service academies helped draw so many crack high school girls into coed institutions that two-thirds of the nation's 298 women's colleges either went coed or closed their doors. But today the surviving 101 boast that undergraduate enrollment is surging, despite a declining pool of

high school graduates. Last week a preliminary survey of 64 schools, conducted by the Women's College Coalition, showed that the number of entering freshmen this semester has risen an average of 6.6% above last year, with some notable peaks around the academic landscape. The head count at California's Mills College is up 20%; freshman enrollment at the College of New Rochelle in New York has jumped from 92 to 144. At Bryn Mawr in Pennsylvania, early-admissions applications increased 50% to help make the freshman class of 345 the biggest in the school's 102-year history. "Our applicant pool is up, the quality of students is up, and we're doing quite well," exults Martha Morris, admissions director at Chicago's Mundelein College.

Why this dramatic turnaround? "We're doing a better job of getting out the message on how well women's colleges train women for careers," asserts Nicole Reindorf, the WCC's associate director. Graduates of women's colleges, she points out, generally outperform their coed counterparts. For instance, a 1985 survey of 5,000 women's school alumnae found that nearly half had earned graduate degrees (vs. one-third for all graduates from coed institutions). Of women listed in *Who's Who in America*, women's college alums outnumber coed-school graduates by more than 2 to 1. And the bottom line turns out to be the bottom line: two years ago, the median salary

for graduates of all-female colleges from the classes of '67 and '77 was $25,000, about $8,000 more than for coed-school alumnae.

These figures come across loud and clear to some of the sharpest of today's college-bound women, 24% of whom say they are interested in pursuing a business major—twice the proportion 20 years ago and only 2% lower than the men's figure. Some are also aware of studies suggesting that female egos take a subtle but destructive pounding in coed classrooms. A report released last fall by the Carnegie Foundation found that "even the brightest women students often remain silent" in mixed classes. "Not only do men talk more, but what they say often carries more weight." By contrast, at women's colleges, notes Wellesley President Nannerl Keohane, female students not only enjoy "equal opportunity, but *every* opportunity." This pays off, she insists, when graduates go out into the real and frequently sexist world: "When they do hit their first mound of prejudice, instead of saying, 'I'm not ready for this,' they will say, 'I know I can do this. I did it at Wellesley.'"

They learn leadership by example: top administrators at women's colleges tend to be women and, on average, the faculty is 61% female, in contrast to 27% for all higher-ed schools. Without the intimidating male presence, notes WCC's Reindorf, students at all-female colleges are more apt to venture into

Education

such traditionally male fields as engineering, physics and economics. At Bryn Mawr, for example, the percentage of physics majors is 20 times as great as the national average for all women students.

Recruiters for women's colleges have been working hard to bring these advantages to the attention of high school students, some of whom continue to regard single-sex schools as anachronisms or even convents. Not all are succeeding. A number of small isolated Roman Catholic women's colleges continue to struggle against stagnant enrollments. And over the past two years, Wheaton College in Massachusetts and Goucher in Maryland have abandoned the battle and gone coed. Russell Sage in New York was considering conversion last spring, but after completing a 15-month study of other colleges that had gone coed, administrators decided not to tamper with 71 years of tradition.

Russell Sage is among the most aggressive and innovative recruiters of female applicants. Among its techniques: assigning every arriving freshman an upper-class "big sister," along with a faculty mentor and a student ad-

viser, and weaving "old-girl networks" to create the same kinds of career opportunities for its graduates that "old boys" have traditionally held out to young men. Russell Sage also puts its seniors in touch with alumnae executives who provide career advice and arrange job contacts.

Other women's colleges offer similar programs. Many promise applicants "the best of both worlds" through cross-registration arrangements with nearby coed colleges. "This is no cloistered enclave," says Barnard President Ellen Futter. "Our students have an absolutely coeducational life by virtue of our participation in Columbia University." Yet the best women's schools remain shrewdly protective of the special position they occupy in the highly competitive college market. Many educators, and some alumnae as well, believe that schools like Skidmore and Vassar, once bellwether women's colleges, have slipped in both status and educational quality since they decided to admit men.

"To go coed makes you one more small, non-name-brand liberal arts college," says Reindorf. "Theoretically, you get twice as

many students, but you trade off your market niche."

Bryn Mawr President Mary Patterson McPherson believes single-sex institutions play an important role by contributing to a pluralistic approach to education. She frets about the sameness of so many American colleges: "There aren't many institutions anymore that have a very clear image." Futter concurs, "We are dealing with an increasingly franchised commodity. This isn't hamburgers; this is education." Finally, educational leaders are far from convinced that the women's movement has erased the prejudices that gave rise to women's colleges in the first place. "Maybe there will come a day when women and men will be able to work equally professionally across the board," says Wellesley's Keohane. "Perhaps when that day comes, our mission of educating women alone will be accomplished. I don't think it's going to happen soon."

By Ezra Bowen.
Reported by John E. Gallagher/New York and Pat Karlak/Chicago

QUESTIONS AND ACTIVITIES

Comprehension Questions

1. What happened to the majority of women's colleges during the 1960s and 1970s?

2. What percentage of graduates of women's colleges earn advanced degrees? What percentage of female graduates of coed institutions earn advanced degrees?

3. What is the median salary for recent graduates of women's colleges? What is the median salary for female graduates of coed institutions?

Discussion Questions

1. Some women's colleges claim to offer "the best of both worlds." Do you think this is an accurate description? Why or why not?

2. Do you agree that single-sex institutions (either all-male or all-female) play an important role in society? Why or why not?

Group Activities

One prominent educator has stated, "Not only do men talk more, but what they say often carries more weight." In groups of five or six, discuss this statement. See if your group can reach a consensus.

Individual Work

Have you attended an all-female or an all-male school? If so, what did you like and dislike about the experience? If not, would you like to? Why or why not? Be prepared to present your answers to the class or to write a one-page summary of your opinions.

Article Five

BACKGROUND NOTES

for **Silver Bullets for the Needy**

Preview

Students have often been accused of being self-centered. Today, however, many students across the country are volunteering to help others in need.

Culture

Appalachia [ˌæpəˈletʃə]: an economically poor, mountainous region of the east central United States

big brother: a young man (not a biological brother) who acts as a friend and companion to a boy. Big brother organizations exist throughout the country.

Lone Ranger [ˈlon ˈrendʒɚ]: the main character in a popular television series of the 1950s and 1960s. He was a masked man who did good deeds without reward in the American West of the 1800s; he always left a silver bullet as his trademark.

Peace Corps [. . . kor]: an organization developed during the Kennedy administration in the 1960s. Peace Corps volunteers serve in a number of countries throughout the world as teachers, health-care workers, and agricultural assistants.

ROTC: Reserve Officers Training Corps. ROTC students are enrolled full-time in a college or university. They receive tuition assistance from a branch of the military (e.g., the U.S. Air Force); in exchange, they serve in the military for a specified number of years after graduation.

spring break: a week-long school holiday usually occurring near Easter. Many college students traditionally travel to the beaches of Florida for spring break.

YMCA: Young Men's Christian Association. YMCAs offer short-term inexpensive housing and other community services.

Vocabulary

activist [ˈæktəvəst]: a person who actively supports a cause or an ideal. There were many social and political activists during the 1960s and 1970s.

bum rap: a bad deal; an unfair criticism (slang)

burn out: to become exhausted and discouraged as the result of overwork or excess enthusiasm (slang)

careerist: a person who cares about nothing except his or her career

entrepreneurship [ˌɑntrəprəˈnurˌʃɪp]: the act of developing and managing a business. One who does so is called an entrepreneur.

goad: a prod; a motivation

imbued [ˌɪmˈbjud]: filled with; characterized by

mandatory [ˈmændəˌtori]: required; obligatory

network: an interconnected system; a system used especially for communications

selfless: unselfish; having no concern for oneself

tangible [ˈtændʒəbəl]: real; material

undergrad [ˈəndɚˌgræd]: an undergraduate; a student in one of the four years of undergraduate school. Undergrads are working toward a B.A. or B.S. degree. (colloquial)

unsoftheaded: practical; clearly thought out

volunteerism [ˌvɑlənˈtɪrɪzəm]: a movement in which people perform services for others free of charge

Vanderbilt volunteer gardens with Cambodians in Nashville

Silver Bullets for the Needy

Campuses are seeing a renewal of student volunteerism

Ah, spring break. The traditional time to shed campus cares and haul hormones off for some sun and fun. But as the recess started last week at Vanderbilt University, one group of students was off in pursuit of more serious exertions. A score went to a Sioux reservation in South Dakota to do painting, tiling and light carpentry at a Y.M.C.A. center; a dozen arrived in Juárez, Mexico, to help build a *"serviglesia,"* a church to serve the poor; another twelve headed for Appalachia's "Valley of Despair" to plant fir trees and work on construction and furniture-building projects. Says Vanderbilt Senior Ethel Johnson, 21, who stayed in Nashville with another team sowing gardens, making curtains and teaching English in a community of Cambodian refugees: "Students are vastly underestimated. They have a real desire to get out there and do something to try to help and to have their eyes opened."

Vanderbilt's Alternative Spring Break is simply one rustling of a new spirit of volunteerism blowing across campuses. In California, 40 Stanford volunteers took time out two weekends ago to paint an elementary school gym in East Menlo Park. In Boston, Wellesley undergrads tend to homeless women every

night at Rosie's Place, a local shelter. At Northwestern in Evanston, Ill., volunteers have started an "adopt a grandparent" program to aid the elderly. Students at the University of Michigan in Ann Arbor help low-income people with tax returns.

No one can say exactly how many are involved overall; the best estimate is that 15% to 25% of collegians engage regularly in some form of public service. Many campus volunteer agencies are finding that interest is higher than it has been since the early '70s. Declares Stanford University President Donald Kennedy: "Everybody's view of this generation was that they were careerist, that they were yuppies in the making. I always thought that was a bum rap."

Today's volunteers, however, are no throwback to the '60s activists. "It's not enough to say peace, love and happiness," notes Brown Sophomore David Graff, who worked in a storefront school in Harlem and is now a big brother to a youngster in Providence. "We need to be realistic about our expectations so we don't burn out." Linda Chisholm, co-director of the Partnership for Service Learning, an organization that has sent students to

assist schools in Jamaica and Ecuador, explains, "They haven't decided who is right and who is wrong. And they aren't saying that others should change. They're saying, 'I'll change. I'll do it.' " The Peace Corps is enjoying an increase in applicants who are college graduates, and Spokeswoman Alixe Glen characterizes most of them as "realistic idealists."

Another difference: today's volunteerism is imbued with an '80s entrepreneurship and conservatism that include carefully defined goals and evaluation procedures. Schools such as Rice University and Georgetown have hired full-time service coordinators to foster student involvement and match volunteers with community agencies and projects. Networks have been established to pass along information. Campus Compact, started in 1985 by three university presidents, now comprises 259 colleges. COOL, Campus Outreach Opportunity League, run by a former Harvard volunteer, embraces 250 schools. Harvard's Phillips Brooks House Association, the nation's oldest college community-service organization, is a model of how unsoftheaded the approach now is. Students must not only dream up the projects (which now number 50) but write detailed proposals for how to fund and operate them. Last week the city of Cambridge awarded a $23,000 contract to the association, rather than other social service agencies, to run a 20-bed shelter for the homeless.

Many colleges give academic credit for public service. Some, like Brown and Harvard, provide fellowships. Educators and politicians have proposed offering other tangible rewards to volunteers, many of whom are accumulating high tuition debts and feel pressure to earn wages. Rhode Island Democratic Senator Claiborne Pell will introduce a bill this month that would give ROTC-like tuition assistance to students doing community service. Thanks, say some, but no thanks. "Volunteerism should be selfless," explains M. Richard Rose, president of Rochester Institute of Technology. "Ideally you should be like the Lone Ranger. You do a good deed, then you leave a silver bullet and move on."

Making volunteer work mandatory sparks more controversy. Proposed legislation in California would require all four-year students enrolled in state schools or receiving state aid to devote time to community projects. But, argues Robert Pollack, dean of Columbia College in New York City, "required service is not service, it is servitude." Besides, say participants, the spirit of giving does not need that goad. The personal satisfaction, the real-world exposure, the "chance to give something back," as dozens of volunteers put it, is enough. "In class, we study the big questions," says Georgetown Student Elaine Rankin. "At the homeless shelter we live the big questions."

By Anastasia Toufexis.
Reported by John E. Gallagher/New York and Melissa Ludtke/Boston

QUESTIONS AND ACTIVITIES

Comprehension Questions

1. What percentage of college students are believed to be doing volunteer work?

2. What kinds of public service projects are students participating in?

Discussion Questions

1. How does today's volunteerism differ from that of the 1960s? What do you think accounts for the differences?

2. Have you ever done volunteer work? If so, what did you do? If not, would you like to? What kind do you think you would like to do?

Group Activities

1. Some colleges and universities give academic credit for volunteer work. In small groups of four or five, discuss the pros and cons of this practice.

2. Some colleges and universities are considering requiring students on financial aid to do volunteer work. In the same groups of four or five, discuss the advantages and disadvantages of such a practice.

Individual Work

Interview a teacher or another student. Find out whether that person has ever done volunteer work. If so, what were the benefits of the experience? If not, what kind of volunteer work would he or she like to do, if any? Report your findings to the class.

Article Six

BACKGROUND NOTES

for **Stop the Student Presses**

Preview

The Supreme Court recently ruled that a public school district has the right to censor a student newspaper. Some argue that freedom of speech is being denied.

Culture

American Civil Liberties Union (ACLU): a private organization whose purpose is to safeguard individual liberties. Attorneys working for the ACLU often file lawsuits on behalf of individuals and groups of individuals.

Bill of Rights: the first 10 amendments to the U.S. Constitution. The Bill of Rights lists fundamental rights guaranteed to people by the federal government.

First Amendment: the first amendment to the U.S. Constitution. This amendment guarantees the right to freedom of expression, whether spoken or written.

Supreme Court: the highest court of the United States. The nine justices of the Supreme Court are appointed by the President and serve for life once appointed.

underground newspaper: a secretly produced publication; a clandestine newspaper. Underground newspapers often flourish when a government suppresses information.

Vocabulary

auspices ['ɔspəsəz]: protection; guidance

censor ['sɛnsɚ]: to delete written or recorded material that is thought to be objectionable in some way. Television censorship is usually stricter than other forms of censorship.

curtail [kɚ'tel]: to shorten; to lessen; to abbreviate

disrupt: to disturb the proceedings of something; to cause disorder

feistier ['faɪstiɚ]: more aggressive; more exuberant

impact ['ɪm,pækt]: an effect

innuendo [,ɪnju'ɛndo]: a veiled reference; a hint

lament [lə'mɛnt]: to mourn; to regret strongly

pedagogical [,pɛdə'gɑdʒəkəl]: pertaining to education; instructional

principal: the person in charge of an elementary or secondary school. Principals oversee teachers, students, the school building, and the curriculum.

profane [,pro'fen]: irreverent; debasing what is considered holy. What one person considers profane often differs from what another person does.

pseudonym ['sudənɪm]: a pen name; a false name used by the writer of an article or book. Female writers in the 1800s often used male pseudonyms.

vulgar ['vəlgɚ]: lacking in good taste; coarse; common

warrant ['worənt]: a legal document that gives permission to police to search someone's property or to make an arrest

All the news the principal deems fit: *Spectrum* staffers at work

Stop the Student Presses

The Supreme Court says educators can censor school newspapers

The Bill of Rights isn't stamped "for adults only." The U.S. Supreme Court has said as much in the past, acknowledging that public school students do not give up their constitutional rights when they step onto school property. But the Justices have also recognized that the need for an orderly school environment sometimes imposes limits on those rights. In recent years, for example, the majority has voted to permit the search of student possessions without a warrant and has allowed school officials to suspend a student for making sexual innuendos in a speech. The Justices were in that mood again last week when, in a 5 to 3 ruling, the court upheld a high school principal's right to censor a student newspaper.

The case, *Hazelwood School District v. Kuhlmeier*, involved a publication called *Spectrum*, produced every few weeks by journalism students at Hazelwood East High School near St. Louis. In May 1983, Principal

Robert Reynolds summarily ordered two articles deleted from the paper. One featured the experiences of three Hazelwood students who had become pregnant; the second dealt with the impact of parental divorce on students. Though the girls in the first piece were given pseudonyms, Reynolds believed that they were identifiable, that the article was too frank for younger students and that its overall picture of teenage pregnancy was too positive (sample quote: "This experience has made me a more responsible person. I feel that now I am a woman"). In the second article, a student complained that her father was "always out of town on business or out late playing cards with the guys." Reynolds objected that the piece failed to give the father's viewpoint.

Three students who worked on the *Spectrum* brought suit, alleging a violation of their First Amendment right to free expression. They had some reason to suppose that the

courts might agree. In its landmark 1969 *Tinker* decision, the Supreme Court held that a school acted unconstitutionally when it suspended students for wearing black armbands to class in protest against the Viet Nam War. Schools may curtail those rights, the court ruled, only when the student expression substantially disrupts schoolwork or discipline, or invades the rights of others.

Writing for the majority in last week's case, Justice Byron White saw a distinction. While the First Amendment prevented a school from silencing certain kinds of student expression, he said, it did not also require a school actively to promote such expression in plays and publications produced under its auspices. White, who had joined the majority in the *Tinker* case, ruled this time that educators may exert editorial control in such instances "so long as their actions are reasonably related to legitimate pedagogical concerns." Such concerns, he noted, might extend to work that is "poorly written, inadequately researched, biased or prejudiced, vulgar or profane, or unsuitable for immature audiences."

Justice William Brennan, in a dissent joined by Justices Thurgood Marshall and Harry Blackmun, strongly rejected the notion that school-sponsored speech was less worthy of protection than any other. He complained that the new ruling might permit school officials to censor anything that personally offended them. "The young men and women of Hazelwood East expected a civics lesson," he lamented, "but not the one the court teaches them today."

Educators were happy with the decision and discounted fears of a wave of high school repression. "The only thing this will do is make principals feel more comfortable in exercising control when they see it as necessary," says Ivan Gluckman, attorney for the National Association of Secondary School Principals. For his part, Principal Reynolds says he has no plans to increase his oversight of the *Spectrum,* and insisted that the paper would not shy away from sensitive issues.

Andrea Callow, the student who wrote the article on teenage pregnancy, was more concerned. "If student journalists want to write about a subject like teen pregnancy, they are going to be hesitant," says Callow, now a journalism student at the University of Missouri.

The ruling is especially troubling, says Steven Shapiro of the American Civil Liberties Union, because there was nothing vulgar about the censored articles. "Here we are dealing with clearly serious and responsible student speech."

Ironically, the decision may help create the conditions for a feistier kind of student journalism. The court did not give schools the power to suppress independently produced student publications. The underground newspaper, a familiar sight in many schools 20 years ago, may be ripe for a comeback.

By Richard Lacayo.
Reported by Anne Constable/Washington

QUESTIONS AND ACTIVITIES

Comprehension Questions

1. What was the issue in the *Hazelwood School District v. Kuhlmeier* case? What was the Supreme Court's decision?

2. What was the reaction of educators to the decision?

3. What was the reaction of students to the decision?

4. How did the ACLU react to the case?

Discussion Questions

1. Do you think that it is appropriate for secondary school newspapers to print articles about teenage pregnancy? Would it be an appropriate topic for college and university newspapers? Why or why not?

2. Do you believe that divorce is an appropriate topic for an article in a secondary school newspaper? Why or why not?

3. Does your school have a student newspaper? Do controversial articles ever appear? If not, why do you think not? If so, what are some of the topics that have been dealt with? If your school does not have a student newspaper, do you think there is any interest in having one?

Group Activities

Students should form groups of four or five. Half the groups will choose the first statement below to discuss and defend. The other half will discuss and support the second statement.

    a. Students should be allowed to print whatever they want in a public school newspaper.

    b. Public school officials should have the final authority over what is printed in a school newspaper.

Be prepared to defend your group's position to the opposing groups.

Individual Work

Which of the two positions discussed in the Group Activity do you personally support? Write a brief statement (one page maximum) explaining why you support the position you do.

Environment

Article One

Background Notes

for **Tick, Buzz, It's That Time Again**

Preview

Once every 17 years a group of cicadas emerges from the earth for three weeks. Scientists are still puzzled by the mysterious behavior of these insects.

Culture

Methuselah [mə'θuzələ]: the oldest man mentioned in the Bible. Methuselah supposedly died at the age of 969.

Old Testament: the first part of the Christian Bible. The Old Testament contains a history of Israel and a summary of its laws.

Pilgrim: an English Puritan who came to New England in the 1600s. The Pilgrims sought religious freedom.

softball: a game similar to baseball. Softball is played with a larger, softer ball that is pitched underhand. A softball game has seven innings rather than nine.

Vocabulary

appendage [ə'pɛndədʒ]: a limb; a lesser body part

brood [brud]: the young of an animal; the offspring of an animal born and cared for at the same time

cacophony [kə'kɑfə,ni]: harsh sounds; discordant sounds

carapace [kɛrə,pes]: a hard outer covering; an animal's protective covering. The shell of a turtle is an example of a carapace.

decibel ['dɛsə,bɛl]: a unit of measurement of the loudness of sounds. The least audible sound for humans is one decibel.

entomologist [,ɛntə'mɑlədʒəst]: a specialist in entomology. Entomology is a branch of zoology concerned with insects.

glinting: gleaming; sparkling

glistening ['glɪsənɪŋ]: shining; sparkling due to moisture on the surface

infested: swarming (with something); overpopulated (with something)

nuisance ['nusəns]: a pest; an annoyance

nymph [nɪm(p)f]: an immature insect; a larva of an insect

plague [pleg]: pestilence; a destructive influx

pruning: the trimming of a bush or tree

racket: confused noise; loud or clattering noise

sojourn ['sodʒɚn]: a temporary visit; a stay that is not permanent

staccato [stə'kɑ,do]: disconnected; characterized by short-spaced notes

subterranean [,səbtə'reniən]: underground; hidden

twig: a very small branch of a tree or bush

vulnerable: open to attack; capable of being damaged

wane [wen]: to become less powerful; to lessen in intensity

wax: to become more powerful; to increase in intensity

They're back: cicadas on a favored spot

Mysterious and "amazing" complexity.

Tick, Buzz, It's That Time Again

Locusts? No, it's the 17-year cicada, creating a racket

One of the first to spot the invasion in the South was retired Textile Worker Hugh Salmons, who on May 9 saw the glistening bodies on the willow oaks in his front yard in Elkin, N.C. The next morning, Judy Carpenter, 32, of Blairsville, Ga., was in the backyard playing softball with her daughter when she saw the intruder, its red eyes glinting in the sun and its clawed front feet pulling it through the grass. Within 24 hours she had collected 21 of them in a jar from the rhododendron bush in front of the house.

After nearly two decades of a subterranean existence, one of the two largest broods of the 17-year cicadas (pronounced suh-*kay*-duhs) is back. During the next few weeks and continuing through early July, the Eastern U.S. from Georgia to New York and as far west as Illinois will become infested with these mysterious insects, which emerge from the ground every 17 years to mate and die. This year, as in previous appearances, their numbers are likely to reach into the millions to the acre. The greatest concentrations are expected in the suburbs of Bal-

timore, Washington, Philadelphia and Cincinnati, where the days will be filled with a cacophony of ticks and buzzes that will wax and wane with the heat of the sun. A population in full song can exceed 100 decibels, roughly the level of a circular buzz saw at full throttle.

Many people still call the cicadas "locusts," because that is what the Pilgrims first called them, thinking no doubt of the locust plagues described in the Old Testament. Actually, those biblical insects were migratory grasshoppers, which even today cause extensive crop damage in Africa, Asia and South America. In contrast, the 17-year cicadas are reasonably harmless bugs whose only sins are sucking sap out of trees for nourishment and killing small branches by laying eggs in them. They also mess up lawns with their 2-in.-long bodies. Vulnerable sapling oaks and fruit trees can easily be protected with a covering of cheesecloth. "They're more of a nuisance than anything else," says Douglass Miller, an entomologist with the Agricultural Research Ser-

vice in Beltsville, Md. "They do less damage than a good pruning."

Compared with the average bug, which goes from birth to death in less than a year, the 17-year cicada is Methuselah: it has the longest life cycle of any known insect. In all, there are twelve distinct broods of 17-year cicadas, each of which emerges in a different year. This year's group is referred to by scientists as Brood 10. The other large group, Brood 14, is due to make its next appearance in 1991.

What triggers the insect's emergence from the ground exactly on cue in the final months of its life cycle is one of nature's continuing mysteries. Scientists assume that hormones play a role. The creatures also appear at about the time the soil temperature reaches 68°F to 70°F, which is why they are first seen in the South. Says University of Michigan Biologist Thomas Moore: "It's an amazing demonstration of biological complexity."

In its long sojourn underground, subsisting on sap in tree rootlets, the cicada nymph passes through five growth stages, or instars, each of which ends with the insect throwing off its carapace. About two months before it is ready to emerge, the nymph tunnels its way upward, lying at the surface and building a protective earthen turret if the ground is too damp. This final rest stop is truly character building: it apparently enables the insect to develop adult claws and flight muscles to help it cope with life aboveground. "Their bodies undergo a major transformation, especially of muscle structure," says Miller.

As a safeguard against predators, the cicadas usually first crawl out of the ground after sunset. Their main defense, though, may be sheer numbers: birds, raccoons and skunks can crunch up only so many insects. After climbing the nearest vertical object—a tree or post, for example—the insects take their last step toward adulthood. They hook their needle-like claws into the surface, arch their backs to break their skin and then wiggle free. A day later they are ready to fly away. All of this is merely a prelude to courtship, with the male cicadas seeking to attract mates with their staccato siren song, produced by vigorously vibrating two drumlike appendages on the abdomen.

The final hours of the cicada's three-week life aboveground are played out as the female deposits hundreds of eggs in a series of pockets cut in twigs. Nine weeks later the microscopic nymphs hatch, drop to the ground and burrow down as far as 2 ft., where they grow, eat and await their coming-out 17 years hence. The fact that this brood will not reappear until 2004 is one reason scientists are reluctant to put too much of their time into unlocking the cicada's secrets. As Richard Froeschner, a research entomologist at the Smithsonian Institution, points out, "Enthusiasm and curiosity tend to wane between generations."

By David Brand.
Reported by Andrea Dorfman/New York and Joseph J. Kane/Atlanta

QUESTIONS AND ACTIVITIES

Comprehension Questions

1. Are the 17-year cicadas harmful in any way?
2. When is the next large group of cicadas due to appear?
3. Why are the cicadas first seen in the South?
4. What is the purpose of the cicadas' three weeks above ground?

Discussion Questions

1. If you were an entomologist, what would you like to discover about the cicadas?
2. Why do you think scientists have not devoted as much research time to cicadas as to other animals?

Group Activities

Form dyads (groups of two people). One person in each group will be a homeowner; the other will be an official for the city health department. Role-play a situation in which the homeowner calls the health department to complain about the noise and "destruction" being caused by the "locusts" in the neighborhood. The health department official must try to calm the homeowner down and explain about the "locusts." After you and your partner have practiced your role-play, you may be called upon to present it to the whole class.

Individual Work

Write a brief (one page maximum) description about an unusual animal that lives in the region you are from.

Article Two

Background Notes

for **New Life Under the Volcano**

Preview

*Nature is rebuilding the area around the Mount St. Helens volcano.
Some wonder whether people should assist nature in this process.*

Culture

national monument: an area reserved by the federal government as public property. Canyons and mountains are often designated as national monuments.

U.S. Forest Service: a federal agency charged with the maintenance and preservation of the country's public lands

U.S. Geological Survey: a federal agency that is concerned with geological research. The USGS studies earthquakes and volcanos, among other things.

Vocabulary

belch: a sudden expulsion of gas

burrower ['bɜ·oɚ]: an animal that digs tunnels in the earth

canopied ['kænə,pid]: protected, as if by a canopy; covered by the uppermost branches of trees in a forest

dormant: inactive; at rest. Things lying dormant have the capability of becoming active.

ecologist: a specialist in ecology. Ecology is the study of the relationships between organisms and their environment.

epicenter ['ɛpə,sɛntɚ]: the center of activity. The part of the earth's surface directly above the source of an earthquake is called the epicenter.

facsimile [,fæk'sɪməli]: a duplicate; an exact copy

fauna ['fɔnə]: animals; the animal life of a region

flora: plants; the plant life of a region

magma: molten rock expelled by a volcano

nutrient ['nu,triənt]: food; a substance that provides nourishment

pumice ['pəməs]: volcanic glass. Pumice stone is often used to smooth and polish another object.

regeneration [,ri,dʒɛnə'reʃən]: renewal; restoration; reformation

seismometer [,saɪz'mɑmədɚ]: an instrument that measures movements of the earth's surface

silviculturalist [,sɪlvə'kəltʃɚələst]: a specialist in silviculture. Silviculture deals with the development and care of forests.

spume [spjum]: froth; foam

sylvan ['sɪlvən]: wooded; related to the woods or forest

tiltmeter: an instrument that measures the slope or incline of the earth's surface

ubiquitous [ju'bɪkwədəs]: being everywhere at the same time; omnipresent

untutored: untrained; untaught

volatile ['vɑlədəl]: explosive; tending to erupt violently

A landscape being reborn: against a backdrop of Mount St. Helens, new growth covers a hillside

New Life Under the Volcano

Hikers and scientists glimpse a mountain on the mend

In the seven years since Mount St. Helens exploded in a spume of gas, ash and pumice, there have been 24 additional eruptions at the volatile peak in the Cascade Range. The last, a small explosive belch of magma that added 85 ft. to the height of the lava dome inside the crater, occurred eight months ago. As a result, the U.S. Forest Service, cautious guardian of the 110,000-acre Mount St. Helens National Volcanic Monument, has decided to let the general public have a closer look at a postvolcanic environment. Since early May, some 100 climbers a day have been issued permits to slog across solidified mudflows, or lahars, and up through snowfields to the lip of the crater.

What they observe is nothing less than a landscape being reborn. Nature is laboring mightily to transform the scoured flanks of the mountain, its debris-filled river systems and chemically polluted ponds and lakes into a facsimile of the sylvan setting that existed before the eruption. To the untutored eye, the evidence

of devastation still seems overwhelming. Scientists, however, see a glass filling itself up slowly but surely. Says James MacMahon, head of the biology department at Utah State University: "It's not a forest yet, but the rate of progress is amazing."

That progress encompasses both flora and fauna. Inside the boundaries of the monument, where by law people are not allowed to assist regeneration, a mammalian equivalent of the bulldozer has been the pocket gopher. Colonies of these tiny industrious burrowers have helped mix the nutrient-poor ash and pumice with rich, pre-eruptive soil, creating a more hospitable turf for windblown seeds. Deer mice, ants and beetles have also assisted in the regeneration of the soil. Flowering lupine, with root nodules that convert nitrogen into compounds necessary for plant growth, has seized a foothold on the pumice plain, along with the ubiquitous fireweed and timothy grass.

Farther from the epicenter, in hummocky fields of loose volcanic ash and fine pumice pebbles, willows, red alder and an occasional Douglas fir have taken root near small ponds. At the waters' edge, Pacific tree frogs and salamanders now flourish. Large bodies of water like Spirit Lake, which was filled with organic debris and robbed of its oxygen by accompanying bacteria during the eruption, have made even more rapid recoveries. Algae, zooplankton and freshwater crustaceans have all recolonized the lake, prompting authorities from the state department of game to push for the restocking of such game fish as rainbow and brown trout.

But others oppose the plan, arguing that the volcano has provided them with an unprecedented opportunity to watch unhindered regeneration. Says Cliff Dahm, a biologist at the University of New Mexico: "It would be foolish to short-circuit nature's experiment."

Outside the monument, where nature is allowed an assist from man, recovery has been even more striking. The Weyerhaeuser Co., which lost 60,000 acres of timber when Mount St. Helens blew, finished replanting conifers last fall. In Clearwater Canyon, nine miles from the center of the blast, one-acre test plots set up in 1981 are flourishing. Douglas, noble, grand and Pacific silver firs planted by the Forest Service staff have enjoyed an almost 90% survival rate. Some are already 12 ft. tall. "The trees are growing faster than normal," says Eugene Sloniker, a Forest Service silviculturist. The impressive growth rate of these species is partly attributable to the fact that they were the first ones reintroduced. Explains Sloniker: "They have had less competition."

The reopening of the mountain worries scientists at the U.S. Geological Survey.

Reason: the vulnerability of sensitive, untended monitoring equipment that provides a constant readout of the peak's vital signs. Hikers are given a handout warning that tampering with seismometers, tiltmeters and other equipment would cripple the USGS early-warning system and could lead to the reclosing of the mountain. Although geologists feel comfortable with their ability to predict the behavior of Mount St. Helens itself, they freely admit that the inner workings of the volcano are still a mystery. Says Research Geologist C. Dan Miller, who assesses volcano hazard for the USGS: "We learn as we go along. There is really no alternative to studying each volcano."

Geologists who have been monitoring Mount St. Helens' hiccups since 1980 have predicted all but one volcanic event and believe they can continue to do so. As long as the volcano remains dormant, more and more people are certain to come and marvel at what Jerry Franklin, the Forest Service's chief plant ecologist, calls "the resilience of nature." Since the $5.3 million Mount St. Helens visitor center opened in nearby Silver Lake last December, more than 150,000 people have paraded through its exhibits. Now they can see the mountain for themselves. "We've got quite a way to go yet," says Franklin. "We're 10% along the way. In another hundred years, we'll have a canopied forest."

By Paul A. Witteman/
Mount St. Helens

QUESTIONS AND ACTIVITIES

Comprehension Questions

1. In what year did Mount St. Helens erupt?
2. Why did the U.S. Forest Service decide to reopen the area to the public?
3. What group of animals is helping the area to recover? How?
4. Why are the scientists of the U.S. Geological Survey worried about reopening the area to the public?

Discussion Questions

1. Do you think that it is safe to reopen the area around Mount St. Helens to the public? Why or why not?
2. Do you think that the printed warnings to the public about the sensitive scientific equipment in the area are sufficient? Why or why not?

Group Activities

In groups of approximately four or five, choose one of the following two positions to defend. (Note: Half the groups should choose the first statement; the other half should choose the second.)

a. The rule that man should not assist nature in the restoration of the area damaged by the volcano is a good one and should not be changed.
b. Man should be allowed to help restore the area damaged by the volcano by restocking the lakes and reforesting the land.

In your small groups, identify arguments in support of the statement chosen. Be prepared to have your group present the arguments to the whole class.

Individual Work

Would you be interested in visiting Mount St. Helens or another area where a volcano has recently erupted? Why or why not? Summarize your reasons in a brief written report (one page maximum).

Article Three

Background Notes

for **Tubers, Berries and Bugs**

Preview

The first official release of man-made microbes into the environment has taken place. This act marks another stage in the long controversy over environmental safety.

Culture

Chernobyl [ˌtʃɚˈnobəl]: the site of the recent disaster at a nuclear reactor in the Soviet Union. Radioactive fallout from the accident reached many European countries.

genetic engineering [dʒəˈnɛɑk ˌɛndʒəˈnɪrɪŋ]: scientific experimentation in which an organism's genes are altered for specific purposes. Genetic engineering is a controversial procedure.

watchdog: an individual or group that monitors the activities of another individual or group. Those being observed are believed to be engaged in activities that might threaten the health, safety, or political well-being of others.

Vocabulary

acre [ˈekɚ]: a unit of measurement of a piece of land, about 0.4 hectares

alienate [ˈeliəˌnet]: to cause to become unfriendly or hostile

biodegradable [ˌbaɪoˌdiˈgredəbəl]: able to be decomposed by nature. Biodegradable products are thought to be harmless to the environment.

clamber [ˈklæmbɚ]: to climb awkwardly

deleterious [ˌdɛləˈtɪriəs]: harmful; capable of causing damage

frost: a covering of ice crystals on a surface. Frost kills fruits and vegetables.

haywire: out of order; chaotic (colloquial)

knack [næk]: a talent; an ability

legitimate [ləˈdʒɪdəmət]: justified; rightful; fair and appropriate

microbe [ˈmaɪˌkrob]: a germ; a microscopic organism

mutant: produced by mutation; changed due to alterations in the genes

parasite [ˈpɛrəˌsaɪt]: an organism that lives in or on another organism. Some parasites are harmful; others are helpful.

pesticide [ˈpɛstəˌsaɪd]: insecticide; chemicals used to destroy pests. Certain kinds of pesticides are harmful to the environment.

recombinant [ˌriˈkɑmbənənt]: characterized by genetic recombination; having a new formation of genes

symptomatic [ˌsɪmptəˈmædək]: showing symptoms; characteristic

toxic [ˈtɑksək]: poisonous

transgression: a wrongful act; a violation of the law

tuber: a fleshy underground stem. The potato is an example of a tuber.

Tubers, Berries and Bugs

Scientists release man-made microbes into the environment

In a dusty half-acre potato patch near the tiny (pop. 1,000) farming community of Tulelake, Calif., scientists in canary yellow overalls clambered aboard a tractor last week and began what looked like a workaday farmyard chore. They were planting ordinary potatoes, 2,000 tubers in all, that had been treated with an extraordinary additive: a genetically altered bacterium designed to inhibit the formation of frost. This experiment—and a similar one performed only five days earlier—marked a turning point in the efforts of scientists to apply the advances of recombinant DNA technology to agriculture: the first authorized release of man-made microbes into the environment.

The routine Tulelake operation stood in marked contrast to the more dramatic previous test, 350 miles away in a Brentwood, Calif., strawberry field. There, technicians wrapped in head-to-foot "space suits"—required by federal regulations governing airborne use of potentially toxic substances—sprayed 2,400 strawberry plants with a slightly different strain of the same ice-inhibiting bacterium. The event drew a crowd of reporters and government officials, who arrived with elaborate devices to sniff the air and taste the dirt around the test site. The start of the experiment was delayed for an hour because of an act of sabotage: the night before, vandals, apparently expressing their disapproval of the experiment, cut through a chain-link fence and uprooted some 2,000 plants.

The uninjured berries were quickly replanted, and the project proceeded without further incident, but the protest was symptomatic of the fierce controversy surrounding the open-air trials. They have become the focal point of a bitter debate over the creation of new organisms and the risks involved in releasing them. Most biologists have argued that the outdoor tests are a necessary first step that may help reduce the $1.5 billion lost by U.S. farmers each year to frost and may someday lead to the replacement of chemical fertilizers and pesticides with biodegradable, nonpolluting microbes.

Opponents, captained by Washington-based Activist Jeremy Rifkin, have raised legitimate questions about how well these experiments are regulated and monitored. But Rifkin and his supporters have also played on public fears by painting the specter of a biotech Chernobyl—an experiment gone haywire, spreading man-made germs that could ruin crops, change rain patterns and render large swatches of California uninhabitable.

The current experiments, almost everyone agrees, do not pose any such threat. They involve a modest bit of genetic engineering on the bacterium *Pseudomonas syringae,* a common parasite that lives on the bark and leaves of many plants. The bacterium produces a protein that serves as a seed for the formation of ice crystals when the temperature drops below 32°F. By snipping the seed-making gene from the DNA of the microbe, Berkeley Plant

Pathologists Steven Lindow and Nickolas Panopoulos created a mutant form of *P. syringae* that does not promote frost. They call their new microbe "ice-minus." In the laboratory, leaves coated with the microbes have briefly withstood temperatures as low as 23°F.

In 1982 Lindow and Panopoulos applied for permission to treat potatoes with ice-minus. They failed to anticipate Rifkin. A former antiwar activist with a fertile imagination and a knack for using the bureaucratic process, Rifkin organized what may be the longest-running regulatory battle ever. One of his victories: a 1984 temporary injunction against Lindow and Panopoulos issued by Federal District Judge John Sirica of Watergate fame.

There have been excesses and lapses on both sides. Rifkin, who makes his living speaking against genetic engineering, sowed fear and doubt among the public even after his supporters had concluded that the experiments were safe. But the scientists have not been blameless. Advanced Genetic Sciences Inc., the Oakland-based start-up firm that conducted the strawberry tests, managed to alienate most of California's Monterey County in 1986 when its closely held plans to test the microbes in that area were uncovered by a local newspaper. While that issue was being debated, Rifkin revealed that AGS scientists had already injected mutant bacteria into fruit and nut trees growing on the roof of their Oakland labs—a violation of federal and state regulations. AGS was fined $13,000 for its transgression.

AGS learned its lesson. This month's experiments were preceded by a well-orchestrated campaign that included public meetings, mounds of explanatory literature and plant tours for county officials. The final legal hurdle fell the day before the first test. "The court is convinced," said Sacramento Superior Court Judge Darrell Lewis, "that [the experiments] are not unleashing some deleterious bacteria that are going to consume the city of Brentwood or anywhere else."

It was a setback for opponents of such research, and for Rifkin in particular. But it does not mean smooth sailing for the genetic engineers. Strict guidelines are now in place, and as long as there are industry watchdogs, every experiment will be closely checked. Rifkin shows no signs of giving up. "We will battle every step of the way," he promised last week. "This protest is not going to go away." For Lindow, however, the long battle was over. Said he, when the tubers were finally in the ground: "It's quite a relief to finally see science progress."

Spraying the strawberries

By Philip Elmer-DeWitt.
Reported by Cristina Garcia/Tulelake and Dick Thompson/Washington

QUESTIONS AND ACTIVITIES

Comprehension Questions

1. What is the purpose of the "ice-minus" microbe? How is it made?
2. Where is the man-made microbe being tested?
3. Why did people vandalize the strawberry fields?
4. Who is Jeremy Rifkin? What are he and his supporters protesting?

Discussion Questions

1. Do you think the testing of the "ice-minus" microbe should have been allowed? Why or why not?
2. Should a government establish the rules and regulations regarding the testing of genetically engineered material, or should scientific researchers be in charge of this? Or should there be no rules and regulations? Explain your answer.

Group Activities

In groups of four or five, decide which of the statements given below best describes your collective viewpoint. After you reach a consensus, develop arguments in support of your group's position. Be prepared to defend your opinions to the entire class.

    a. No genetic engineering research whatsoever should be allowed.
    b. Genetic engineering research should be allowed only on plant life.
    c. Genetic engineering research should be allowed on plant life and all nonhuman animal life.
    d. Genetic engineering research should be allowed on all forms of life, including humans.

Individual Work

Poll five to 10 people to learn their opinions on the following question:
    Are you in favor of scientific research in genetic engineering? Why or why not?
Record the answers you receive and tally the results. Summarize your findings in a brief written report (one page maximum).

Article Four

Background Notes

for **Shrinking Shores**

Preview

Erosion is a critical problem in all coastal areas.
Efforts to stop the process have had little success.

Culture

dune buggy: a four-wheeled open vehicle designed for use on beaches. Dune buggies are outlawed in many areas because of the destruction they cause.

Great Lakes: the collective name for Lake Superior, Lake Michigan, Lake Ontario, Lake Huron, and Lake Erie. The Great Lakes are located in the Midwest.

Hurricane Gloria: a 1985 tropical storm that hit the southeastern part of the United States. Hurricanes are named in alphabetical order as they occur. Gloria was thus the seventh hurricane in 1985.

parish ['pɛrɪʃ]: a division of a state similar to a county. Louisiana is the only state that is divided into parishes.

robbing Peter to pay Paul: using one part of a system to aid or repair another part of the system. Such a procedure may help at first, but rarely provides a satisfactory, permanent solution.

Vocabulary

bluff: a cliff; a high steep bank

chunk: a large piece

devastating ['dɛvəˌstedɪŋ]: causing destruction; bringing ruin

dredge [drɛdʒ]: to dig; to remove large portions of earth

driftwood: wood that is deposited by water onto beaches

dune: a hill of sand formed by the wind

dynamic [ˌdaɪ'næmək]: active and changing; not static

encroaching [ˌɛn'krotʃɪŋ]: trespassing; advancing beyond what is expected or desired

erosion: the process of wearing away. Wind and water both cause erosion.

exacerbated [əg'zæsɚˌbedəd]: made worse; made more severe

formidable ['fɔrmədəbəl]: difficult to overcome; having qualities that discourage action

fractionalized ['frækʃənəlaɪzd]: divided; having many parts

gale: a very strong wind. Gales are often accompanied by severe rainstorms.

instinct ['ɪnˌstɪŋkt]: an innate tendency; an animal's hereditary responses

larceny ['lɑrsəˌni]: theft; stealing

ominous ['amənəs]: threatening; foreshadowing disaster

precipice ['prɛsəpəs]: an overhang; a piece of land that drops steeply to the land or water below

replenishment [ˌri'plɛnəʃmənt]: replacement; an act of building up or filling up something again

scourge [skɚdʒ]: a widespread affliction; distress that is felt by many

scouring ['skaurɪŋ]: rubbing caused by a strong force of water

BOLINAS, CALIF.

PACIFIC OCEAN

San Francisco

A partially collapsed house perches on the edge of a bluff damaged by storms and high tides

Shrinking Shores

Overdevelopment, poor planning and nature take their toll

Patricia and Francis O'Malley bought their summer home in Long Island's fashionable Westhampton Beach four years ago. "There used to be a dune in front and a beach in front of that," Patricia recalls. "The very first winter we had a horrible storm, and we lost the dune." Two years later gale-force winds blew the house's roof and top floor off. "We rebuilt a whole new house. Since then, we've lost 8 ft. of sand." Now, she complains, "there's water under the house. The steps are gone. The houses on both sides of ours are gone." She adds bitterly, "And they say you can't lose in real estate." The O'Malleys figure their home will wash away completely by next year. The potential loss: hundreds of thousands of dollars.

Jan and Bill Alford's troubles began during the devastating winter storms of 1982. That January a 15-ft. chunk of earth slid away from in front of their bluff-top home in Bolinas, Calif., about 30 miles north of San Francisco, and crashed to the beach below. A year later another 15 ft. vanished, leaving the house just a few feet from the edge of a 160-ft. cliff. So, in the summer of 1984, the Alfords moved their 1,300-sq.-ft. house 32 ft. back from the edge. Then came Valentine's Day 1985. Following unusually high tides, 30 ft. of land dropped into the sea. The foundation of the house remained just a foot from the precipice, with nothing but air between the guest-room deck and the surf below.

"We loved the lot," says Jan. "On a clear day, you could see all the way to San Francisco. We tried everything to save it, but the erosion just didn't stop." Last autumn the Alfords moved their home again, this time hauling it a third of a mile to a new site more than 300 ft. from the cliffside. The cost of the two moves: $80,000.

The problem is hardly limited to New York and California. The scourge of coastal erosion is felt worldwide, especially in such countries as Britain, West Germany and the Netherlands, where ocean-front property has been heavily developed. In the U.S., entire coastal areas are disappearing into the sea. Virtually every mile of shoreline is affected in every state that borders an ocean, as well as those on the five Great Lakes, where large chunks of waterfront property have been lost or damaged due to record-high water levels in recent years. Some 86% of California's 1,100 miles of exposed Pacific shoreline is receding at an average rate of between 6 in. and 2 ft. a year. Monterey Bay, south of San Francisco, loses as much as 5 ft. to 15 ft. annually. Cape Shoalwater, Wash., about 70 miles west of Olympia, has been eroding at the rate of more than 100 ft. a year since the turn of the century; its sparsely settled sand dunes have retreated an astounding 12,000 ft., or more than two miles, since 1910.

Parts of Chambers County, Texas, have lost 9 ft. of coast to Galveston Bay in the past nine months. Louisiana has shrunk by 300 sq. mi.

since 1970; entire parishes may disappear in the next 50 years. At Boca Grande Pass, an inlet on the Gulf Coast of Florida, some 200 million cu. yds. of sand have been carried seaward by the tidal currents. In North Carolina, where erosion this year alone has cut into beachfront property up to 60 ft. in places, the venerable Cape Hatteras lighthouse is in peril of the encroaching sea. Soon it must either be moved or surrounded by a wall. Otherwise, it is likely to suffer the fate of the Morris Island light, near Charleston, S.C. Once on solid land, it now stands a quarter of a mile offshore.

Coastal erosion is only one of the natural processes that have altered the world's shorelines ever since the oceans first formed some 3 billion years ago. Over geologic time, the daily scouring action of waves and the pounding of storms, as well as the rise and fall of ocean levels, have changed coastlines dramatically. "Sandy beaches are dynamic. They are meant to erode," says Richard Delaney, chairman of the Coastal States Organization, a group that advocates better coastal management in 30 states (including those that border the Great Lakes) and five territories. The problem, however, is Americans' passion for living and vacationing at the seashore. That has led to a boom in the development of U.S. coastal areas since World War II. "When you put a permanent structure onto a piece of land that is by nature mobile," says Delaney, "you have a very serious problem."

"If we had known 30 years ago what we know now, New Jersey and much of the rest of the country would be in better shape," admits Governor Thomas Kean, a strong believer in shoreline protection. "We wouldn't have built in those areas, and we wouldn't allow people to build in those areas." Even now, however, billions of dollars worth of coastal development—some would say runaway overdevelopment—cannot simply be abandoned. Says Chris Soller, management assistant of the National Park Service's Fire Island National Seashore, off Long Island: "It's a tough tightrope to walk. Our whole concept of property rights clashes with the natural process."

Along with property, receding U.S. coastlines threaten the survival of shore-dwelling wildlife. Florida's sea turtles, for example, including loggerheads, green turtles and others, cross hundreds of miles of ocean to lay eggs on the same sections of the same beaches. If the beach has eroded badly, a turtle is forced by instinct to use it anyway, dooming the eggs to be washed away or eaten by seabirds and raccoons. Least terns, Gulf Coast shellfish and beach-spawning fish, like the California grunion, are also in danger.

In the past few decades, as property owners began to demand that coastal areas stay put—by buying up seaside property and erecting multimillion-dollar beachfront houses, condominiums, hotels and resorts on the shifting sand—the natural process of erosion began to matter to growing numbers of Americans. Along with the roads, parking lots, airfields and commercial interests that serve them, development projects not only put more people and property in harm's way but also unwittingly accelerated the damage to U.S. coastal areas.

How? On the West Coast, houses perched atop cliffs create new runoff patterns for rainfall and irrigation; combined with seepage from septic systems, the drainage weakens the land itself. On the East and Gulf coasts, the major problem is destruction of beaches and sand dunes that normally check the ocean's force. Of particular concern are the 295 barrier islands—strips of sand dune, marsh and sometimes forest—that protect most of the U.S. coast from Maine to Texas. Not surprisingly, they are considered prime development spots: Atlantic City, N.J., Virginia Beach, Va., and Hilton Head, S.C., among others, were all built on barrier islands.

It is mainly the dunes, explains the National Park Service's Soller, that keep coastal areas, including barrier islands, intact. "The natural process is for dunes to roll over on themselves," he says. When the ocean breaks through, "what was once the secondary dune becomes the primary dune. The beach retreats as the ocean level rises. When you have houses on the beach, there's no place for the dunes to move."

In Ocean City, Md., developers hoping to reinvent Miami Beach, where a single mile of oceanfront is now worth an estimated $500 million, began building high-rises on the dune line in the 1970s. So that people on the lower floors could have an unimpeded view of the ocean, the dunes were simply bulldozed away. Since then, the ocean has come to see the tourists: beneath many buildings, pilings are exposed to the waves. At Garden City, S.C., just south of Myrtle Beach, where big condos dot the waterfront, crumbled seawalls and wrecked swimming pools testify to the power of storms unchecked by protective dunes.

Sand dunes can also be destroyed in subtler ways. For a dune to form in the first place, sand must somehow be trapped, much as a snow fence traps drifting snow. That something is dune grass. After the dunes form, the roots anchor the sand in place. "Dune grass is pretty hardy stuff," explains Stephen Leatherman, a University of Maryland coastal-erosion expert. "It can take salt spray and high winds. But it just never evolved to take heavy pedestrian traffic or dune buggies." Since the plants depend on chlorophyll in their green leafy parts to convert sunlight into food, he says, and since there is only so much food reserve in the roots, "a couple of weekends with a few hundred people walking back and forth to the beach, or a single pass from an off-road vehicle, kills off the dune grass."

Shoreline erosion, however, is exacerbated by less well understood—and perhaps more ominous—factors. Over the past 100 years, the ocean has risen more than a foot, a rate faster than at any time in the past millennium. Sea-level fluctuations are part of a natural cycle, but scientists suspect that this one may be different. They believe it is magnified by a fundamental change in world climate caused by a phenomenon called the greenhouse effect. Since the Industrial Revolution, people have been burning greater quantities of fossil fuels, such as coal, oil and gas. One by-product is carbon dioxide, which has entered the atmosphere in ever increasing amounts.

While carbon dioxide allows the warming rays of the sun to reach the earth, it blocks the excess heat that would normally reradiate out into space. As a result, the atmosphere is gradually growing warmer, thus melting the polar ice caps and raising sea levels. It may be years before scientists determine just how significant the greenhouse effect is—but they know the process is accelerating. Sea levels are expected to rise at least a foot in just another half-century.

For all the danger, people still want to own seafront property. And why not? They are still protected—and encouraged—by knowing that they can write off storm damage on their taxes.* In many cases, they can depend on federal flood insurance for at least partial reimbursement in case of disaster. Environmentalists believe the insurance program actually encourages building in high-risk locales. Says Town Councilman Neil Wright, of Surfside

Beach, S.C.: "It's an incentive to build in dangerous places. The feds need to change the rules."

Federal flood insurance has traditionally reimbursed owners for rebuilding, rather than for relocating houses to safer ground. The owners of the Sea Vista Motel on Topsail Island, N.C., whose property was damaged in 1985 by Hurricane Gloria, wanted to move inland, but their federal insurance would not cover the $150,000 cost. It would, however, pay $220,000 for repairs and renovations. The motel stayed put. Then came last winter's New Year's storm, which tore out all 15 of the first-floor units. Says Manager Frances Ricks: "There's a feeling we can't win."

That does not stop people from trying. The growing damage to oceanfront property has generated a host of makeshift solutions to erosion. On Galveston Bay, desperate ranchers have positioned junked cars on the shore to prevent the waters from washing away roads. Conservation officers are planting dense patches of cordgrass just offshore in an effort to buffer the bay's clay banks from the relentlessly lapping waters. To protect the transplants until they take hold, conservationists have jury-rigged a protective barrier of old Air Force parachutes in the water to absorb and attenuate the force of the waves. Harry Cook, a Texas shrimper, is considering wire mesh and old tires to keep the bay waters from chewing away any more of his bluffs, which he is losing at the rate of 10 ft. yearly. On Long Island, beach residents shore up dunes with driftwood and old tires. And in Carlsbad, Calif., the community has come up with a number of ideas, from planting plastic kelp to laying a sausage-like tube along the beach in order to trap sand normally washed away during high tide.

There are more substantive approaches to beach protection. When properly designed and built, they can slow beach erosion. Nonetheless, most are ineffective in the long run and can actually exacerbate damage. A seawall, for example, may protect threatened property behind it, but it often hastens the retreat of the beach in front as waves dash against the wall and scour away sand. Louis Sodano, mayor of Monmouth Beach, N.J., knows the process firsthand. "When I moved here 28 years ago, you could walk the whole beach," he remembers. "Now the waves slap against the wall. We've lost 100 ft. of beach in the past 28 years."

A variant on the seawall that can also hasten erosion is riprap—rocks and boulders piled into makeshift barriers to absorb the force of incoming waves. While seawalls and riprap run parallel to the beach, groin fields extend directly out into the water. Made up of short piers of stone extending from the beach and spaced 100 yds. or so apart, they can slow erosion by trapping sand carried by crosscur-

---

*Since damage lowers the value of an investment, owners can deduct the amount as a capital loss.

The sea in full fury: Hurricane Gloria batters homes on Long Island Sound in 1985

rents. But down current, the lack of drifting sand can result in worse erosion. "It's like robbing Peter to pay Paul," says Leatherman—a concept the O'Malleys of Westhampton Beach understand all too well, since it was a neighboring groin field that robbed their beach of replenishing sand.

Jetties can cause beach larceny on an even grander scale. Long concrete or rock structures, they jut out into the water to keep inlets and harbors navigable by keeping sand and silt from drifting in. Like groin fields, jetties can keep sand from replenishing beaches down current. The construction 90 years ago of a pair of jetties to improve the harbor at Charleston, S.C., altered currents and natural sand drift so drastically that there is no beach left at high tide at nearby Folly Beach. In Florida an estimated 80% to 85% of the beach erosion on the state's Atlantic Coast is caused by the maintenance of 19 inlets, all but one of them made or modified by man to link the open ocean and inland waterways.

There is one anti-erosion scheme, however, that can be effective: beach nourishment, which simply involves replacing sand that has washed away. Between 1976 and 1980, a ten-mile stretch of Miami Beach was rejuvenated with a brand-new, 300-ft.-wide beach. Oceanside, Calif., has struggled for more than 40 years to maintain its sandy beaches, ever since the creation of a boat basin at nearby Camp

Pendleton during World War II interrupted the flow of sand down the coast. More than 13 million cu. yds. of sand have been dredged from offshore or trucked in from nearby rivers to replenish the Oceanside beaches.

Beach nourishment, however, is expensive. Just off the southern tip of Key Biscayne, Fla., an Army Corps of Engineers' hydraulic pump ran 24 hours a day, from mid-April to early July, sucking up sand from the ocean bottom and piping it to the beach half a mile away. By the time the dredge had finished, it had moved some 400,000 cu. yds. of sand at a cost of $1.55 million, much of it from the pockets of local businesses. In the early 1980s, the Army Corps brought in sand to widen the dwindling strip at Wrightsville Beach, N.C., by 200 ft., as well to construct and regrass new dunes. Price tag: $2.95 million. That is small change, however, compared with a program begun in 1976 for the New York City Rockaway beach project. Total cost for the twelve-year, 11.5 million-cu.-yd. project: $52 million in federal, state and city funds.

But even beach replenishment is a temporary measure. At the sprawling resort complex of Myrtle Beach, S.C., the community had little choice but to haul in 854,000 cu. yds. of new sand along ten miles of beach that had dwindled to a 10-ft. width in places, creating a glistening 100-ft.-wide strip at high tide. Ex-Mayor Erick Ficken says the community will

be paying for the $4.5 million project over the next ten years. Naturally, he wonders, "How long will it last?" There are no guarantees. John Weingart, director of coastal resources for New Jersey's department of environmental protection, recalls one of that state's first replenishment projects. The 2 million-cu.-yd., $5 million nourishment of the beach at Ocean City was unfortunately timed; it was completed just before the stormy fall season. "Within ten days of finishing," he says, "we had several really bad local storms. Over 60% of the sand was washed away."

A major problem in the battle against coastal erosion is the lack of statewide coordination. Says Dick McCarthy, a member of the California coastal commission: "We have a series of fractionalized local efforts that has each community involved in its own projects, often without taking into account the effects its protective measures may have on adjacent areas."

One problem with getting the Federal Government involved in coastal management is that there is no single responsible Government agency. The Army Corps of Engineers comes closest, but it is often hamstrung by its dual mission: it is charged with both protecting vulnerable wetlands and keeping waterways navigable. In Louisiana, complains Environmental Lawyer Houck, when there is a conflict, the waterways win every time. This does not have to be the case, contends Bill Wooley, planning chief for the corps's Galveston office. While he concedes the task is formidable, he insists that "we can manage both. It's a matter of how much we want to spend."

The simplest and most effective response to coastal erosion would be to prevent people from living at the edge of the sea. The nonprofit, Washington-based Nature Conservancy encourages just that by buying threatened coastal areas and refusing to develop them. The group has made 32 separate purchases in eight states, sheltering more than 250,000 acres, including 13 barrier islands off the coast of Virginia that it bought for $10 million. Says

Orrin Pilkey, a Duke University geologist and one of the country's top experts on beach erosion: "Retreat is the ultimate solution. Property owners must pack up and move."

That is not likely. "Abandonment is a joke," scoffs Folly Beach Mayor Richard Beck, noting that his island is almost completely developed and that tourism is just too valuable an income source. Indeed, unless it is voluntary, any restriction of land use, even for good environmental reasons, must respect property rights. Two recent Supreme Court decisions served as timely reminders that local governments have a constitutional responsibility to protect property owners. Even so,

those who resist a balanced policy of coastal management, whether they are motivated by greed or by genuine concern for the well-being of coastal communities, will probably lose in the end—to the sea. Says Coastal Geologist Griggs: "In the long run, everything we do to stop erosion is only temporary." John Tesvich, a Louisiana oysterman, perhaps puts it more feelingly, "The land has shrunk. It looks like a lake out there. My heart sinks to see the land get lost to the sea."

By Michael D. Lemonick.
Reported by Christine Gorman/New York, Nancy Seufert/Bolinas and Richard Woodbury/Topsail Island

QUESTIONS AND ACTIVITIES

Comprehension Questions

1. What accounts for the excessive development of coastal areas?

2. What else besides property do the receding coastlines threaten?

3. What purpose do sand dunes serve? What happens if they are destroyed?

Discussion Questions

1. Is erosion a problem in any place you have lived? If so, what efforts have people made to slow the process? Have they been successful?

2. What is the greenhouse effect? What has caused it? Do you think it accounts for the rising levels of the seas?

3. Environmentalists believe that federal insurance programs designed to help homeowners in high-risk areas actually contribute to the destruction of these areas. Explain their thinking. Do you agree with them? Why or why not?

Group Activities

In groups of five or six, list and discuss the various methods mentioned in the article to slow coastal erosion. Do any of them seem effective? Can your group add any solutions to the list? Do you think such efforts are a losing battle against nature? Be prepared to summarize your group's discussion for the whole class.

Individual Work

Do you think that people should be allowed to build on coastal areas? Do you think that people already living in coastal areas should be encouraged or forced to leave? Explain your answers in a written summary (one page maximum) of your position on this issue.

Article Five

Background Notes

for **Coming Back from the Brink**

Preview

*Leopards and alligators, once threatened with extinction,
now exist in large numbers. Many other endangered species,
however, have not had such successful comebacks.*

Culture

Crocodile Dundee [ˈkrɑkəˌdaɪl dənˈdi]: the main character in an Australian movie of the same name. Crocodile Dundee had great skill in capturing crocodiles.

endangered list: an official listing of the plant and animal species in danger of extinction. Every year more species are added to the list.

U.S. Fish and Wildlife Service: a federal agency responsible for the maintenance and preservation of non-domesticated animals

Vocabulary

assault [əˈsɔlt]: an attack

assiduously [əˈsɪdʒuəsli]: diligently; with constant attention

bayou [ˈbaɪˌ(j)u]: a marshy body of water; a creek that leads to a river or larger body of water

catastrophe [kəˈtæstrəˌfi]: a disaster; a tragic event

coax [koks]: to persuade gently; to influence in a kind manner

consciousness [ˈkɑnʃəsnəs]: awareness

elimination: the act of getting rid of something

feline [ˈfiˌlaɪn]: any member of the cat family. Lions, tigers, and leopards are all felines.

flagrant [ˈflegrənt]: conspicuous; unable to go unnoticed

habitat: the location where a kind of plant or animal naturally lives. Numerous animal habitats are being destroyed by man.

harvest: a killing of animals. Normally the term **harvest** refers to a gathering of food crops at the end of the growing season.

indifference: a lack of concern; a lack of interest; apathy

phenomenal [fəˈnɑmənəl]: amazing; remarkable; extraordinary

poacher: a person who illegally captures or kills animals. Poachers who are caught receive severe penalties.

rebound: to recover; to spring back

recategorize [ˌriˈkædəgəˌraɪz]: to put into a different classification; to reclassify

tanning factory: a place where animal skins are treated for use. Leather is produced in tanning factories.

Coming Back from the Brink

Alligators and leopards are no longer seen as endangered

To animal preservationists, leopard coats and alligator shoes have long ranked among the most flagrant symbols of human indifference to the fate of wild animals. Even among the general public, consciousness has been raised high enough so that anyone sporting finery made from the skins of endangered animals runs the risk of at least verbal assault.

The attackers may have to shift emotional gears, however. Last month the U.S. Fish and Wildlife Service formally announced that the American alligator is no longer an endangered species. And, at a meeting this week in Ottawa, the U.N.'s Convention on International Trade in Endangered Species will release a report urging not only that the common leopard be removed from its list of endangered animals but that legal hunting be resumed.

While the alligator's recovery has been "phenomenal," according to David Klinger of the FWS, it seems that the spotted feline may never have faced a catastrophe in the first place. Unlike its truly rare cousin the Himalayan snow leopard, the common leopard made the list, in the 1970s, largely for emo-

tional reasons. Worries about shrinking habitats and excessive hunting were "clearly overblown," admits Jaques Berney, deputy secretary-general of CITES. "Leopards are not like cheetas," he observes. "They're highly adaptable animals."

The push to recategorize the leopard is based on a five-month study, conducted in 23 countries by Rowan Martin, chief ecologist for Zimbabwe's department of national parks and wildlife management, and Belgian Biologist Tom de Meulenaer. The pair used eyewitness accounts and statistical computer modeling to estimate Africa's leopard population at a healthy 700,000 to 850,000. The 75- to 150-lb. cats have even been sighted recently on the outskirts of Nairobi. The biologists went so far as to recommend the resumption of international trade in leopard skins. The best approach to leopard management, they argue, is to legalize a limited "harvest," diverting revenues from poachers and providing an estimated $29 million to "governments and law-abiding citizens."

The reclassification of the alligator,

however, is a true victory. Twenty years ago, the toothy reptiles had been so assiduously hunted, says FWS Director Frank Dunkle, "that many believed the species would never recover." Skin-seeking poachers had killed the animals by the tens of thousands. In 1966 Congress passed the first of the Endangered Species Acts, which banned hunting any animal at risk of elimination over a major part of its range. Such legislation was spectacularly successful for the gators, thanks in large part to the FWS agents who enforced it.

One of the heroes was David Hall, an agent who went undercover for nearly ten years in the swamps and bayous of the South. Hall would get to know the locals and start buying alligator hides from traders; at one point, he operated a tanning factory for more than a year. "The big traders would bring their skins to me in 18-wheel trucks," says Hall, "and we'd bust them on the spot. I know the real Crocodile Dundees, and I've arrested about half of them."

Alligator populations rebounded rapidly. Says Klinger: "All we had to do was stop the poachers, and the gators did the rest." In

New surveys suggest the spotted feline was never at risk in the first place

Alabama, for example, biologists reported a tenfold increase in alligators between the mid-1970s and the early '80s. By 1985 the FWS declared the animal no longer endangered in Louisiana, Florida and Texas, where 90% of the animals live, and last month it extended that decision to the seven other states where gators are found. "We've got more alligators than we know what to do with," exclaims Klinger, who says there may now be several million.

The alligator is not the only FWS success: the brown pelican, once in danger, is now off the list in several states. The bald eagle is up from its 1963 low of 417 active nests in the lower 48 states to some 2,000 breeding pairs this year—not enough to be declassified but an impressive return for the national symbol. Unfortunately not all protected species can be coaxed into bouncing back. Despite government protection, there are no known California condors left in the wild; the remaining 27 are in captivity. And in 70 years of trying to save the whooping crane, the population has grown from a low of 15, in 1941, to just 170 birds. Nor can deletions from the endangered list begin to keep pace with the new additions. At the moment, 449 animal and plant species remain listed in the U.S.; 37 of them were added in 1987 alone.

By Michael D. Lemonick.
Reported by Jerome Cramer/Washington and Robert Kroon/Geneva

QUESTIONS AND ACTIVITIES

Comprehension Questions

1. Why has the alligator been taken off the endangered species list? What accounts for the large numbers today, especially in the South?

2. Why was the leopard put on the endangered list? What are some scientists recommending regarding the leopard? Why?

3. What are some other animal species that have larger populations now than a generation ago?

4. How many plant and animal species are on the endangered list for the United States?

Discussion Questions

1. Do you think a limited legal harvest of leopards should be allowed? Why or why not?

2. Do you believe that protecting species of plants and animals is necessary and important? Why or why not?

3. Can you think of any other endangered species besides those mentioned in the article? If so, what is their habitat? Is there hope that their numbers will increase?

Group Activities

In groups of five or six, select the statement below that best describes the position of the group:
   a. Any kind of fur should be used for clothing.
   b. Only furs from unendangered species should be used for clothing.
   c. Only furs from domesticated animals, such as rabbits and minks, should be used for clothing.
   d. No furs of any kind should be used for clothing.
Once a consensus is reached, discuss reasons in support of your group's position. Be prepared to present your position to the entire class.

Individual Work

Poll five to 10 people to learn their reactions to the following question:
   If you could afford to, would you buy a fur coat? Why or why not?
Tally the responses and summarize your findings in a brief written report (one page maximum).

Background Notes

for **Stalagmites and Stunning Vistas**

Preview

*After more than 100 years of attracting visitors, the
Great Basin Area has become a national park. Local
residents are providing suggestions for its management.*

Culture

"multiple use" privileges: an official designation that allows for various uses of public lands. The uses might include mining, oil drilling, and livestock grazing, for example.

town-hall meeting: a meeting of the citizens of a town to discuss business of concern to them. Town-hall meetings are characteristic of rural areas.

Vocabulary

cirque [sɚk]**:** a basin on a mountain shaped like half a bowl. Cirques have very steep sides.

conservation: the preservation and protection of a natural resource

dignitary [ˈdɪgnəˌtɛri]**:** an official; an important person

foothills: small hills at the base of a mountain

frolic [ˈfrɑlək]**:** to play happily

grazing: feeding done by animals, such as sheep or cattle, in a field

limestone: a kind of rock formed by organic remains, such as shells. Caves are often formed in limestone.

overture [ˈovɚtʃɚ]**:** a proposal; a suggestion that something be done

sediment [ˈsɛdəmənt]**:** material left behind by water, wind, or glaciers

sledgehammer [ˈslɛdʒˌhæmɚ]**:** a kind of large, heavy hammer. Two hands are needed to use a sledgehammer.

stalactites [stəˈlækˌtaɪts]**:** a formation hanging from the roof of a cave. Stalactites resemble icicles.

stalagmites [stəˈlægˌmaɪts]**:** a vertical formation on the floor of a cave. Stalagmites are formed by the dripping of water containing certain minerals.

tundra: a treeless plain found in arctic and subarctic regions

Ancient and awesome beauty: rock formations of Lehman Caves and towering Wheeler Peak highlight the natural splendors of Great Basin Park

Stalagmites and Stunning Vistas

Great Basin is Nevada's majestic new national park

Rising abruptly from the eastern Nevada desert, snow-capped Wheeler Peak has long been a regional attraction. Visitors began arriving in 1885, after Rancher Absalom Lehman discovered vast limestone caves in the neighboring foothills. Swinging a sledgehammer to cut paths through forests of stalactites and stalagmites, Lehman then led candlelight tours through the caves for a dollar a head. After President Warren G. Harding declared the caves a national monument in 1922, Manager Clarence Rhodes rented them out for weddings, dances and initiation ceremonies for the Knights of Pythias, who frolicked in clouds of sulfurous smoke wearing costumes.

Last week, beneath the majestic 13,060-ft. mountain, Nevada Governor Richard Bryan and former Senator Paul Laxalt, along with other dignitaries, dedicated the surrounding 120 sq. mi. of wilderness as Great Basin National Park, the country's 49th. Named by Explorer John C. Frémont, the area known as the Great Basin stretches across northern Nevada, touching California, Oregon, Utah and Idaho. Once an inland sea, it was formed 20 million

years ago by geologic plates thrusting sediment layers upward into mountain ranges. The relatively small national park contains nearly all the Great Basin's ecosystems, from desert to arctic-alpine tundra, encompassing 3,000-year-old bristlecone pines, glacial lakes and one of the continent's southernmost permanent ice fields. As recently as 10,000 years ago, bowl-like cirques in the park's mountains were sculpted by glaciers, which left in their wake gray carpets of rock known as taluses.

Federal agencies have managed the area since 1932, but efforts to make the caves and neighboring mountains into a national park were frustrated by local ranching and mining interests. Great Basin Park, however, is good news for nearby White Pine County, a dusty patchwork of small towns, ranches and mines. Indeed, merchants from Ely (pop. 7,000) convinced Nevada's congressional delegation last summer that the park was desperately needed. For decades, Kennecott Copper Corp., which provided thousands of jobs at an open-pit mine near Ruth, had argued that the mountains might be mineral rich. By 1980 the mine was

closed, undercut by cheap foreign copper. Unemployment skyrocketed. The new park, they hoped, would bring paying guests for hotels, restaurants and other services. Conservation suddenly began to look like good business.

At Laxalt's urging, the Reagan Administration, normally cool to such environmental overtures, went along. One reason: Laxalt helped negotiate "multiple use" privileges for cattle grazing and valid mining claims. Even so, it will take years for the new park to become fully operational, says Superintendent Al Hendricks. Hiking paths are barely marked, roads often too bumpy for cars, and campsites have no potable water. Rangers are still taking inventory of plant and animal life, charting soil types and reviewing mining claims. The public has taken a role in park planning through a series of town-hall meetings. Among the suggestions: erecting campsite fences to keep out cows and banning fat-tired all-terrain bicycles from trails.

By James Willwerth/
Great Basin National Park

QUESTIONS AND ACTIVITIES

Comprehension Questions

1. Where is the new Great Basin National Park located?
2. What are some of its interesting geological and ecological attractions?
3. For many years what prevented the Great Basin Area from becoming a national park?
4. What benefits will the national park have for the nearby residents?

Discussion Questions

1. Have you ever visited a national park, either in the United States or in another country? If so, which one? Describe it to the class.
2. What are the advantages and disadvantages of an area of a country being set aside as a national park?

Group Activities

Imagine that a new national park is being established in your area of residence. Imagine also that a citizens' group is being allowed to provide ideas for management of the park. In groups of four or five, decide on rules for use of the park. You may wish to discuss the following issues in your group:

a. Will the park have unlimited access? Or will only a certain number of people be allowed to use it at one time?
b. Will you permit hiking and camping? What about hunting and fishing?
c. Will the park be open all year or only during certain seasons?

Be prepared to present your list of rules to the entire class.

Individual Work

Choose one of the following activities to do:

a. Identify an area of your home country that you think deserves to be a national park. Write your reasons for your choice (one page maximum).
b. Using a map of the United States, find the national parks. Make a list of at least 15 parks and their locations. Compare your list to those of the other students. Did they locate any national parks that you did not?

Science & Technology

Article One

Background Notes

for **Games That Grownups Play**

Preview

Computer games were at first designed for children and teenagers. Now, however, businesspeople are major consumers of computerized entertainment.

Culture

coffee break: a short period of relaxation given to employees during their workday. Coffee breaks may be as short as 10 minutes or as long as 30 minutes.

computer buff: a fan; an enthusiast. Computer buffs are growing in numbers now that personal computers are readily available.

corporate rat race ['korp(ə)rət . . .]: the high-pressured competition and resultant frenzied activity that exist in large corporations. The corporate rat race can be very stressful.

Donkey Kong: an extremely popular video game

Pac-Man: an extremely popular video game

R-rated: one of several ratings used to indicate appropriate audiences for films. An R-rating indicates that the film is for restricted viewing due to explicit language or content that is violent or sexual in nature.

Vocabulary

alien ['eliən]: a being from another planet. Aliens are frequent subjects of science fiction books and movies.

bollixed up ['bɑləkst əp]: confused; disordered (slang; tends to be old-fashioned)

cockpit: the part of an airplane where the pilot and crew sit to fly the plane

decompressant [ˌdikəm'prɛsənt]: something that reduces pressure; something that lessens mental distress

exploit [ɛk'sploɪt]: to take advantage of; to use for one's own ends

geek: a strange and/or socially inept person. The stereotypic geek is a student interested only in science. (slang)

hole in one: the lowest possible score for one hole of golf. A hole in one is very rare.

lewd [lud]: obscene; coarse; sexually explicit

novice ['nɑvəs]: a beginner; a learner

pimple: a small swelling of the skin from a clogged pore, usually on the face. Pimples usually occur during the teenage years.

sand trap: a hazard to be avoided while playing golf

simulation [ˌsɪmjə'leʃən]: something that gives the appearance of something else; a representation

sly, on the: secretly; furtively (colloquial)

software: operating programs for computers. The equipment itself is called hardware.

suppress [sə'prɛs]: to discourage the production of; to stop the development of

tolerant: accepting; allowing

zap: to strike down; to destroy by shooting

Games That Grownups Play

Business machines loosen up and have a bit of fun

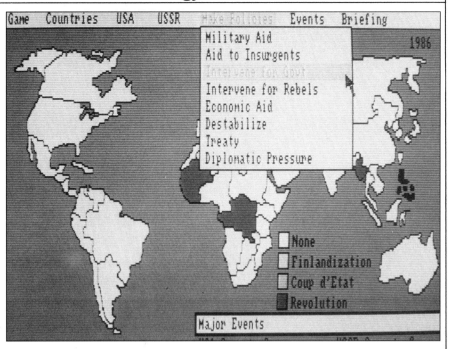

Balance of Power: countering the global Soviet threat

Jim Cantrell, the chief financial officer of a San Diego diving-suit manufacturer, has been known to drive ten miles to his office on a Saturday just to play Starflight on his IBM Personal Computer. Jim Bonevac, a senior economist for the state of Virginia, likes to spend lunch hours playing APBA Baseball and other games on his Leading Edge computer. Peter, a San Francisco marketing representative, uses lunch breaks to get in rounds of Mean 18 golf on an IBM PC Model AT, although he feels guilty enough about fooling around on the company computer to shut off the game the moment he hears the boss coming his way.

Who said office computers could only be used for work? Machines designed to juggle equations, balance budgets, process words and draw graphs are now also capable of bringing a little fun and adventure to the corporate routine—either after hours or on the sly during the workday. Of the 15 million personal-computer games sold in the U.S. last year, according to Ingram Software, a leading game distributor, nearly 40% were designed for the most popular business machines: the IBM PC, the Apple Macintosh and such IBM-compatible brands as Compaq, Epson, Leading Edge and Tandy. In 1985, by contrast, only about 15% of the games sold would run on business computers. When 750 U.S. executives were polled by Epyx, creator of Winter Games and Temple of Apshai, nearly 40% admitted that they had used their office computers for entertainment. Says Will Rodriguez, assistant manager of a B. Dalton's Software Etc. shop in Torrance, Calif.: "We sell an awful lot of games to people in business suits."

Traditionally, game publishers steered away from business computers. Games that ran well on Atari or Commodore machines could not be easily adapted to the IBM PC, primarily because it did not come equipped with a joy stick. The more versatile Macintosh was better suited to game playing, but Apple, which was eager to have the machine accepted as a serious business computer, discouraged independent game developers and even suppressed some early staff-written entertainment programs.

More important, software companies feared that games written for business computers would not sell. "The thinking was that the average player was a 17-year-old geek with pimples who wanted to blow up spaceships," says Chris Crawford, a former game designer at Atari who now writes programs independently for both business and home computers. "Publishers are just beginning to realize there is another market out there."

To exploit that market, software houses are busy developing adult-oriented games that are more sophisticated than Pac-Man and Donkey Kong and can be played as easily on a keyboard as with a joy stick. Programmer Crawford's best seller, for example, is Mindscape's Balance of Power ($49.95), a foreign policy simulation in which the player tries to check Soviet expansion in 62 different countries without starting a nuclear war. In Starflight by Electronic Arts ($49.95), players explore some 270 star systems and 800 simulated planets, zapping aliens all the way. Infocom has even come out with an "R-rated" adventure game called Leather Goddesses of Phobos ($34.95) to $39.95), which features Martian sirens bent on turning earth into their "private pleasure palace." The game comes in three levels: tame, suggestive and lewd.

Many of the top-selling games for business computers are based on adult pastimes. In Accolade Inc.'s Mean 18 ($44.95 to $49.95), armchair golfers can hit a sand trap or score a hole in one without ever stepping into the hot sun. Software Toolworks' popular Chessmaster 2000 (160,000 copies sold at $40 to

$45) offers players up to 20 levels of difficulty, from novice to grand master. The classic of business-computer games is Microsoft's Flight Simulator ($49.95), which puts Walter Mitty pilots in the cockpit of a Gates Learjet or a Cessna 182. During the past five years, more than 500,000 copies have been sold.

Computer buffs maintain that managers should be tolerant of employees who want to sneak a small amount of computerized relaxation into their workday. Stewart Alsop, a computer columnist for *PC World,* argues that game playing can serve as a "decompressant" for people caught up in the corporate rat race. Says he: "You get all bollixed up, you play a game, it clears your mind, and you start over again." One executive who agrees is David Winter, president of Living Videotext, a software publisher that does not put out games: "I don't want my employees playing all day," he says, "but I certainly don't object to an occasional play. We have coffee breaks, why not have computer-game breaks?"

Knowing that most bosses might take a different view, software companies have equipped many games with a "panic button." When the boss approaches, a player can hit a single key, thereby stopping the game instantly and bringing rows of businesslike figures to the screen. Such a feature is available on every game produced by Les Crane, a popular TV talk host of the '60s turned software publisher. Says he: "I hate to think we're seriously hampering the productivity of America. But, on the other hand, what the heck!"

By Philip Elmer-DeWitt.
Reported by Linda Williams/New York and David S. Wilson/Los Angeles

QUESTIONS AND ACTIVITIES

Comprehension Questions

1. What percentage of computer games were designed for use on business computers?

2. What percentage of executives interviewed said that they use their office computers for entertainment?

3. Why did publishers of computer games stay away from business computers?

4. What are some of the best-selling computer games? What is their average cost?

Discussion Questions

1. Have you ever played any computer games? If so, which ones? Describe the purpose of the game(s) to the class. If not, would you like to play computer games? Why or why not?

2. What games would you like to see developed for computers? Describe them.

Group Activities

In groups of six to eight, choose one of the statements given below to defend. Half the groups should choose the first position; the other half should choose the second.

    a. Employees should not be allowed to use office computers for games.

    b. Employees should be allowed to use office computers for games during their lunch hours and coffee breaks.

In your small group, select arguments in support of the position you have selected. Be prepared to present your arguments to the entire class.

Individual Work

1. Select one of the following activities to do:

    a. Visit a computer store. Make a list of the games available. Are there any you would like to play? Which one(s)? Why?

    b. Talk to someone you know who has a computer at the office. Is the person allowed to use the computer for games? Why or why not?

    c. If you worked in an office, would you like to be allowed to use the office computer for games? Why or why not?

Be prepared to give an oral report of your findings to the class (five minutes maximum).

2. Select another of the choices given in Individual Work 1 above. Give a brief oral report of your findings to the class.

Background Notes

for **In Arizona: White-Knuckle Astronomy**

Preview

Astronomy is a science that is both fascinating and frustrating. Bad weather, equipment failure, and a scarcity of telescopes all contribute to astronomers' problems.

Culture

little girl with the curl: a character in a nursery rhyme. The verse reads:
There was a little girl who had a little curl
Right in the middle of her forehead;
When she was good, she was very, very good,
And when she was bad, she was horrid.

Pillsbury Doughboy: the trademark character of Pillsbury bakery products. The Doughboy is very
['pɪlz,bɛri 'do,bɔɪ] plump.

Vocabulary

arduous ['ɑr,dʒuəs]: difficult; marked by great labor or effort

array [ə're]: a precise arrangement; a large number

balky ['bɔki]: refusing to act as expected; uncooperative

brutal [brudəl]: severe; cruel; unpleasantly incisive

commiseration [kə'mɪzə,eʃən]: sympathy; an expression of compassion

copious ['ko,piəs]: abundant; plentiful

crunch numbers: to perform statistical analyses of data. A person who does this is often called a "number cruncher."

cryptically ['krɪptək,li]: mysteriously

galaxy ['gælək,si]: a system of stars, planets, and other matter.

ire: anger

joker: one in a deck of playing cards. The joker, when used, can be played in place of any other card. Thus, a joker represents the unpredictable.

outhouse: an outdoor toilet facility. Outhouses are relatively small structures.

oversubscribed: requested in too large an amount

pirouette [,pɪrə'wɛt]: to turn completely. **Pirouette** is a ballet term meaning to turn fully on the toe or the ball of one foot.

post-doc: a person who already has a doctorate (a Ph.D.) and is pursuing a specialized course of study or doing research. Post-docs are usually based at prestigious research universities.

proposal: a written request for funding or other kinds of support for a professional project. Proposals are usually judged competitively.

smear: to stain or to smudge by spreading over a surface

summit the highest point; the top

trundle ['trəndəl]: to move on wheels

vista: a view, especially a wide and impressive one

white-knuckle ['waɪt 'nəkəl]: nerve-wracking. People who fear flying often call themselves "white-knuckle flyers." (Their knuckes turn white from gripping the arm rest.)

In Arizona: White-Knuckle Astronomy

Marcia Rieke sits on a mound of dirt on a cold mountaintop, nearly two miles up in the clear Arizona sky, watching the sun go down and worrying. A shadow slowly creeps past her, cast by a nearby tan, four-story building that looks like a gigantic bread box. Inside the bread box is the Multiple Mirror Telescope, the world's third and most powerful telescope. It looks like no other. There is no glistening dome; it might be a four-story barn. But there are 800 tons of it, and it turns. The whole structure can pirouette 360°, enormously simplifying the aiming of the instrument. It is probably the world's only building with snowplow blades on its corners to clear a path as it rotates about a circular track.

When its doors open, they reveal not a sleek, tubular telescope, but a six-eyed monster, a hexagonal array of half a dozen 72-inch mirrors, the sum of whose images equals the capacity of a single mirror 176 inches across.

None of which bears directly on the reasons why Rieke, a professor of astronomy at the University of Arizona, is worrying. She's been planning for this night for most of a year. Her invitation was an intriguing one: ''If you want to see some real white-knuckle astronomy, be out here on the 14th.'' Astronomy isn't normally considered as nerve-racking a profession as, say, commodities trading or the high wire. This is a mistake. There is great tension, and it comes from scarcity. The mountains around

Tucson, the ''astronomy capital of the world,'' may bristle with telescopes, but they are mighty rare in the remainder of the world. There are about 500 American astronomers who publish at least one scholarly paper a year; there are only eight telescopes large enough to see the extremely faint and faraway objects of interest to many of them.

Rieke has driven to the mountaintop with her husband George, also a professor of astronomy at the University of Arizona. The two of them are part of a team that made headlines around the world this winter when it announced the discovery of what appeared to be new galaxies farther out in space and back in time than any other yet seen. Tonight they plan to use the experimental Red Channel Spectrograph, which ''sees'' deep red light when looking at a galaxy known as M82. Their ''eyeball,'' the spectrograph, is supposed to analyze light that has passed through the telescope, pick out energy in the deep red frequencies coming from the galaxy, and display it on a television screen in symbols that may help the Riekes understand what is going on out there. Deep red light passes through galactic dust more easily then most other colors, and the Riekes are hoping to use the telescope and the spectrograph to penetrate the dust obscuring what they believe is a nursery of new stars. Explains Marcia Rieke: ''This galaxy has made a whole lot of new stars, and very recently.'' Furthermore, she notes, ''this guy is in the neighborhood, close by, at 10 million light-years.'' The edge of the universe is, by some estimates, 15 billion light-years out there, and the M.M.T. can cover four-fifths of the distance.

Before a stargazer can even think about reaching those distances, it is necessary to get to the Arizona mountaintop. That's a tough trip, and one with two parts. First, the observer, who can be astronomer, physicist, mathematician or even chemist, applies well ahead of time to a screening committee of scientists. If the proposal is new, interesting and most likely doable, it is considered. ''Most nights are oversubscribed by 50%,'' says Rieke, ''and it can run as high as four times.'' Then there is a joker in the deck. If you as an applicant are approved and given a night or nights, that is your time. If it rains or clouds over, it is nevertheless still your night, and there are no second chances. You go back to the end of the line. On these mountains Mother Nature bats last.

The second part of the trip to the telescope is equally arduous. Marcia and George and their companion had just spent nearly two bone-shaking hours in a four-wheel-drive carryall with a light-year of mileage on it. The telescope perches on the summit of the mountain on a rocky outcrop that looks as if it were reproduced from a Chinese print. The road would intimidate a mountain goat. Two-thirds of the way up the 18 kidney-crushing miles to

Marcia Rieke and the six-eyed monster: patience helps

the summit we start running into snow on the road, and it is cold.

But then come Marcia's worries, and they are manifold: there are vigorous-looking clouds about, and it is cryptically announced that there are "some problems" with the Red Channel Spectrograph. Marcia has expressed earlier concern about the gadget, "about as big as a small outhouse," which contains a million transistors and costs $200,000.

A word here about the process of astronomy:

▶Rarely, rarely, does anyone actually look with an eye through one of these big telescopes. The "eye" now most probably is a charge-coupled device, the same electronic "film" that makes home video cameras work—except this electronic film is of extraordinary sensitivity.

▶Nobody wears tidy white laboratory coats. It is bloody freezing cold in the mountains, and the entire crew pads about swathed in layers of wool and copious amounts of down, like multicolored Pillsbury Doughboys.

"Some problems" with the Red Channel Spectrograph has but a single translation: the miserable thing won't work. It was performing perfectly in the Tucson lab, but it is being balky here at the telescope. These edge-of-the-possible electronic devices resemble the little girl with the curl: when they work, they can be wondrous, opening up both vistas and questions; when they quit, they can make you crazy.

Because the Red Channel Spectrograph is ailing and the Riekes are sharing the night with another astronomer, who is going first, there is nothing to do for a while. We drive a couple of hundred yards down to the common room, a comfortable building that houses a kitchen, a pool table, a satellite-dish TV, chairs and couches, and a library. After a quick microwave dinner, the Riekes go back to the M.M.T., where things are still not going well. Glaring at a spectrograph that has smeared a useless mess across the screen, George mutters, "This run is slightly snakebit," "Snakebit?" Marcia asks. "More like cobrabit." It's now 8:45. Marcia's object, M82, is due to become visible in a little more than four hours, and still the red channel isn't working. Marcia retreats to a corner in one of the labs, produces a hand-held calculator and a big stack of printouts, and proceeds to "crunch numbers." By 9:15 she becomes restless and wanders back downstairs. "I'm gonna see what those guys are doing." The red channel is having all its circuit boards replaced one by one. The changes do no good. Next the cables are switched about, likewise to no avail. 10:02. Marcia: "We're getting to a time where we're going to have to make a brutal decision."

10:12. Marcia: "This ain't a winner. I thought all we had to worry about was the weather." 10:20. Marcia: "We're dead in the water." The Riekes make a decision: they are going to give up their section of the night to the other astronomer, who's not using the red channel of the spectrograph. "This is the first time this has happened to me in a long time," says Marcia. "We'll just apply again." Back to the end of the line. Marcia and George go down to the common room for a little commiseration—and get it. A small, very late-night toast is offered. Morning arrives, and after too few hours of sleep in the mountaintop's minimotel, the equanimity of the night before has given way to a little ire. "A night like this could be career damaging to a 'post-doc,'" explains George. "They have only two years and, if lucky, ten viewing nights to prove their merit as astronomers."

George and Marcia prepare to head down the mountain and home. The day is clear and still cold. They drive back up to the M.M.T. to gather their equipment. Marcia, her arms full of tapes, papers and a computer, sidles over to the spectrograph, now completely sealed in its hard case, and delivers a small, satisfying kick. Then the Riekes climb into the truck and trundle down the mountain.

By Stephen Northup

QUESTIONS AND ACTIVITIES

Comprehension Questions

1. Where is the world's third most powerful telescope? What is it called?

2. What was the Riekes' famous discovery? What piece of equipment do they need to do their current work?

3. Why is it so difficult to get to use a telescope? What procedures must be followed to get to use the M.M.T.?

4. What happens if there is bad weather or an equipment problem the night an astronomer is allowed to use the M.M.T.?

Discussion Questions

1. According to George Rieke, "a night like this could be career damaging to a post-doc." What does he mean by this? Do you think this is true?

2. Given the long waits involved in using a telescope, why do you think people want to be astronomers?

Group Activities

Form groups of six to eight. Discuss the procedures for use of the M.M.T. presented in the article. Do you think these procedures are fair? Do you have any suggestions to improve the process? After your discussion, be prepared to present your suggestions to the class.

Individual Work

Poll five people to learn their opinions about the following question:

Do you think research in astronomy is important? Why or why not?

Write a brief summary (one and a half pages maximum) of their responses. In addition, be prepared to tell the class what you learned from the people you polled.

Background Notes

for **Dreaming the Impossible at M.I.T.**

Preview

The future is happening now at the Massachusetts Institute of Technology Media Lab. Dozens of research projects are expanding the uses of mass media.

Culture

counterculture: relating to a group opposed to the principles of the group in power. The 1960s and 1970s were marked by a strong counterculture movement.

Whole Earth Catalog: a catalog of tools and ideas originally published in the late 1960s and recently revised. The *Whole Earth Catalog* appealed to members of the counterculture.

Vocabulary

bankrolled: financed; supported financially

concave [ˌkɑnˈkev]: rounded inward. The inside of a bowl is **concave.**

culled [kəld]: selected; chosen

customize: to construct according to individual taste; to design according to one's needs

flattering: complimentary; showing praise

gadget [ˈgædʒət]: a mechanical item; a device. The term **gadget** is often used when one doesn't know the name of something.

groundbreaking: revolutionary; new and inventive

laser [ˈlezɚ]: a device that makes beams of light stronger. Laser is an acronym for *light amplification by stimulated emission of radiation.*

lurking: lying hidden; staying persistently in the background

maze: a confusing network of passages

mesmerizing [ˈmɛzməˌraɪzɪŋ]: fascinating; spell-binding

razzle-dazzle: a colorful or gaudy display intended to impress (colloquial)

seductive [səˈdəktɪv]: tempting; alluring

sponsor [ˈspɑnsɚ]: one who financially supports the work of a person or organization. Sponsors are always needed for research projects.

visionary: existing in one's imagination; not yet realized

Dreaming the Impossible at M.I.T.

In the Media Lab, the goal is to put the audience in control

What if television sets were equipped with knobs that let viewers customize the shows they watch? If they could adjust the sex content, for example, or regulate the violence, or shift the political orientation to the left or right? What if motion pictures were able to monitor the attention level of audiences and modify their content accordingly, lengthening some scenes while cutting others short if they evoke yawns. What if the newspapers that reach subscribers' homes every morning could be edited with each particular reader in mind—filled with stories selected because they affected his neighborhood, or had an impact on his personal business interests, or mentioned his friends and associates?

There are a lot of "what ifs," but none of these is mere futuristic fantasy. All of them, in fact, are the goals of research projects now under way at the Media Laboratory, a dazzling new academic facility at the Massachusetts Institute of Technology. The lab's unique mission is to transform today's passive mass media, particularly TV, into flexible technologies that can respond to individual tastes. Because of advances in computers, says Nicholas Negroponte, 43, the co-founder and director, "all media are poised for redefinition. Our purpose is to enhance the quality of life in an electronic age."

Two years ago, when the lab first opened its doors in Cambridge, Mass., the announced intention of "inventing the future" seemed like an impossible vague undertaking. But Negroponte has made believers of much of the corporate and academic establishment. Bankrolled by more than 100 business and government sponsors, he has filled his $45 million facility with a group of 120 gifted re-

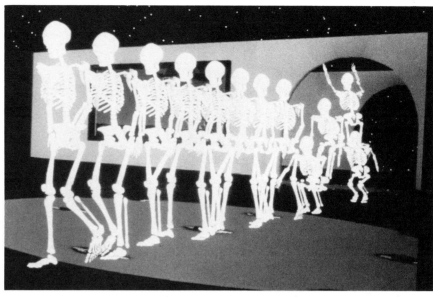

Automated actor: trying out a scene without hiring a cast

searchers that includes some of the brightest and quirkiest minds in computer science: Marvin Minsky, dean of artificial-intelligence research; Seymour Papert, disciple of Child Psychologist Jean Piaget and a leading advocate of computerized education; Alan Kay, one of the most influential designers of personal computers.

Some of the projects are still in the visionary stage, but several investigative teams have come up with working products and prototypes. In many cases, research relating to electronic media has led to spin-offs that could have wide applications for both individuals and businesses. Consider the following:

▶The lab's Conversational Desktop is a voice-controlled computer system that acts like an automatic receptionist, personal secretary and travel agent—screening calls, taking messages, making airline reservations. "Get me two seats to the Bahamas," says Research Scientist Chris Schmandt to his computer. "When do you want to go?" replies the machine.

▶NewsPeek is a selective electronic newspaper made of material culled daily from news services and television broadcasts. By sliding their fingers across the screen of a computer terminal, viewers can ask to see lengthier versions of particular stories, roll selected videotapes or call up related articles. The computer remembers what it has been asked to show and the next day tailors its news gathering to search for similar stories. Says Associate Director Andrew Lippman: "It's a newspaper that grows to know you."

▶The lab has developed the world's first computer-generated freestanding hologram—a three-dimensional image of a green Camaro sedan suspended in midair. Unlike most holographic images, which are put onto flat photographic plates, the Camaro is recorded on a concave plate and projected into the air by laser beams. The hologram was designed with funding from General Motors, which still painstakingly builds scale models of new car designs out of clay. In the future, GM and other automakers may be able to use holograms to see what a car will look like before it is actually manufactured. Eventually, such images may be made by laser-age copying machines for a few dollars apiece.

▶In the field of fine arts, the world-class music research center in the lab has already produced

Synthetic accompanist: responding to the slightest change in tempo

Talking head: next best thing to being there

Creating TV that may be too seductive.

the Synthetic Performer, a computerized piano-playing accompanist. The system not only plays along with soloists but also adapts to changes in their tempo and cadence without losing a beat. The project is part of an ongoing effort to explore the mysteries of harmony and composition by teaching music appreciation to computers.

Negroponte began raising funds for the Media Lab in 1980 with the help of Jerome Wiesner, former, M.I.T. president. The two men sought out publishers, broadcasters and electronics manufacturers whose businesses were being transformed by the advent of VCRs, cable television and personal computers. Then they hinted broadly that the faculty at M.I.T. knew precisely where all this was headed. Money came in from such leading sponsors as IBM, CBS, Warner Communications, 20th Century Fox, Mitsubishi, Time Inc. and the Washington *Post*. Sponsors can send scientists and other observers to the Media Lab and make commercial use of any of the facility's research. Though many of the projects may never yield commercial or educational applications, only one company, Toshiba, has failed to renew its funding.

Visitors to the lab, a sleek four-story maze of gadget-filled work areas, are assaulted by strange sights. In a 64-ft.-high atrium, 7-ft.-long computer-controlled blimps may be flying overhead—part of a project to develop stimulating science activities for elementary and high schools. In another area visitors encounter computers that can read lips. After spending three months at M.I.T. last year, Stewart Brand, the counterculture guru who originated the *Whole Earth Catalog*, was impressed enough to write a flattering book titled *The Media Lab*, published by Viking Press.

But the lab's high-tech razzle-dazzle masks plenty of serious business. Investigators are experimenting with new forms of teleconferencing. One idea involved projecting video images of individuals onto plaster casts of their faces. The resulting "talking heads" were so lifelike that people using the system felt they were "meeting" with colleagues who were actually in another city. A major effort is also being made to enhance computer animation. Assistant Professor David Zeltzer, building on research he started at Ohio State, is developing new ways of simulating human figures and movement. One application would allow playwrights to see just how scenes would look without having to hire live actors to try them out.

Within the Media Lab there is a lurking fear that the research might prove too successful. Some of the scientists, who point to TV's mesmerizing impact, worry about creating new media so powerfully seductive that they might keep many viewers from venturing into the real world. Minsky, for one, has given that a lot of thought. "Imagine what it would be like if TV actually were good," he told Brand. "It would be the end of everything we know." Yet he and his groundbreaking colleagues seem more than willing to take that risk.

By Philip Elmer-DeWitt
Reported by Robert Buderi/Cambridge

QUESTIONS AND ACTIVITIES

Comprehension Questions

1. What is the mission of the Media Lab at M.I.T.?
2. Who funds the research at the Lab?
3. What is the Conversational Desktop?

Discussion Questions

1. What is NewsPeek? Do you think it's a good idea? Would you use it? Why or why not?
2. What are some of the other research projects at the Lab? Give your reactions to these projects. Do they seem interesting and important? Why or why not?

Group Activities

In small groups of four or five, brainstorm media ideas of your own. Be as imaginative as possible. Be prepared to present your list of ideas to the rest of the class. Once each group has presented its ideas, select the three best from the entire class.

Individual Work

The article suggests that the media will become so seductive that viewers will not want to venture into the real world. Do you think that there is any possibility that this may happen? Why or why not? Present your reactions in a brief written summary (one page maximum).

Article Four

Background Notes

for **Steps Toward a Brave New World**

Preview

*Experimental brain implants have helped treat
certain neural disorders. With these successes have
come ethical and technical problems.*

Culture

brave new world: the world of the future. *Brave New World* is a satirical novel written by Aldous Huxley that portrays the negative social results of scientific experimentation.

Frankenstein: the main character in a novel by the same name written by Mary Shelley. Frankenstein was a student who created a monster from corpses.

Boris Karloff: a 20th-century actor. Karloff is best known for his villainous roles in numerous horror films.

right-to-life: a movement of individuals who oppose abortion under any circumstances

science fiction: a category of literature devoted to speculation and imaginings on the impact of science on society. Science fiction has numerous fans.

Vocabulary

awed [ɔd]: filled with wonder; amazed

circumvent [ˌsɚkəm'vɛnt]: to avoid as a result of cleverness; to use skill or ingenuity to get around an obstacle

ethical ['ɛθəkəl]: moral; relating to particular standards of behavior. Ethical principles vary from culture to culture.

graft: living tissue that is surgically implanted. Grafts are often rejected by the body.

havoc ['hævək]: destruction; great disorder

heartening: encouraging; causing hope

immune system [ˌɪ'mjun ˌsɪstəm]: the body's natural defenses against diseases

implant ['ɪmˌplænt]: living tissue that is introduced surgically into other tissue

neural ['nɚəl]: pertaining to the nerves

optimistic: having a positive outlook; expressing a hopeful attitude. Pessimistic is the opposite of optimistic.

prelude: an introductory event; a happening that occurs before a more important occurrence

revived: made active again; restored to life

symposium [ˌsɪm'poziəm]: a (usually scholarly) meeting devoted to a single topic or related topics

tentatively ['tɛn(t)ə,tɪvli]: hesitantly; uncertainly

ultimate ['əltəmət]: final

wreak [rik]: to cause; to inflict

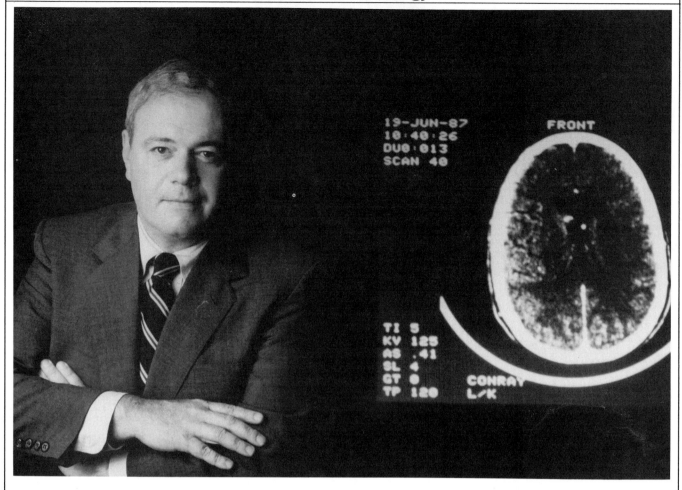

Vanderbilt's Allen with brain scan showing region of experimental adrenal-cell implant

Steps Toward a Brave New World

The rush is on to treat neural disorders with brain implants

For more than a year, Tess Follensbee had found it easier to start moving her rigid muscles if she walked backward, so pronounced was her Parkinson's disease. In May, all that changed. The 39-year-old mother of four was one of the first half a dozen Americans to undergo experimental brain surgery for Parkinson's at Vanderbilt University Medical Center in Nashville. Last week some 500 medical researchers, gathered at a symposium sponsored by the University of Rochester in New York, watched a videotape of Follensbee in awed silence as she triumphantly, if tentatively, propelled herself forward. Says the patient, who still suffers from slight tremors: "I have hope where there was no hope before."

The surgery that preceded Follensbee's partial recovery—the transplanting of tissue from one of her adrenal glands to her brain—may be only a prelude to even more remarkable developments. Several scientists at the Rochester meeting, citing promising research on animals, predicted that human fetal tissue

would eventually be implanted in brains not only to treat Parkinson's but Huntington's and Alzheimer's diseases as well as other brain disorders. Given the rapid surgical advances recently, there is no question that the rush is on to try adrenal-cell implants to correct Parkinson's, a neural disorder that afflicts an estimated 1 million Americans. At the Rochester conference, doctors from China to Mexico reported successes in dozens of adrenal implants. At least four U.S. medical centers, including New York University in Manhattan and Rush-Presbyterian-St.Luke's in Chicago, are planning to perform the operation on at least 30 Parkinson's victims in the next six months.

Parkinson's disease, which causes trembling and muscular rigidity, stems from the still unexplained gradual death of most of the cells in a tiny, darkly pigmented area of the brain called the substantia nigra. The cells produce dopamine, a chemical that helps transmit impulses from the brain through the nervous system to the muscles. The Vanderbilt

operations, adapting a technique that was developed in Sweden and first used successfully in Mexico last year, involve transplanting dopamine-producing tissue from one of the patient's two adrenal glands (located atop the kidneys) into the brain. Since the cells are the patient's own, there is no danger of rejection by the immune system. They are accepted by the brain and begin producing the needed dopamine.

Despite the heartening Parkinson's results reported in Rochester, doctors at the symposium were cautious. "In my mind, there is no question that the patients get better," said Dr. René Drucker-Colín, a leader of the transplant team at Universidad Nacional Autónoma de México, in Mexico City. "The real question is: For how long will they get better? Obviously, if the answer is six months, it would be less important to do this operation." Admitted Dr. George Allen, chairman of the department of neurosurgery at Vanderbilt, where twelve more operations are planned later this year: "This is still very much an experimental procedure. It is too early to tell if the improvement is due to the operation.''

Whether or not the recoveries prove to be long lasting, University of Rochester Neurobiologist John Sladek and Yale Psychiatrist Eugene Redmond see a braver new world ahead. The two scientists reported reversing the effects of Parkinson's in adult African green monkeys by implanting cells from the substantia nigra of monkey fetuses, and believe that fetal brain grafts offer a better bet for Parkinson's patients. Vanderbilt researchers, using fetal nerve-tissue implants in experiments with rats, also reported progress in reducing chemically induced symptoms of Huntington's disease, a fatal genetic brain disorder. Others expressed hope that once the underlying causes of Alzheimer's disease are determined, it too might be brought under control by implants of fetal tissue.

Despite some optimistic statements, most scientists are aware that ethical dilemmas as well as technical difficulties stand in the way of successful fetal-cell therapy. Many church leaders and right-to-life advocates oppose the use of tissue from artificially aborted fetuses. And doctors worry about using tissue from spontaneously aborted fetuses, which often have serious genetic defects. In any event, Sladek believes animal research on fetal tissue should continue for several more years before fetal-cell transplants are even attempted in humans. He and Redmond plan to treat monkeys and observe them for two to five years in order to detect any unexpected long-range effects. Still, Sladek is optimistic. Says he: ''I just know it's going to work.''

Another Rochester Neuroscientist, Timothy Collier, has already begun looking into freezing and storing fetal brain tissue for use in implants. He reported last week that he had successfully transplanted frozen-and-revived fetal neural tissue in both rats and monkeys. The next step: implanting the thawed tissue into monkeys afflicted with Parkinson's. The ultimate aim is to create neural-tissue banks that surgeons will be able to draw on for future operations.

Animal research may help answer some basic physiological questions about fetal brain implants. Will the brains of Parkinson's victims, most of whom are middle-aged or elderly, integrate with fetal tissue? Could a virus that found its way into the brain, which is nor-mally unaffected by the immune system, accidentally set off an abnormal immune response that would destroy the graft? And even without viral intervention, would the foreign fetal cells be rejected? Moreover, surgeons will have to know precisely how much tissue from what stage of development should be used in each transplant. Taking the tissue too early, for example, might result in runaway cell growth that could wreak havoc in the brain.

Sladek, for his part, believes that technology may circumvent some of these dilemmas. ''We may someday be able to genetically engineer the cells we need—add the genes for dopamine to cells, grow them in culture and use them in the brain. Whatever happens,'' he says, ''it will be exciting.'' Notes New York University Neurologist Abraham Lieberman, who will assist in N.Y.U.'s first adrenal-cell transplant this week: ''Five years ago, when you talked about brain transplantation, you were talking about Boris Karloff and Frankenstein. Today it's no longer science fiction.''

By Leon Jaroff.
Reported by Andrea Dorfman/Rochester and Christine Gorman/New York

QUESTIONS AND ACTIVITIES

Comprehension Questions

1. What kind of surgery has helped victims of Parkinson's disease?

2. Why are some doctors cautious about these surgical successes?

3. What other diseases may be helped by brain implants?

Discussion Questions

1. What are the potential problems—both moral and technical—regarding the use of fetal tissue for brain implants?

2. Do you think animals, such as monkeys, should be used for experimental brain surgery? Why or why not?

Group Activities

In groups of four to six, select one of the following positions to defend. Try to have each of the positions defended by at least one group.

a. No experimental brain implants should be done.

b. Experimental brain implants involving the patient's own cells are acceptable.

c. Experimental brain implants using cells from spontaneously aborted fetuses are acceptable.

d. Experimental brain implants using cells from artificially aborted fetuses are acceptable.

Individual Work

Which of the positions discussed in the Group Activity do you support? In a written summary (one and a half pages maximum), present your reasons for holding that position.

Article Five

Background Notes

for **Red for La Guardia, Brown for J.F.K.**

Preview

*Computer advances are aiding air-traffic control.
The successes are attracting the attention of other
federal agencies.*

Culture

Apollo [ə'pɑˌlo]: a brand of computer workstation

Max Headroom: the main character in a popular late 1980s television show. Max Headroom is a computerized image.

Vocabulary

alleviated [ə'liviˌedəd]: lessened; relieved

blip: an image on a radar or computer screen

choke point: an area of congestion; a point where traffic is clogged

fascinated ['fæsəˌnedəd]: awed; filled with wonder

interception: prevention of progress; a stopping of action

intervention: interruption; interference

intricate ['ɪntrəkət]: complicated; having many parts

linkup: a hookup; a connection

looming: impending; appearing as something about to occur

merge: to join; to unite

overburdened: overworked; having too many duties and responsibilities

pardonable: able to be forgiven or excused; capable of being ignored or overlooked

piecemeal: one piece at a time; in parts

precision: exactness

primitive: unsophisticated; characteristic of an early stage of development

unprecedented [ˌən'prɛsəˌdɛn(t)əd]: without precedent; having no previous example; one of a kind

virtuosity [ˌvɚtʃu'ɑsədi]: great technical skill

Red for La Guardia, Brown for J.F.K.

An intricate system augurs a new era for air-traffic control

At first glance, the image that flashed on the 19-inch computer screen looked like an ordinary road map. Then John Richardson, acting manager of the Federal Aviation Administration's Central Flow Control Facility in Washington, began tapping at his keyboard. With one stroke he zoomed in to an aerial view of the New York Metropolitan area, divided not along town or county lines but along sectors of airspace. With another keystroke he eliminated hundreds of tiny black dots showing the location of low-flying aircraft and private jets. What remained on the screen were larger, winged symbols representing commercial airliners. With a few more key taps he color-coded the jetliners according to their airport destination: red for La Guardia, green for Newark, brown for John F. Kennedy.

To computer buffs at ease with the graphic virtuosity of Max Headroom, the FAA demonstration might seem primitive. But to air-traffic professionals gathered in the agency's sixth-floor "war room," it represented a technological breakthrough. Prior to last week, FAA radar data showing the location of planes flying over the U.S. could be shown only piecemeal on computer screens at one or more of the aviation agency's 20 regional control centers. Now, all that information has been merged and displayed on a single cathode-ray screen, giving the nation's air-traffic controllers an unprecedented view of overhead traffic patterns as they unfold from coast to coast. Exclaimed the FAA's Richardson, with pardonable pride: "It's unbelievable!"

Well, at least impressively intricate. Last week's display—more evolutionary than revolutionary—involved the funneling of data on aircraft position, altitude, speed and identification from each of the regional air-traffic control centers to the FAA's Washington headquarters. There the information is merged into a manageable whole by an assembly of Apollo workstations and displayed via custom-designed software on as many as three dozen screens. The objective of the system is to provide centralized management of traffic problems as they may build up at any of the country's 12,500 airports. Cost of the new computer operation so far: about $2 million. The FAA's ultimate goal, though, is a multibillion-dollar air-traffic control system so highly automated that it can monitor flights and direct pilots with little or no human intervention.

Such a system is far in the future, but the new linkup may have arrived just in time. A badly overburdened U.S. air-traffic system has pushed control tower errors and airborne near

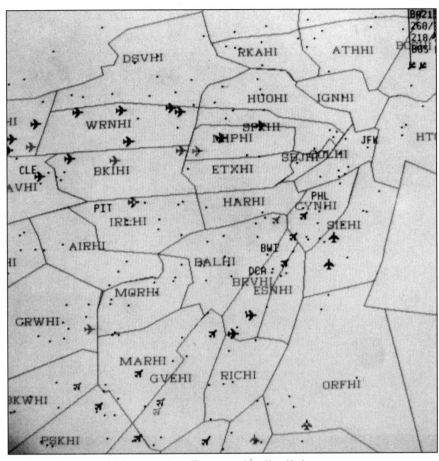

What the FAA sees: midafternoon air traffic approaching New York

misses to record levels. In the first three months of 1987, midair close calls increased 13%, to about 215, while errors by overtaxed air controllers jumped 18%. The looming safety crisis prompted James Barnett, chairman of the National Transportation Safety Board, to recommend earlier this month that the FAA take "immediate action" to reduce air traffic at key airports before the anticipated summer air-travel crush.

FAA officials say that with their new control system they will be able to meet those recommendations without reducing the number of flights entering or leaving the critical choke points. Using the new computers, supervisors can monitor with greater precision specific sections of airspace that are becoming dangerously overcrowded. Traffic jams can then be alleviated or prevented by shifting the altitude of some flights or rerouting others so that they bypass congested areas. By this fall, when more complex computer programs should be in place, controllers hope to be able to predict at least two hours in advance when

an airspace sector is about to become saturated, and thus prevent delays. Says Jack Ryan, director of the FAA's Air Traffic Operations Service: "We will be ready to head off problems before they occur."

The FAA's glowing new capability is attracting curiosity from other federal agencies. The Defense Department, which must monitor the flow of aircraft into the U.S.'s air defense identification zone, is said to be fascinated by the new system. So is the Drug Enforcement Administration, which desperately seeks to know the identity of every aircraft entering U.S. airspace, especially those from the south. They are particularly impressed with an FAA feature that allows controllers to place an electronic cursor over an individual blip, press a key and see all the available aircraft data displayed on the screen. Any blip that fails to provide information has not registered a flight plan with the FAA and may be fair game for interception.

By Philip Elmer-DeWitt.
Reported by Jerry Hannifin/Washington

QUESTIONS AND ACTIVITIES

Comprehension Questions

1. What is the purpose of the air-traffic control system described in the article?

2. What is the use of the color-coding feature of the system?

3. What other kinds of flight information can be displayed with this system?

Discussion Questions

1. What other federal agencies are interested in the FAA's new air-traffic control system? Do you think these agencies would make appropriate use of the system? Why or why not?

2. Some say that there is a safety crisis in air-traffic control. Do you think that this is true? If so, what do you think are the causes of the problems? If not, do you anticipate that there will be problems in the near future? Why or why not?

Group Activities

In groups of five or six, brainstorm solutions to heavy air traffic. You may wish to consider the following potential solutions, among others:

  a. build more airports
  b. reduce the number of flights
  c. develop better computer systems to track flights
  d. raise the prices of airfares to reduce the number of passengers

Be prepared to present your recommendations to the whole class.

Individual Work

What do you personally think are the best solutions to the problems of heavy air traffic and overworked air-traffic control systems? Summarize your recommendations in a brief (one and a half pages maximum) written report.

Article Six

Background Notes

for **Examining the Limits of Life**

Preview

Medical advances have resulted in longer human life-spans. However, at least one medical ethicist believes that the quality of life should be more important than its length.

Culture

living will: a document in which a person requests that no "heroic" medical measures be taken if he or she is terminally ill or otherwise has no hope of surviving a disease or injury. Doctors may choose to ignore living wills.

Pandora's box: something that appears valuable, but is actually a curse. In Greek mythology, Pandora possessed a gift that was never to be opened; when it was, all the evils of the world were released.

surrogate mother ['sɚəgət]: a woman who bears a child for a couple when the wife is unable to conceive. The woman is artificially inseminated. Surrogate motherhood is legally and ethically controversial.

think tank: an organization of individuals whose purpose is to deliberate over critical societal issues and to propose solutions. Some think tanks are conservative in their orientation; others are liberal.

Vocabulary

austere [ˌɔ'stɪr]: severe; serious; grave

battlement: a structure of a castle used for defense

chide [tʃaɪd]: to scold; to show disapproval of

chronic ['krɑnək]: characterized by a long duration; characterized by frequent recurrences

eccentric [ək'sɛntrək]: unusual; strange

eloquence ['ɛləkwənts]: forceful expression; moving discourse

euthanasia [ˌjuθə'neʒə]: the painless putting to death of an incurably ill person

exotic [əg'zɑdək]: unusual; strikingly different

forthrightness ['forθˌraɪtnəs]: honesty; frankness; openness

grapple: to struggle; to wrestle

inexorably [ˌɪn'ɛksɚəbli]: relentlessly; inflexibly

insatiable [ˌɪn'seʃəbəl]: unable to be satisfied

provocative [prə'vakətɪv]: stimulating discussion; inspiring interest or anger

relentless [ˌri'lɛntləs]: unyielding; unlessening

stance: a position; an intellectual opinion

unflinching: steadfast; not moving or changing

withering ['wɪðɚɪŋ]: devastating; serving to destroy

Examining the Limits of Life

A medical philosopher argues that longer is not always better

Americans have an "insatiable appetite for a longer life," complains Daniel Callahan, 57. They should be "creatively and honorably accepting aging and death, not struggling to overcome them." Medicine, Callahan chides, ought to "give up its relentless drive to extend the life of the aged," who in any event are often "being saved from death for chronic illness, with Alzheimer's as a tragic example." It is time to honor a "natural lifespan" that normally winds down in the late 70s to mid-80s, he says. "How many years do we need to have a reasonably decent life, to raise a family, to work, to love?"

A provocative argument: longer is not better. But Americans have shied off from similar points made in recent years. When former Colorado Governor Richard Lamm spoke out in 1984 about the terminally ill's "duty to die," his forthrightness seemed eccentric. In his writing, the late Dr. René Dubos urged more emphasis on the quality rather than the length of life, but his eloquence failed to generate sustained debate. Callahan, arguably the nation's leading medical ethicist, means to make discussion of the subject inescapable. For 18 years, as director of the Hastings Center in Briarcliff Manor, N.Y., he has grappled with the tide of problems arising from biomedical advances. In a new book called *Setting Limits* (Simon & Schuster; $18.95), he makes his hard case with a care that is feeling but unflinching.

The fastest growing age group in the U.S. proportionately is the over-85s, he reports, and children born this year can expect to live 16 years longer than their grandparents born in 1930. Such statistics prompt visions of a lifespan beyond 100 years, a prospect Callahan finds alarming. In the past two decades, the amount of the federal budget spent on those over 65 leaped from 15% to 28%; and the $80 billion spent in health care for the old in 1981 is expected to pass $200 billion by the year 2000. The result is a serious threat to the economics of health care.

Author Callahan at the Hastings Center

The elderly should be "accepting aging and death."

Callahan's long-term limits—medical, economic and social—will seem harsh to many. He would have Congress restrict Medicare payments for such procedures as organ transplants, heart bypasses and kidney dialysis for the aged. States should give legal status to "living wills," allowing individuals to demand that they not be kept alive artificially. Respirators would not be used for the terminally ill. On the emotional issue of extending life by use of feeding tubes, he reasons that as external life extenders in some cases, they also should be treated as artificial intrusions. His logic moves inexorably on to the withholding of costly antibiotics.

The author firmly opposes euthanasia, however, which involves active steps toward direct killing. And he would have doctors provide the elderly with greater relief of their suffering and more home care and support. He would also increase medical resources devoted to defective newborns, the now hopeless victims of AIDS or any nonaged patient with slim chances of recovery. "A 35-year-old has not had a chance to live out a full life-span," he says. "Some research may come along in time to save them—we don't know that they are all going to die." Callahan carefully avoids setting a flat cutoff age, preferring to let the condition of the patient, the judgment of the doctor and the wishes of the individual interact.

Part of his argument rests on a deep concern about "intergenerational equity." There are "better ways to spend money than indefinitely extending life," he charges. Long treatment of the elderly drains funds from the health needs of other groups and from urgent social problems. He also has withering views about many of the non-ill elderly: the "young-old" who deny age and indulge an "it's-my-turn" attitude. Their lives, says Callahan crustily, would gain meaning "if instead of taking a cruise, they work for a cause."

He knows that rationing health resources on the basis of age is an "austere thesis," but he takes to the intellectual battlements willingly. Thinking through the fundamental moral and practical problems of life is the unique concern of the Hastings Center, which he co-founded with Psychiatrist Willard Gaylin in 1969. Reared in a comfortable Roman Catholic family in Washington, Callahan earned a Ph.D. in philosophy from Harvard in 1965. By then he was a leader in the effort to liberalize Catholic thought as an editor of the Catholic weekly *Commonweal*. But about 1968 "I started fading from Catholicism," he says without elaboration. "I ceased being a believer." His wife Sidney, a psychology professor and writer on religion and feminism, converted to the church and remains active in it; they have six children.

Writing a book in 1968 on the morality of

abortion—he describes his stance as "conservative pro-choice"—Callahan hit on the idea for a think tank on biomedical ethics. At the start, Callahan and Gaylin wondered if there would be enough moral issues to keep them busy. But since an initial project on the definition of death, Hastings researchers have dealt with organ transplants, artificial reproduction, surrogate motherhood (Callahan opposes it; some of his colleagues approve), AIDS testing and privacy, genetic engineering—a never-ending list.

The center, which now has twelve professionals and a support staff of 15, is housed in a stucco mansion on the Pace University campus and runs on an annual budget of $1.6 mil-lion, met largely through foundation grants and contributions from its 11,000 members. In addition to publishing regularly, the Hastings ethicists develop model legislation, draw up guidelines for public policy, consult in such tortured cases as Karen Anne Quinlan's fate and assist universities in setting up ethics departments. "People used to think of medical ethics as between doctor and patient at the bedside," says Callahan. "We consider wider public policy, how Government spends its money, issues that affect millions of lives, as well as the exotic issues where the number is small."

He puts artificial reproduction and genetics at the top of his list of emerging concerns. The possibility of selecting a child's sex, he contends, has "profound social implications." Advances in genetic screening that identifies whether the unborn individual will be subject to heart disease or cancer or schizophrenia raise a new round of issues. Would altering the defective genes in utero be ethically permissible, given the risk of unforeseen results for future generations? The moral dilemmas spawned by the high-tech world of biomedicine—closer to salvation or Pandora's box?—are sufficient to keep Callahan and his Hastings associates busy for a lifetime. A natural life-span, of course.

By Bonnie Angelo/New York

QUESTIONS AND ACTIVITIES

Comprehension Questions

1. What is Callahan's definition of a "natural life-span"?

2. Proportionately, what is the fastest growing age group in the United States?

3. What is Callahan's position on euthanasia?

4. Currently, what are two main topics of interest at the Hastings Center?

Discussion Questions

1. Do you agree with Callahan that the non-ill elderly should work for causes instead of taking cruises and participating in other "selfish" activities? Why or why not?

2. Have you ever heard of a living will before? What is its purpose? What potential problems are associated with living wills?

Group Activities

1. In groups of five or six, develop a list of up to 10 ethical problems raised by biomedicine. You may use some of the issues mentioned in the article, as well as others you think of. Why are these important societal issues? Present your list to the whole class, and have other groups present their lists. Then, as a whole class, make a list of the 10 most critical issues identified.

2. In groups of five or six, select one of the 10 issues identified by the class. Discuss the pros and cons of the topic. Attempt to reach a consensus in your group. Be prepared to report your group's position on the issue to the entire class.

Individual Work

1. Pick one of the 10 issues selected by the class in Group Activity 1. (Do not choose the same one your small group discussed in depth.) Present your opinion of the issue in a written statement (one and a half pages maximum).

2. Choose another of the 10 issues identified by the class. Poll five people to learn their reactions to the issue. Summarize your findings in a written report (one and a half pages maximum). Be prepared to report orally to the class as well.

Article Seven

Background Notes

for **In Case You Tuned In Late**

Preview

Impressive technological advances have occurred in televisions and video recorders. It may be some time, however, before the public catches up with these developments.

Culture

Moonlighting: a popular television comedy/mystery series of the 1980s. "Moonlighting" is known for its innovative writing and broadcasting.

MTV: Music Television. MTV is a cable channel that broadcasts only rock videos.

Vocabulary

blow someone away: to amaze someone; to greatly impress someone (slang)

distortion: an inadequate reproduction; an altered copy

fare: to succeed; to get along

frame: a transmitted image; a single picture in a series of pictures in a movie or video

hurdle: a barrier; an obstacle

mar: to spoil; to damage

radical: extreme; drastic

scheme [skim]: a plan; an outline

sluggish: slow moving

snow: light spots on a television screen that resemble snow

surmount [sɚ'maʊnt]: to overcome

top-of-the-line: the best of a category of items; the best of what is available

undulating ['əndʒə,ledɪŋ]: moving with a wavelike action

In Case You Tuned In Late

TV's flashy new features are just a preview of coming attractions

Steven Minskoff, 28, a Manhattan real estate executive and a card-carrying member of the TV generation, thought he had seen and heard it all, from *Moonlighting* on a 35-in. screen to MTV in surround-sound stereo. Then he saw a store demonstration of Panasonic's new "picture in picture" VCR system, which lets viewers watch two or more programs on the same TV screen. As a salesman tapped on a remote control, new stations began appearing, one at a time, until the screen was filled with nine equal-size panels, each showing a different channel. "My mouth dropped," says Minskoff. "It totally blew me away."

Minskoff is not alone. Anyone who has shopped for a TV or VCR this season knows that television is going through some dramatic changes. The immediate effect is a flood of models endowed with high-tech conveniences, enormous screens and dazzling special effects. Waiting in the wings is a new generation of TV sets that are ready, once economic and political hurdles have been surmounted, to deliver images comparable in quality to those of a wide-screen motion picture. Says William Glenn, director of video research at the New York Institute of Technology: "This is the most exciting period in television history since the invention of color TV."

At the heart of the new features are computer circuits that change standard analog TV signals, which are broadcast as a series of undulating waves, into digital impulses—strings of 0s and 1s. The digital signals can then be transformed by microprocessors—tiny computers on silicon chips—to achieve a variety of exotic effects. When the processing is complete, the signals are changed back to analog for display on an ordinary TV picture tube.

When video signals take numerical form, all sorts of manipulations become possible. In addition to displaying multiple channels, the circuits can freeze frames or zoom in for close-ups. Digital VCRs can repeat sequences in slow motion or fast-forward without the distortion that mars conventional machines. Standard broadcast images can also be improved, up to a point. One video recorder made by NEC reduces interference by using microprocessors to compare successive image frames. By subtracting random elements that appear on one frame but not the other, the circuitry removes snow before it shows up on the screen.

None of this comes without cost. VCRs with digital features sell for $700 to $1,400, up to $1,000 more than conventional models. Digital TVs run from $1,500 to $3,000, in contrast to $1,800 for a top-of-the-line nondigital set. Given these prices, sales have been understandably sluggish. Digital VCRs will account for less than 3% of the 15 million videocassette recorders sold this year, and the high-tech TVs are not expected to fare much better. Observes

Feast for the eyes: Are four channels better than one?

David Lachenbruch, editorial director of *TV Digest:* "Consumers are not prepared to pay twice as much for one set with two pictures. They would rather buy two sets with one picture each." That could change quickly, of course, as the cost of the electronic components falls. "In the future," says Shinichi Makino, an executive at Toshiba, "digital will be mainstream."

On the horizon are more radical improvements in TV image quality that will come from attacking the problem at its source: the broadcast signal. American television is transmitted as a succession of images, each containing 525 horizontal lines, that follow one another at 30 frames a second. Japan's public broadcasting system, NHK, has developed a new standard called high-definition television, which widens the screen and more than doubles the number of lines, to 1,125. The result is a picture of extraordinary clarity that compares favorably with 35-mm film.

The problem with HDTV is that its signal cannot be squeezed into the narrow space allocated each channel in the TV broadcast spectrum. For the U.S. to switch to the new system, every television station would have to replace its equipment, and the country's 140 million TV sets would have to be scrapped, an unlikely prospect at present.

Nonetheless, several U.S. production companies have bought Japanese-made HDTV equipment for shooting movies, commercials and music videos. Reason: videotape is easier and cheaper to edit than film. *Crack in the Mirror,* a new action movie starring Robby Benson, was shot entirely on HDTV videotape, and will be transferred to 35-mm film for theatrical release early next year. Rebo High-Definition Studio in New York City, which produced the feature, estimates that its costs were 30% lower than if it had shot and edited the movie on film.

Various schemes have been put forth to make HDTV more widely available. One proposal is for cable TV operators to provide the higher-quality images as an added service for their subscribers. Another is to distribute HDTV programming on high-capacity videodisks, much as videotapes are distributed today. A third approach involves splitting the HDTV signal into two parts and transmitting it over two separate broadcast channels. Old TV sets could utilize enough of the signal to provide a standard-quality picture, while an HDTV receiver could display the higher-resolution image.

As U.S. broadcasters ponder what to do, the Japanese are making HDTV available on an experimental basis. Next year they will begin special coverage of the Seoul Olympics, which can be viewed in Japan only on HDTV sets. In 1990 Japan will launch a communications satellite designed to carry HDTV signals, capable of transmitting them anywhere in the world. But experts predict that it could be five years or more before the slow-moving U.S. networks begin to offer HDTV broadcasts of their own.

By Philip Elmer-DeWitt.
Reported by Kumiko Makihara/Tokyo and Thomas McCarroll/New York

QUESTIONS AND ACTIVITIES

Comprehension Questions

1. What features are available on the new generation of televisions and video recorders?
2. What are the prices of the new VCRs? of the new TVs?
3. Have sales of these new items been good?
4. What country is planning to use the HDTV technology in the near future?
5. What is preventing U.S. broadcasters from using the new HDTV technology?

Discussion Questions

1. Do you think you would have use for a television set that shows numerous channels at once? Why or why not?
2. Do you think the new VCRs will become popular? Why or why not?
3. Do you think HDTV will become widely used in the United States? Why or why not? What about in other countries?

Group Activities

In groups of six to eight, brainstorm ideas for other developments in TVs and VCRs. Use your imagination. At the end of your discussion, present your list of ideas to the whole class. Once every group has presented its list, have the class select the three most interesting and unusual ideas suggested.

Individual Work

Write a brief description (one and a half pages maximum) of what you think televisions will be able to do in the year 2010. Be as imaginative as possible.

Health & Fitness

Background Notes

for **Oh, Wow, Water Beds Are Back**

Preview

Water beds were once associated with the free-spirited lifestyle of the 1960s. Today most buyers are middle-aged and middle-class.

Culture

Jane Fonda: an award-winning contemporary actress. In many of Fonda's early roles, she portrayed mindless, sexy women. Later she accepted more challenging roles; in addition, she has starred in and produced a number of exercise videos.

Vocabulary

arthritis: an inflammation of the joints of the body. There are several different causes of arthritis.

baffle: a device to check the flow of something

blissfully: extremely happily

emblem: a symbol; an identifying mark

infamous ['ɪnfəməs]: notorious; having a very bad reputation

insomnia [ˌɪn'sɒmniə]: an inability to sleep well. Insomnia refers to a long-term problem, not just a single night's poor sleep.

orthopedist [ˌorθə'pidəst]: one whose specialty is orthopedics. Orthopedics deals with the treatment and prevention of skeletal problems.

scanty: in short supply; insufficient

sloshy ['slɑʃi]: moving with a splashing motion; characterized by a slapping of liquid

stumped [stəmpt]: puzzled; perplexed (colloquial)

therapeutic [ˌθɛrə'pjudək]: medicinal; having the effects of medicine; serving as a remedy

thermostat ['θɚmə,stæt]: a device that regulates the temperature of something

tout [tɑut]: to praise strongly; to publicize greatly

Resting happily: Arthritis Sufferer Nancy Wallrich and Husband Bert atop therapeutic mattress

Oh, Wow, Water Beds Are Back

A symbol of hippiedom is reincarnated in suburbia

Quiz time. Besides Jane Fonda, what sex symbol of the '60s has become a health emblem of the '80s? Stumped? Try the water bed. Yes, that infamous fixture of hippie pads has been transformed in just two decades into an increasingly popular middle-class therapeutic aid. Kathleen Hetland and her husband Darwin of Osakis, Minn., both 56 and arthritis sufferers, sleep blissfully on a water mattress that their children sent them as a gift. Says she: "I absolutely love it, and I wouldn't know what to do without it."

Today the water-bed industry is not only a $2 billion business (compared with about $13 million in 1971), but it is also the fastest-growing segment of the bedding market, accounting for 21% of all mattress sales. Last year 4 million water beds were sold (price: $100 to $600), nearly three-quarters of them to buyers over age 30. About one-fourth of purchasers now cite health reasons for choosing a water bed. The most common complaints are back pain, arthritis and insomnia.

The most popular water bed is still the original water-filled vinyl bag set within a plastic or wooden frame. Fast gaining in appeal, however, is the soft-sided bed made of vinyl with foam baffles, cells or cylinders inside that reduce wave motion. Water temperature can be varied by a thermostat-controlled heater mat that plugs into a wall socket.

The liquid system provides more even support than conventional bedding, say enthusiasts, contouring to body shape and thus easing stress on the buttocks, shoulders, elbows, hips, calves and heels. "It's just more support in the right places without exerting pressure on the wrong places," explains Stacy James, head of advertising for Land and Sky, a Lincoln, Neb., water-bed manufacturer. Sloshy cushions, say advocates, keep the spine in proper alignment and, along with the heat, help blood circulation. Ads now tout water beds as good for the whole family, from children to the elderly.

As yet, though, scientific proof for such claims is scanty. Water beds are helpful in the prevention of bedsores, a problem that afflicts up to 30% of patients in chronic-care facilities; some hospitals also endorse the use of flotation mattresses to help premature infants breathe more normally. Opinion is mixed, however, on whether water beds are good for back pain. Orthopedist Steven Garfin of the University of California at San Diego gives cautious approval. "Patients tend to do a little better in terms of range of motion and comfort on the water bed than conventional bedding," he says. But Dr. Rene Caillet, a rehabilitation specialist at Santa Monica Hospital Medical Center, is unconvinced. "If you lie on your stomach, the water bed allows you to increase the sway or the sag of the back," he notes.

Nonetheless, satisfied users abound. Nancy Wallrich, 56, a homemaker in Santa Fe Springs, Calif., who has had rheumatoid arthritis for 30 years, says her water bed has brought her uninterrupted sleep. It has also improved her sex life. "For me, many positions and movements had become difficult," she observes. "Now I am able to move around more." That sounds a lot like what water beds were famous for way back when.

By Anastasia Toufexis.
Reported by Beth Austin/Chicago and Bill Johnson/Los Angeles

QUESTIONS AND ACTIVITIES

Comprehension Questions

1. What percentage of mattress sales do water beds account for?
2. What age group buys the majority of water beds?
3. What therapeutic benefits do some believe water beds to have?
4. Is there scientific evidence for the benefits cited?

Discussion Questions

1. Have you ever slept on a water bed? If so, did you enjoy it? Why or why not? If not, would you like to? Why or why not?
2. Do you believe that there are therapeutic effects from sleeping on a water bed? If so, which ones? If not, why not?
3. Would you ever buy a water bed? Why or why not?

Group Activities

In groups of four or five, work together to write a commercial announcement for television or radio that advertises water beds for the Dreamland Bedding store. Once every group is finished, read the commercials to the entire class.

Individual Work

Take a poll of 10 people. Have them select the ending to the statement below that best describes their opinion of water beds.

I think water beds are
   a. good for one's health
   b. a fun novelty
   c. a waste of money

Summarize the results of your poll and present them to the class in a brief oral report.

Article Two

Background Notes

for **Snip, Suction, Stretch and Truss**

Preview

*Cosmetic surgery was once performed mainly on the wealthy and the aged.
Today numerous young clients are lining up for the services of plastic surgeons.*

Culture

baby boomer: a person born during the post-World War II period from the mid-1940s until the early 1960s. Because of their large numbers, baby boomers have caused many societal trends.

chop shop: a place where stolen cars are disassembled or disguised. A chop shop is characterized by fast and careless work, not attention to skill.

Goya ['gɔɪə]: a Spanish painter and etcher who lived from 1746 to 1828. Many of his paintings are known for their unflattering but realistic views of his subjects.

Me generation: the youth of the late 1960s and 1970s. The term resulted from the societal perception that the group was extremely self-centered.

Michelangelo [ˌmɑɪkəl'ændʒəlo]: an Italian painter, sculptor, architect, and poet who lived from 1475 to 1564. His sculptures are noted for their beauty and their anatomical accuracy.

Vocabulary

charlatan ['ʃɑrlətən]: a medical impostor; a fraud

collagen ['kɑlədʒən]: a protein occurring in the connective tissue of vertebrates

cosmetic surgery: surgery performed to improve one's appearance
[ˌkɑz'mɛdək 'sɚdʒɚi]

crow's-feet: tiny wrinkles around a person's eyes. Crow's-feet develop with age.

dermatologist [ˌdɚmə'tɑlədʒəst]: one whose specialty is dermatology. Dermatology concerns the structure and diseases of the skin.

grand-slam: total; complete. The term comes from baseball: A grand-slam home run drives in three men on base, in addition to the batter, for a total of four runs.

hype [hɑɪp]: excessive publicity (slang)

jowl [dʒɑʊl]: loose skin on the lower jaw or throat

moan: to complain; to lament

outpatient: characterized by medical treatment in a doctor's office, not in the hospital; characterized by treatment in a hospital that does not require an overnight stay

quack [kwæk]: one who pretends to be a doctor

rage: a fashion; an extremely popular item, issue, or practice

rehab ['rihæb]: rehabilitation; reconstruction. Usually used in reference to housing construction.

trussed: bound; secured tightly. Turkeys are trussed for cooking by binding their legs close to the body.

wizardry ['wɪzɚdˌri]: magic; extreme skill

Snip, Suction, Stretch and Truss

America's Me generation signs up for cosmetic surgery

A nip here, a tuck there, and the face you have at 40 is no longer the face you deserve but the face you can afford. In the past five years, thanks to new surgical wizardry, media hype and the laws of gravity exerting their inevitable effect on baby boomers, cosmetic surgery has soared in popularity. Last year some half a million Americans were snipped, suctioned, stretched and trussed, compared with 300,000 in 1981. Once the province of aging screen stars and wealthy matrons, cosmetic surgery now attracts middle-class office workers, many in their 30s and 40s, and many of them men. Los Angeles Plastic Surgeon Richard Grossman describes the phenomenon as "another transition" for the restless Me generation: "They protested against the wars, and now they're protesting against the mirrors."

More often than not, today's face-lift clients are fitness buffs who view a little surgical correction as the finishing touch to their efforts at the health club. "These people are in great shape and aware of their diet, yet their faces look older because of sun exposure," observes Dr. Stephen Kurtin, a New York City dermatologist. Michael, 46, a lean Manhattan executive typifies the trend. Over the past six months he has undergone a grand-slam rehab: eye lift, face-lift and collagen shots to plump out his facial wrinkles. "I had a body by Michelangelo and a face by Goya," he says. "No matter how much exercise I did, the face didn't respond."

According to the American Society of Plastic and Reconstructive Surgeons, the number of men seeking cosmetic correction has increased 35% in the past two years. They often cite professional image and job marketability as the reasons for smoothing creases or trimming jowls. Explains Dr. Melvyn Dinner, director of the Center for Plastic Surgery in Cleveland: "The 40-year-old who has lost his job is competing with a young hotshot. It's the competitive demand to look youthful."

Improving one's looks surgically has never been easier. A number of quick procedures can be done on an outpatient basis and require a short recovery period. Tops on the list, for women, is suction lipectomy, an operation developed in France and introduced in the U.S. in 1982. Also called liposuction, it entails the insertion under the skin of a hollow, blunt-ended tube that is attached to a high-powered suction machine that vacuums out the fat. The procedure can take 30 minutes to three hours, depending on how many problem areas are worked on. Removal of saddlebag thighs runs about $2,000; love handles, $1,500; saggy jowls, $1,300; and baggy knees, $1,200. Observes Dr. Jack D. Norman, a Miami plastic surgeon: "Twenty years ago, it was the nose job. In the 1970s, it was silicon implants. Now the rage is lipectomy."

An even newer trick, called lipofilling, makes use of the fat removed by liposuction to build up other areas, such as filling out cheeks on the face or redefining a jawline. The inspiration for the idea came from patients, says

Beverly Hills Plastic Surgeon Ian Brown. "They kept coming in and moaning, "Why can't you just take some from here and put it in there?'" he recalls. "Now we are doing just that." Steven Soll, 38, a Los Angeles financial planner, is looking forward to having fat suctioned from under his double chin and reinserted to strengthen his jawline. "I could go out and spend $20,000 on a car to make myself feel better," he explains, "or I could spend $3,000 to change something that has always bothered me." An older, simpler method to smooth the skin involves the injection of protein collagen into scars and wrinkles. This procedure usually requires several treatments plus an annual booster. Cost: $750 to $1,000.

Such readily available quick fixes for cosmetic problems have fostered a remarkably casual attitude toward plastic surgery. "I see it as a little investment in health, like owning an electric toothbrush," says Joyce Nesbit, 32, a Los Angeles psychologist who has enthusiastically undergone several procedures. But cosmetic repair has greater risks than a day at Elizabeth Arden. Collagen shots are painful; they can cause twelve to 18 hours of swelling and sometimes provoke allergic reactions. After liposuction, bruises and discomfort can last for weeks. Moreover, there are risks with any operation. Last March, Patsy Howell, 39, a Texas mother of two, died of a severe infection three days after undergoing lipectomy. At least two other deaths from infections have been reported.

The best protection against disaster is choosing the right doctor. Despite an abundance of qualified plastic surgeons, the $250 million-a-year industry has attracted numerous charlatans and quacks working in "chop shops." Doctors advise prospective patients to seek board-certified surgeons who have admitting privileges at reputable hospitals. Says Dr. Carl Korn, assistant professor of dermatology at the University of Southern California: "Choosing a surgeon is tricky, tricky, tricky. Walk into the office and look around at the others there who have had work done, and then only go in yourself if you like what you see."

Doctors debate whether or not public enthusiasm has gone too far. At Johns Hopkins, Dr. John Hoopes turned away a 23-year-old woman "who felt she would feel better if she had an eye lift." Hoopes estimates that he and his colleagues reject about 25% of those seeking cosmetic surgery, often because they are too young. But New York Plastic Surgeon Gerald Imber encourages preventive surgery for clients in their 30s and 40s: "The results are better when the raw materials are fresher." Indeed, so many eager candidates are intent on preserving their youthful looks that crow's-feet and turkey gullets may soon become endangered species.

By Martha Smilgis.
Reported by Jennifer Hull/New York and Nancy Seufert/Los Angeles

QUESTIONS AND ACTIVITIES

Comprehension Questions

1. Why are some young people who are in good physical condition deciding to have cosmetic surgery?

2. Compare the number of men having cosmetic surgery now with the number of men doing so two years ago. What are the reasons for the increase?

3. What cosmetic surgery procedures are currently available?

4. What are the potential dangers in cosmetic surgery?

5. Why do plastic surgeons reject some potential clients?

Discussion Questions

1. Do you think the advantages of cosmetic surgery outweigh the potential problems? Explain your answers.

2. What is your reaction to people in their 30s and 40s having cosmetic surgery?

Group Activities

In groups of five or six, imagine that you are a group of plastic surgeons who share a medical practice. It is the policy of your practice not to accept all applicants for cosmetic surgery. What questions would you ask potential clients to be certain that they are appropriate candidates for surgery? After your group's discussion, present your list of questions to the entire class.

Individual Work

Do you think you would ever have cosmetic surgery done? Why or why not? Present an explanation of your position in a brief (one page maximum) written statement.

Article Three

Background Notes

for **Stealthy Epidemic of Exhaustion**

Preview

Hundreds of people currently suffer from a mysterious fatigue syndrome. Medical researchers and doctors have been unable to identify a cause or to provide a cure.

Culture

Hollywood: a city in California. Hollywood, once known as the "movie capital of the world," still is a major center for the film industry.

support group: a group of people with similar problems who meet on a regular basis in the presence of a counselor or therapist to give assistance and comfort to each other. Support groups are formed for a variety of reasons: to cope with a serious disease or to face the death of a spouse, for example.

Vocabulary

affliction: continued suffering; great pain or distress

anvil ['ænvəl]: a block upon which metal is shaped. An anvil is extremely heavy.

depression: a mental state characterized by inactivity, sadness, and a low self-opinion. Depression sometimes has physical causes.

disproportionate [ˌdɪsprə'pɔrʃənət]: out of proportion; characterized by a lack of proper balance

epidemic [ˌɛpə'dɛmək]: an outbreak of disease affecting many people

epidemiologist [ˌɛpəˌdimi'ɑlədʒəst]: a person whose specialty is epidemiology. Epidemiology is concerned with the occurrence, spread, and control of disease in a population.

flagging: weakening; lessening

hypochondria [ˌhaɪpo'kɑndriə]: a state of mind characterized by imaginary physical ailments. Hypochondriacs generally have an unusual fear of disease.

hysteria [ˌhɪs'tɛriə]: excessive fear; excessive emotional behavior

sap: to weaken; to drain the energy from

stealthy ['stɛlˌθi]: secretive; sly

syndrome ['sɪnˌdrom]: a group of symptoms; a group of indications of a particular condition

virologist: a person whose specialty is virology. Virology is concerned with the study of viruses.

Stealthy Epidemic of Exhaustion

Doctors are perplexed by the mysterious "yuppie disease"

Gerald Kennedy, a high school teacher in Truckee, Calif., first attributed his flagging energies to the extra stress at the end of the school year. Then he developed more severe symptoms, including blinding headaches and painful sensitivity to light. He found it increasingly difficult to stay awake. Says Kennedy: "It was all I could do to get up to go to the bathroom." He was not alone. In the nearby Lake Tahoe area, about 150 others reported similar complaints. Two years later Kennedy has yet to return to work. Says he: "If you push yourself, you pay for it."

Like Kennedy, thousands of Americans believe they are victims of a stealthy epidemic that is draining their physical strength and mental energy. Initially, physicians attributed the mysterious affliction, which often strikes clusters of people, to a mixture of depression, hypochrondria and mass hysteria. It has been called the yuppie disease—because a disproportionate number of its victims have been young, white professionals—chronic mononucleosis or, simply, fatigue syndrome. Hollywood is rumored to be plagued by the disease. Film Director Blake Edwards struggled with it for three years. "Your body starts to collapse," he says. "It was a matter of hell every day."

Decades after it was first reported, fatigue syndrome still lacks a formal name, a cause or a cure. It saps both physical and intellectual reserves, producing symptoms that include swollen glands and fever. Its most devastating physical effect is extreme exhaustion. People use similar words to describe the weakness ("It's hard to lift my coffee cup," "It's like an anvil on my chest"). Many sufferers report suicidal depression and mental impairments, such as flawed memory and inability to read.

Medical researchers remain puzzled by the syndrome. Says Epidemiologist Jonathan Kaplan of the Centers for Disease Control (CDC) in Atlanta, who investigated the 1985 Lake Tahoe outbreak: "We don't know what causes it, and we have a hard time diagnosing it." Still, notes Stephen Straus, a virologist at the National Institutes of Health (NIH), who has interviewed sufferers, "you have to start believing what they're describing."

The symptoms and grouping of victims reminds some virologists of epidemic neuromyasthenia, a polio-like syndrome that occurred in clusters from California to Iceland between 1934 and 1960. Some victims suffered tiredness for years. No organic cause was ever discovered. The latest medical research has focused on several viruses active in fatigue-syndrome sufferers. One frequently cited suspect is Epstein-Barr virus, a member of the herpes family that is carried by an estimated 90% of American adults. Researchers speculate that stress, an immune-system deficiency or even environmental toxins could activate EBV, which is known to cause most cases of infectious mononucleosis and has been linked to Burkitt's lymphoma.

But they are unsure whether EBV causes fatigue syndrome or whether its presence merely reflects an immune system so weakened by another organism that it no longer keeps the virus in check. Two recent reports in the *Journal of the American Medical Association* failed to link EBV to fatigue syndrome. Harvard Researcher Anthony Komaroff, an author of one study, suspects that another virus, perhaps an "EBV mutant," will eventually prove to be the cause.

Of 500 Boston patients studied by Komaroff's team, 21% claimed to have suffered extreme exhaustion for at least six months. None had pre-existing organic illnesses that could account for their symptoms. The second *J.A.M.A.* paper, by Kaplan's CDC team, revealed that only 15 of 134 patients studied in the Lake Tahoe outbreak had "severe, persistent fatigue" of undetermined cause. The remainder either had symptoms that quickly disappeared, missed little or no work because of illness, or had other conditions that could have brought on fatigue.

"There certainly are people who are ill and who can be disabled by this," says the NIH's Straus. "But the percentage is relatively small compared to the claims." Unfortunately for the victims, doctors have few treatments to offer. Stress reduction or sleeping pills may provide some relief. For now, says Gidget Faubion, who runs a 9,000-member support group for the afflicted that is based in Portland, Ore., most sufferers must learn to accept the severity of their condition. Says she: "If you don't change your attitude, you're going to make a suicide call to me within six months."

By Dick Thompson.
Reported by Scott Brown/Los Angeles and Steven Holmes/Washington

QUESTIONS AND ACTIVITIES

Comprehension Questions

1. Why is fatigue syndrome sometimes called the "yuppie disease"?

2. What are its symptoms?

3. What virus may be associated with fatigue syndrome? What may activate the virus?

4. What does the director of one support group believe sufferers of the disease need to do?

Discussion Questions

1. Have you ever heard of this disease before. Do you know anyone who suffers from this disease? If so, in what ways has this person's lifestyle had to change?

2. Why do you think doctors at first disbelieved those who complained of the symptoms associated with fatigue syndrome?

Group Activities

Imagine that you are running a support group for people suffering from fatigue syndrome. In groups of five or six, brainstorm suggestions that you might give the sufferers to help them cope with their illness. Report your ideas to the class.

Individual Work

Imagine that you have begun to suffer from fatigue syndrome. Write how you think your lifestyle would change as a result (two pages maximum).

Article Four

Background Notes

for **Massage Comes Out of the Parlor**

Preview

Massage was once viewed as a suspect activity. Today thousands are discovering its beneficial effects.

Culture

Bible Belt: an area of the southern United States stretching from Texas to the Atlantic coast. Many residents of this area belong to Christian fundamentalist groups who believe that the Bible contains the actual words of God and, therefore, must be obeyed literally. The area is characterized by social conservatism.

Grinch: the main character in a children's book entitled *How the Grinch Stole Christmas* by Dr. Seuss. The Grinch was a nasty and mischievous character who delighted in causing problems in others' lives.

human potential movement: an umbrella term for a group of approaches popular in the 1960s and 1970s that focused on individual self-knowledge and development. Many of the approaches were described as "touchy-feely" because physical contact among the group members was encouraged.

Vocabulary

antidote ['æntə,dot]: a remedy; something that relieves the effects of something else

coo: to make a soft cry of pleasure. Pigeons are said to coo.

dowager ['dɑʊədʒɚ]: an impressive, usually wealthy, elderly woman

frazzled [fræzəld]: upset; nervous (colloquial)

gratify ['grædə,fɑɪ]: to satisfy; to please

handicrafter: one who makes things by hand; one who produces craft items with the use of machinery

knead [nid]: to work and form something with the hands. Dough for bread is always kneaded before baking.

lark: fun; something done spontaneously for pleasure

martini: a kind of cocktail made with gin and dry vermouth. Martinis are stereotypically associated with businessmen's lunches.

masseuse [mə'sus]: a woman who gives massages. A man who gives massages is called a **masseur**.

outré [u'tre]: exaggerated; overdone. (The writer apparently meant *passé* [out of fashion], but has used the wrong word.)

panacea [,pænə'sia]: a cure-all; a remedy for all problems

regimen ['rɛdʒəmən]: a systematic course of therapy

revitalizing: reviving; giving renewed energy to

snared: caught; trapped

stigma ['stɪgmə]: a negative mark; a sign of shame

tactile ['tæktəl]: relating to the sense of touch

Valium: the brand name of a tranquilizer. Valium is obtainable only with a doctor's prescription.

Massage Comes Out of the Parlor

At airports, offices and shopping centers, the rub that refreshes

Susan Gilbert Bryan was 25 and a struggling public relations assistant when, as sort of a lark, she tried one for the first time. She quickly found she had to have it every month. A decade later Bryan, now the owner of an advertising agency in Coral Gables, Fla., finds she requires it twice a week—and insists on having it at home. Husband Jim has also been snared, as well as their two-year-old daughter Vanessa, who coos when she gets it. Admits Bryan without a blush: ''I can go without exercise sometimes, but I can't live without my massages.''

Massage? Isn't that just a high-priced kneading for doughy dowagers or, heh, heh, something offered to men by scantily clad masseuses as a prelude to sex? Not anymore. In the past few years, massage has been moving out of both kinds of parlors and into the mainstream. No longer an embarrassing reminder of those touchy-feely human potential movements of the '70s, massage is fast emerging as Americans' favorite antidote to that current cultural Grinch: stress. Nothing kinky, just a way to get out the kinks. ''It's the ideal therapy for the '80s,'' declares Robert King, president of the Chicago-based American Massage Therapy Association. ''In-

stead of having an extra martini or gulping Valium, people ought to consider a professional massage.''

It is an increasingly popular prescription, one that is eagerly being filled by the nation's 50,000 massage therapists (masseur and masseuse are outré). And they deliver. If health club appointments and at-home visits are inconvenient, don't worry. Therapists will come to the office. No time or inclination for a full-hour full-undress manipulation? Then how about a minimassage? It is brief (ten to 15 minutes), thoroughly proper (clothes stay on) and cheap (a tune-up costs $10 to $15, while a complete overhaul can run $80).

Frazzled urban professionals love them. Once a week Joe Meissner, 39, who runs an executive placement service in San Francisco, reroutes his calls, takes off his vest, loosens his tie and turns himself over to Corporate Stressbusters. They bring the equipment: a stool, a 3-in.-thick black cushion and a pair of hands. ''Stress goes right into my shoulders,'' sighs Meissner. ''They knead it all out of me.'' Portlane, Ore., and Los Angeles boast similar services. In New York City, Attorney Peter Kupersmith calls the quarter-hour sessions devoted to his neck and shoulders ''miraculous

and a crucial part of my weekly regimen.'' Muscle tension under the blue collar is getting attention too. Therapist Pat Malone counts among his clients factory workers outside Chicago, who, in addition to coffee breaks, sometimes schedule a tactile time-out.

Some organizations have even begun to offer massage as a paid employee perk-up. At Vanderbilt University in Nashville, addled workers can get on-site soothing. At Merrill Lynch's Manhattan headquarters, a therapist is on staff. Steve Herfield, president of Manhattan Temporaries, pays for up to two minimassages a week for each of his twelve employees. ''Some were skeptical at first,'' he recalls. ''Now they'd like it every day. It's a real break and a real lift.'' Not always, however. Some therapists report that staffers occasionally are left so relaxed that they nod off at their desks.

Practitioners are successfully digging in at malls. Bob Watt opened Massage Works just six months ago in a plaza in Plantation, Fla., near Fort Lauderdale. Nestled between a VCR repair store and a restaurant, the shop is so busy Watt has had to hire three more therapists. Airports are another new arena. At the Phoenix and Dallas-Fort Worth terminals, tense travelers can drop into the Air Vita health club

Corporate Stressbusters at work in San Francisco

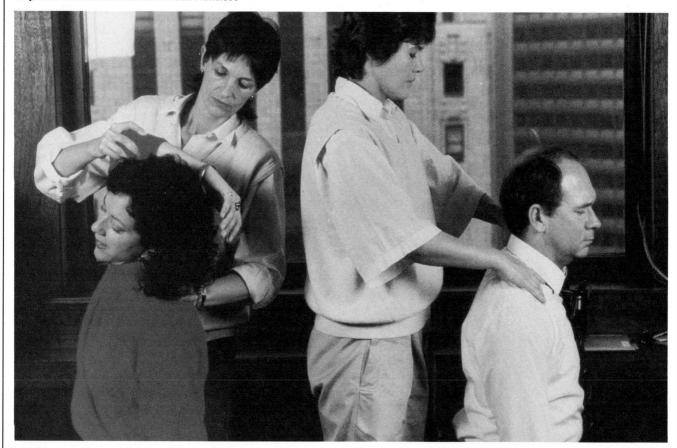

and get a relaxing massage. One satisfied customer, Dr. Steven Jacobson of Madison, Wis., says massage could figure in his future flight plans: "It might be a reason to have a six-hour layover instead of an hour one."

Such enthusiasm gratifies therapists, who five years ago were mumbling the answer when asked what they did for a living. Attitudes began shifting with the fitness boom and with growing recognition of the importance of massage in high-caliber sports. Professional athletes, as well as dancers, have long sworn by its revitalizing effects. Shortly after New York Giant Running Back Joe Morris began getting regular massages this season to relieve hyperventilation, he started to cut loose on his way to a record year. By stimulating blood circulation and oxygen flow through the muscles, therapists explain, massage helps lower blood pressure, speed up healing of injured tissue and aid in keeping muscles supple. But, they caution, it is not a panacea, and it is not recommended for those with circulatory ailments. One thing massage will not do, myths to the contrary, is rub away excess weight.

Different folks can choose different strokes or a combination. Swedish massage, the most familiar technique, uses oils to reduce friction and employs long full strokes, along with kneading and pounding motions. In newly popular Japanese Shiatsu and Chinese acupressure, fingers are pressed along defined paths on the body in order to release *chi,* or trapped energy. Other techniques include deep-tissue or structural massage, and reflexology, which focuses on the foot and hand.

With the stigma lifting and demand growing, massage therapy has become an entrepreneur's dream. Schools are proliferating; there are now about 300. Many therapists are concerned, however, about the lack of uniform training standards: the American Massage Therapy Association has approved only 51 schools. Moreover, the field is poorly regulated by outside authorities. Just 13 states have licensing requirements, and their criteria vary widely. Florida, for example, requires therapists to complete 500 hours of training, while Ohio calls for half that.

Better credentials would certainly add tighter tone. Still, there is no doubt that massage has shed its shady image, even deep in the Bible Belt South. Five years ago, when Therapist Michele Marie Balliet arrived in Murfreesboro, Tenn., "they pictured the places beside I-40 that say MASSAGE," she recalls. Today, though, it seems as if the whole town is beating a path to her table. Not just the doctors, lawyers and bankers, but the factory workers, farmers and handicrafters. Balliet takes cash for her services but occasionally accepts other down-home forms of payment: six dozen eggs, handwoven baskets, clothing. "Massage," she says, "has become a necessary part of their lives."

By Anastasia Toufexis.
Reported by Mike Cannell/New York and B. Russell Leavitt/Atlanta

QUESTIONS AND ACTIVITIES

Comprehension Questions

1. What are some examples of the different places where massages are being given?

2. What are the beneficial effects of massage?

3. For medical reasons, who should not have massages?

4. What various kinds of massage are there?

Discussion Questions

1. Is massage a common practice in your culture? If not, why do you think not? If so, are the therapists generally men or women? Is special training needed to be a therapist?

2. Have you ever had a massage? If so, did you feel it was beneficial? In what way? If not, do you think you would like to have one? Why or why not?

Group Activities

In groups of three or four, write a newspaper or magazine advertisement announcing the opening of a new massage center in your town. Make sure the ad mentions the beneficial effects of massage. When your ad is finished, present it to the entire class.

Individual Work

Do you think it necessary for states to license and regulate massage therapists? Why or why not? Explain your position in a one-page written statement.

Background Notes

for **Total Care at the Ms. Mayo Clinics**

Preview

*Health centers devoted solely to women are appearing across the United States.
In these centers, women receive head-to-toe medical care in pleasant surroundings.*

Culture

health insurance: insurance that helps people pay for their hospital and doctors' bills

Marimekko: a Scandinavian fabric designer. Marimekko fabrics are noted for their bold designs and bright colors and are associated with upscale purchasers.

Mayo Clinic ['mejo 'klɪnək]: a world-famous medical center located in Rochester, Minnesota. The name has become synonymous with the best in health care.

Tupperware: the brand name of a collection of plastic containers used to store food and household items. Tupperware cannot be bought in stores; it is sold only at home demonstration parties.

Vocabulary

accolade ['ækə,led]: an award; a mark of acknowledgment

accommodating: providing what is needed or desired

ameliorate [ə'miliəˌet]: to make better; to improve

bane: a curse; a source of harm

boom: a rapid expansion or development

condescension [ˌkandə'sɛnʃən]: patronizing behavior; an attitude of superiority over another

gynecology [ˌgaɪnəkaləd3i]: a branch of medicine concerned with women and their specific diseases

lumpectomy [ˌləmp'ɛktəmi]: the surgical removal of a tumor or mass of tissue from the breast

mastectomy [ˌmæ'stɛktəmi]: the surgical removal of a breast

oncologist [ˌan'kaləd3əst]: a person whose specialty is oncology. Oncology is a branch of medicine concerned with tumors.

osteoporosis [ˌastiopə'rosəs]: a condition in which the bones become porous and are easily broken. Osteoporosis occurs more frequently in women than in men.

Pap smear ['pæp ˌsmɪr]: a clinical procedure done to diagnose cervical cancer

pastel [ˌpæ'stɛl]: any pale, light color

premenstrual syndrome [ˌpri'mɛnstrəl]: physical and emotional symptoms associated with the female menstrual cycle

solicitude [sə'lɪsəˌtud]: excessive care; extreme attention

specula ['spɛkjələ]: medical instruments used to inspect body passages

stirrups: metal supports on an examining table used to position a patient's feet

test happy: prone to administering too many medical tests

tubal ligation ['tubəl ˌlaɪ'geʃən]: a method of female sterilization in which the Fallopian tubes are cut or tied

woo [wu]: to seek attention; to attempt to gain favor

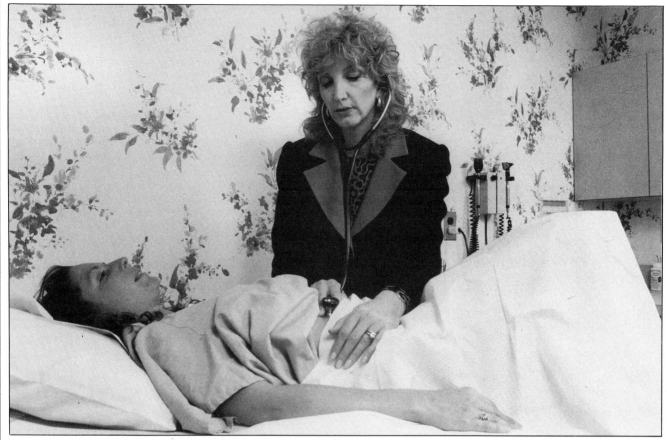

Dr. Budoff examining a patient: afterward, a cup of tea or a carnation

Total Care at the Ms. Mayo Clinics

Women's health centers are one-stop body shops

On the ooh-and-aah scale, it rates a nicely curved 9. Painted *faux* arches on pastel-tinted walls. Plush mauve carpeting. Bathrooms papered with Marimekko designs. Dressing rooms with spacious lockers. Cheerful, friendly staff. And on the way out, visitors receive a single carnation. "It's nice to be treated like a woman," sighs Susan Arcidiacono with pleasure. A ritzy health club? An elegant hair salon? Not at all. The swanky suburban San Diego setup belongs to Women's Health Centers of America and is a model of a hot '80s health-care fashion: the women's clinic.

About 20 centers now dot the nation, and experts predict the number will soar into the hundreds by the end of the year. Many are established by hospitals, either in house or as satellites; others are free-standing clinics or parts of entrepreneurial chains. Frequently they are simply overdressed gynecology practices that differ little from the past segmented service. But, says Dr. Linda Lesky of Women's Health Group in Boston, "there is no anatomic reason why women should be divided at the waist."

Drawing on feminist insights, the best of the new clinics seek to provide total basic care.

They are a kind of one-stop body shop where women can receive a gynecological exam or mammogram; treatment for premenstrual syndrome or osteoporosis; advice on nutrition, weight loss and cosmetic surgery; even counseling for psychological problems. "We have head-to-toe health care," exults Penny Wise Budoff, a family practitioner (and the best-selling author of *No More Hot Flashes and Other Good News*). Her clinic in Bethpage, N.Y., a former Howard Johnson's restaurant painted lilac with yellow columns, has a staff of 13 doctors with a full range of specialties. "We're like a mini-Mayo Clinic," she says. Or a Ms. Mayo Clinic.

The boom is fueled by financial practicalities as well as feminist principles. According to the American Hospital Association, women visit doctors 25% more often than men do and account for 63% of all surgery. Eleven of the 20 most frequent surgical procedures (notably tubal ligations and breast biopsies) are performed only on women. Moreover, women generally choose the family doctor and health-insurance package. Such medical realities have led to fierce and unapologetic wooing. Women's HealthCare and Wellness Center in Oak Park, Ill., signed up Dorothy Hamill, Ann

Jillian and Rita Moreno to promote its opening last November. Intermountain Health Care has spent $800,000 in the past two years to advertise its ten centers in the Salt Lake City area. Says Women's Services Director Marta Clark: "We copy retailers, department stores and hotels in marketing our services."

The centers also use the lures of convenience and comfort. Clinics remain open in the evenings and on weekends; checkups are often booked for an hour instead of the usual 30 minutes. "Doctors shouldn't be able to pat themselves on the back for doing a Pap smear in seven minutes," says Dr. Janet Schwartz of Women's Health Centers. The three W.H.C. clinics in California take pains to ameliorate the two banes of the gynecological exam: icy stirrups on the examining table are covered by foot warmers and vaginal specula are warmed. The clinic at Georgia Baptist Medical Center in Atlanta even offers a small gym and Tupperware-like health parties at which women get to throw questions at a physician. Above all, the centers claim that their largely female staffs are able to treat women without the impersonality and condescension of traditional practices.

Critics wonder whether the new clinics are offering better care or merely fancy wrapping.

Some question the automatic faith in female staffs. "I'm skeptical," says Feminist Judy Norsigian, co-author of *The New Our Bodies, Ourselves,* who notes that because male and female physicians receive identical educations, "the women often come out the same." Others point out that the new centers are geared to affluent women, neglecting the old and the poor. And there is concern about whether the clinics are overly accommodating. Leah Dills, 32, who has visited Woman's Care Center in San Francisco at least eight times in the past six months, says the clinic seems a "little test happy," adding "there's a little bit of a fast-food kind of feel about the place."

Still, many women have found more substantial benefits at women's centers. Long Island Interior Designer Gloria Levine credits Dr. Budoff with saving her from a mastectomy after Levine discovered a lump in one breast: "She told me how to ask my oncologist to find out if I was a candidate for a lumpectomy." Another clinic patient, Delores Burton, reports that after a painful procedure, she was offered tea. "No doctor ever gave me a cup of tea before. It's a different kind of care." That combination of service and solicitude, notes Dr. Budoff, has earned the ultimate accolade. "We don't encourage it," she says, "but a lot of our patients bring their husbands here because they want them to get the same kind of complete care."

By Anastasia Toufexis.
Reported by Cristina Garcia/San Francisco and Christine Gorman/New York

QUESTIONS AND ACTIVITIES

Comprehension Questions

1. How many women's health clinics currently exist?
2. What is the difference between the frequency of men's and women's visits to doctors? What is the difference in the frequency with which they undergo surgery?
3. What marketing devices are women's clinics using to attract patients?
4. What criticisms are the centers receiving?

Discussion Questions

1. Do you think it appropriate or necessary for there to be medical clinics devoted solely to the care of women? Why or why not?
2. Should there be male-only clinics as well? Why or why not?
3. Do you think that female doctors are better for female patients than are male doctors? Explain your answer.

Group Activities

In groups of five or six, develop a list of "wishes" for your visits to a doctor. For example, you might write "I wish I didn't have to wait so long each time I went to see my doctor." When your discussion is finished, present your list to the entire class. Did any item appear on more than one list? What are they?

Individual Work

1. Select the statement that best describes your position:
   a. I prefer to have a doctor who is a woman.
   b. I prefer to have a doctor who is a man.
   c. It doesn't matter to me whether my doctor is a woman or a man.
   Explain the reasons for your position in a brief written report (one page maximum).

2. Poll 10 people to learn their answers to the following questions:
   a. Is your doctor a man or a woman?
   b. If your doctor is a man, would you object to seeing a female doctor? Why or why not?
   If your doctor is a woman, would you object to seeing a male doctor? Why or why not?
   Summarize the results of your poll in a written report (one and a half pages maximum). Be prepared as well to give a brief oral report to the class (five minutes maximum).

Article Six

Background Notes

for **Hands Up and Butts Out!**

Preview

Beverly Hills is one of several towns that now forbid smoking in restaurants and stores. Although many people are pleased about the ruling, some private citizens and business owners are not.

Culture

R. J. Reynolds: the founder of the R. J. Reynolds Tobacco Company. The company produces several brands of cigarettes.

Rodeo Drive: a main thoroughfare in Beverly Hills, California. Rodeo Drive is known for its ultra-expensive boutiques and trendy cafés.

Surgeon General: the chief medical official of the U.S. government

Vocabulary

berserk [bə(r)'zɚk]: crazy; frenzied

bistro: a European-style restaurant or nightclub

booze: alcohol; liquor (a 1930s slang term used mainly for effect)

butt: the unsmoked remainder of a cigarette

emphysema [ˌɛm(p)fə'simə]: a condition of the lungs characterized by overinflation of the air sacs. Heavy smoking is believed to be one cause of emphysema.

fascist ['fæʃəst]: characteristic of a government that is highly centralized and authoritarian. Fascist governments suppress personal freedoms.

gawk [gɔk]: to stare stupidly

mogul: a magnate; a great or important person in a field or profession

nicotine: a poisonous chemical. Nicotine is the chief active agent in tobacco.

ordinance ['ordənəns]: a municipal rule or regulation

posterity ['pɑsˌtɛrədi]: descendents; future generations

setback: a reversal; a defeat

shriek [ʃrik]: to screech; to cry out in a high-pitched voice

snuff: to extinguish the light of a candle; to put out a cigarette or cigar

stoically ['stoəkli]: impassively; indifferently

tranquility [ˌtræn'kwɪlədi]: calmness; quiet

tyrannical [tə'rænəkəl]: oppressive

vigilance ['vɪdʒələns]: a state of watchfulness

vociferous [ˌvo'sɪfɚəs]: given to loud outcries

Hands Up and Butts Out!

Beverly Hills outlaws smoking in restaurants

"It's like the Old West. Whoever draws his gun first wins. Someone lights a cigarette, another person says, 'You can't smoke here.' Then the first says, 'I dare you to do something about it.' And there goes the peace and tranquillity of an evening meal."
— Joe Patti, owner of La Famiglia restaurant

On April 3 a new era began in Beverly Hills: smoking was banned in restaurants and retail stores. Three weeks later many cigarettes remain unlit but scorched tempers are flaring. In cafés and restaurants throughout this clean, orderly city, known for its per capita wealth and celebrity residents, vociferous smokers are shrieking that the new ordinance is fascist, Communist and tyrannical. "It's the People's Republic of Beverly Hills," fumes Irene Robbins, a bookkeeper for the Mandarin, a Chinese restaurant one block from Rodeo Drive. "The smog is ten times worse than anything you're going to breathe sitting through dinner with a smoker," insists Ronnie Fondell, puffing away at an outdoor table at Caffe Roma, a lively bistro where sleek Europeans come to meet and gawk. "Why not take cars off the street, booze off the bar and prohibit anything else anyone ever said was bad for you," grumbles a patron at the Grill, popular with the business-lunch crowd.

More rebellious customers have taken action. At Larry Parker's pricey 24-Hour Diner one recent afternoon, an annoyed patron yanked a woman's hair as he walked out because she refused to put out her cigarette. At Café Beverly Hills, an upscale coffee shop, an elderly man punched his female companion when she told him he must snuff his cigar. "I've been smoking for 92 years," said the patron. "No one is going to tell me where I can smoke."

But such celebrity diners as Actor Carroll O'Connor, owner and occasional piano player at the Ginger Man, and cigar-puffing George Burns are willing to conform. "I'll do whatever the city wants," says O'Connor stoically. Debbie Parker, a ban supporter who has a water pistol emblazoned with the words STOP OR I'LL SHOOT, says, "Smokers have had a lack of consideration for others for a long time. Now the tables are turned." The Beverly Hills police—famed for their vigilance in cracking down on jaywalking, illegal parking and attempted burglary—are so far going slowly. They have made no arrests and answered only two calls; one was a smoking complaint, and the other involved a nicotine lover who went berserk about the ordinance.

The Beverly Hills ban is part of a pulmonary consciousness sweeping the land, fueled by Surgeon General C. Everett Koop's report that secondhand, or "sidestream," smoke can have a negative effect on the health of nonsmokers. Two years ago Aspen, Colo., passed the first law to prohibit smoking in most dining rooms. On May 7 New York State will join the trend, restricting smokers in restaurants with 51 or more seats to designated areas. The Beverly Hills ordinance, passed unanimously by the city council, penalizes disobedient smokers—and restaurants that fail to display no-smoking signs—with fines of up to $500. Mayor Charlotte Spadaro, whose mail is running 2 to 1 in favor of the ban, views it as similar to laws "against pollution and toxic waste, designed to make the environment safe for everyone."

Because the law is directed at residents, not visitors, hotel dining rooms are exempt; restaurant bars and cocktail lounges are also excluded from the ban. "We understand the relationship between alcohol and cigarettes—we're not out to reform human nature," explains former City Attorney Steven Rood. As for hotels, he notes, "French and Italian movie moguls can't do business without a cigarette in their mouth." Such reasoning does not satisfy restaurant owners. Vito Sasso, proprietor of the romantic Romeo and Juliet, argues that he too has foreign customers, citing one wealthy visitor who orders several $500 bottles of wine for a dinner tab of $4,000—which adds up to

a month's rent. "He won't come in anymore because he can't smoke," moans Sasso. "That's like doubling my rent."

A local restaurant survey found that since the ban there has been a 30% drop in business. On the first night of the ban, 36 people called Romeo and Juliet to cancel their reservations. Mr. Chow, a chic Chinese eatery, registered a 17% initial decline and 65% two nights later. At the Beverly Hills Hamburger Hamlet, revenues were slashed by $3,000, while business in the chain's restaurant in nearby West Hollywood was up by the same amount. "The best restaurants are on our borders," says Joanne Le Bouvier, owner of the Saloon, which experienced a 45% setback. "You can just walk from here to another city. What chance do we have?"

Despite a pending lawsuit by the Beverly Hills Restaurant Association, it is unlikely the law will be repealed. "Posterity may find that this ban was well ahead of its time," says Patrick Reynolds, an antismoking activist and Beverly Hills resident who saw his father die of emphysema. He is the grandson of R.J. Reynolds, founder of the famed tobacco company.

By Martha Smilgis.
Reported by Nancy Seufert/Beverly Hills

QUESTIONS AND ACTIVITIES

Comprehension Questions

1. In what locations is smoking banned in Beverly Hills?
2. What have been the reactions to the ban?
3. What has happened to business in some restaurants since the ban?
4. What are the reasons for banning smoking in certain locations?

Discussion Questions

1. Do you smoke? If so, are there certain places where you don't smoke? Why? If not, are you bothered by others smoking near you? Do you ever say anything to the smokers? If not, why not? If so, what have been their responses?

2. Do you think smoking should be banned in any of the following locations?
   a. airplanes
   b. restaurants
   c. public places such as train and bus stations
   d. hospitals
   e. government offices
   Give reasons for your responses.

Group Activities

Form groups of four or five and choose one of the following two statements to discuss and defend. Each statement must be chosen by at least one group.
   a. Governments—whether local, state, or federal—have the right to ban smoking.
   b. Smoking is an individual issue and, therefore, not subject to governmental control.
After your small group discussions, present the arguments in support of your group's position to the entire class.

Individual Work

Interview five people. Ask their opinions of the following questions:
   a. Do you think smoking should be banned on all airline flights?
   b. Do you think smoking should be banned in restaurants?
   c. If you answered *No* to either question, do you think that special smoking sections on planes and in restaurants are the answer to the controversy over smoking?
Summarize your findings in a brief (one page maximum) written report. Be prepared as well to report the results of your poll to the class.

Article Seven

Background Notes

for **How to Get Slim Hips and Catcalls**

Preview

People of all ages are discovering the benefits of aerobic walking. The sport is inexpensive, healthful, and enjoyable.

Culture

Walkman ['wɔkmən]: the brand name of a lightweight portable radio and cassette recorder used with headphones. Walkmans are extremely popular with joggers and bikers.

Vocabulary

aerobic [ə'robək]: any form of exercise whose goal is to strengthen the cardiovascular system by elevating the heart rate to an optimal level, usually between 140 and 180 beats per minute

catcall ['kæt,kɔl]: a noise made to express disapproval. Catcalls are often heard at sporting events.

congenial [kən'dʒi,niəl]: kind; pleasant

consistency: persistence; regularity

faggot ['fægət]: a homosexual (a very derogatory term)

horde: a crowd; a very large group

jeer [dʒɪr]: a taunt; a cry of derision

jogging: running at a fixed pace; running for the purpose of exercise, not racing

lethargy ['lɛθɚ,dʒi]: a lack of energy; an unusual sleepiness

physiologist [,fɪzi'ɑlədʒəst]: a person who specializes in physiology. Physiology is the study of the processes of living matter.

propulsion: the act of propelling; the act of pushing forward

shin: the front part of the leg below the knee

stride: the length of one's step

unfazed: undisturbed; not bothered

How to Get Slim Hips and Catcalls

Aerobic walking is comical, economical and coming on fast

Stepping the light fantastic: walkers learn technique in Manhattan's Central Park

Here she comes at 5 in the morning, following the delivery trucks along Queens Boulevard, her hips rotating, arms pumping and legs jerking straight out in front, looking for all the world like a drunken ostrich on parade. Marian Spatz, a high school administrative secretary from the New York City borough of Queens, is totally unfazed by curious stares, for this is her daily exercise regimen. Not for her the heel-pounding, back-jarring effort of jogging. Instead, she, like many other American fitness enthusiasts, has taken up aerobic walking. If you think mere walking will not keep you in shape, listen to Marian. After three years of pounding the pavement, "the weight has peeled off, along with a tremendous number of inches. I'm aged 50, and I look 42." She does too.

Of course, it isn't mere walking, but a highly energetic, intensive form of exercise that many health experts recommend over jogging because of the lower chance of injury. The National Sporting Goods Association reports that exercise walking in all its forms, whether competitive or just for fitness, is now the second most popular outdoor activity in the U.S. (after swimming), up from fifth place in 1985. American Sports Data, a market-research firm in Hartsdale, N.Y., estimates that there are about 25 million serious walkers of all strides, compared with 13 million runners in 1983, the jogging peak. Actresses Cybill Shepherd and Shelley Hack walk. So do Bob Hope and Walter Matthau. To certify the trend, Jane Fonda will be out next month with two training cassettes—for the Walkman, naturally.

"In exercise, consistency is more important than intensity, and that's the major health message of walking over running," says Cardiologist James Rippe, director of the exercise physiology laboratory at the University of Massachusetts Medical School. Aerobic walking ranges from striding along to race walking, but all forms share the same goal: to give the body maximum propulsion while firming up thighs, hips and bottoms. Coaches like Howard Jacobson, 56, who heads the Walkers Club of America, teach tyro trudgers the race-walking technique. The heel of the front foot must touch the ground before the toe of the back foot pushes off; the leading leg must be straight at the knee as the body passes over it. The arm movement is a sprinter's, pumping diagonally across to the body's center line.

These race-walking movements produce that curious rolling motion of the hips that many bystanders in their lethargy find amusing. "This is not a sport for insecure people," says Julie Morrison, editor of the *Running Journal,* based in Concord, N.C. "People often yell out and call me 'faggot' because I swing my hips," says Jacobson's son Alan,

32, who is a top competitive walker. Shrugging off the stereotypical jeers, Alan Jacobson churns along at 7 m.p.h., compared with the average aerobic walker's 4.5-m.p.h. pace.

Because an aerobic walker's stride is shorter than a runner's, requiring more steps over the same distance, more calories are consumed. At the rate of a mile every twelve minutes, the walker uses up 530 calories an hour to the jogger's 480. The walker also takes fewer risks, according to a number of reports. "We see a lot of runners sent to us with leg and back problems," says Bill Farrell, founder of the Metro Atlanta Walkers Club. "My shins would kill me after running," remembers Elly Christophersen, 30, now a devoted Manhattan walker. "From the standpoint of health and wear and tear on the body, race walking is much better."

The growing interest in aerobic walking has been reinforced by Dr. Ralph Paffenbarger's study of 17,000 Harvard alumni who are now 53 to 90. Paffenbarger, who is at Stanford University's medical school, found that men who walked briskly nine or more miles a week had a 21% lower risk of death from heart disease than those who walked less than three miles a week. Michael Pollock, director of the University of Florida's exercise-science center, recommends exercising at an intensity of 60% to 90% of maximum heart rate for up to an hour. However, notes the physiologist, who wrote the American College of Sports Medicine's *Guidelines for Fitness in Healthy Adults,* "if you choose more moderate train-

ing, you'll have to go longer and more frequently to get good results."

To keep themselves in peak condition, walkers are puffing through city parks and suburban streets. Brad Ketchum, editor of the Boston-based *Walking Magazine,* counts 10,000 walking events taking place this year. Among them: the Boston Stride, the San Francisco Stride (which drew 6,000 last fall) and the Casimiro Alongi International Memorial Racewalk in Dearborn, Mich. To supply this horde, Reebok, Avia and Rockport, even though they are commonly owned, are separately producing a variety of models. Nike says that last year it sold more than half a million pairs of its specially fashioned flexible walking shoes.

Some athletes are alternating their running and walking shoes. Marathoner Clare Hurtel, 25, of San Francisco walks as part of her training regime. "At first I didn't take walking seriously, probably because it didn't hurt," she says. "Now I think it's definitely easier on your structure." So does Etta Hicks, 68, who works with mentally handicapped people in De Kalb County, Ga. She did not take to running, but walking, she says, "has become a way of life." Everyone finds the sport congenial, though not as much as Marilyn Nye, 43, and Paul Perry, 41, who met in a Dearborn race-walking group. In July they will walk, at a normal pace, down the aisle.

By David Brand.
Reported by Georgia Harbison/New York, with other bureaus

QUESTIONS AND ACTIVITIES

Comprehension Questions

1. According to the article, what is the most popular outdoor activity? What is the second most popular outdoor activity?

2. How does aerobic walking differ from regular walking?

3. Which sport uses more energy per hour, jogging or aerobic walking? Which results in fewer injuries?

4. What benefits to the heart does aerobic walking appear to have?

Discussion Questions

1. Have you ever done any aerobic walking? If so, did you enjoy it? If not, would you like to learn? Why or why not?

2. What is your favorite sport to participate in? Why?

3. What is your favorite sport to observe? Why?

Group Activities

Imagine that an aerobic walking class will be offered at your school. In groups of four or five, announce the class by designing a poster that will be placed on school bulletin boards. Be sure to mention the times, dates, and location of the class, as well as the benefits of aerobic walking. Present your poster to the entire class.

Individual Work

Sit in a park for half an hour. Take note of the different kinds of physical activities that people are involved in. You may wish to note the following, among other things:

    a. How many different activities do you see?

    b. How many different age groups are participating?

    c. Is a certain activity more typical of one age group than another?

    d. Are more men than women participating or vice-versa?

Summarize your findings in a brief (five minute maximum) report to the class.

Sports & Entertainment

Article One

BACKGROUND NOTES

for **The Fall and Rise**

Preview

Hours after his sister's death, Olympic speed skater
Dan Jansen fell while racing. In his next race, he fell again,
but his family and the world came to his support.

Culture

gold: a gold medal. Gold medals are given for first place in Olympic sporting events.

Olympics [əˈlɪmpəks]: an international athletic competition held once every four years in both summer and winter. The games are modeled after the original Olympic games of ancient Greece.

Vocabulary

clipping: bumping while passing; bumping someone from behind while both are in motion

crucial [ˈkruʃəl]: decisive; critical

disqualification [ˌdɪsˌkwaləfəˈkeʃən]: an elimination from competition, usually for violating a rule

feuding [ˈfjudɪŋ]: fighting; battling

fiancée [ˌfiˈɑnˌse]: a woman to whom a man is engaged to be married

funeral [ˈfjunɚəl]: a ceremony to honor someone who has died; the observances held for a dead person

grief: sorrow; emotional suffering over a loss

leukemia [ˌluˈkimiə]: a malignant disease of the blood-forming organs. Leukemia is often fatal.

numb [nəm]: emotionless; without feeling

spill: a fall (colloquial)

sprint: a short-distance race that is run at top speed

straightaway [ˈstredəˌwe]: one of the straight sides of an oval track used for racing

stunning: striking; astonishing

sympathy: the capacity to understand and share the feelings of others

The Fall and Rise

Racing just after his sister's death, Dan Jansen took a spill. Four days later, he went down again but rose in the eyes of the world

American Speed Skater Dan Jansen was carrying a weight of grief last week, and he fell. At 22, he was at the top of his form, having won the 500-meter at the world sprint championships near his home in West Allis, Wis., just a week earlier. But at 6 a.m. Sunday, eleven hours before he was to pursue the gold at that distance in Calgary, Jansen was summoned to a phone. It was a call from the hospital room of his sister Jane with the news that she was rapidly losing her year-long battle with leukemia. The eldest of nine children and a speed skater herself, Jane, 27, had urged him to go to Calgary despite her worsening health. While a brother held the phone to her ear, Jansen spoke to her, but she was unable to reply. Four hours later she had died.

It was an anxious and grieving Jansen on the starting line that evening. At the outset he jumped the gun. To avoid a repeat and disqualification, he held back for a crucial moment at the second gun, then bore down to make up for lost time. He went down suddenly in the first turn, clipping Japanese Skater Yasushi Kuroiwa and slamming into the sideboard. Looking back, he said that he might have been pushing too hard. It seemed as likely though that emotional pressure had made a difficult curve impossible.

When he fell the second time, on the straightaway of Thursday's 1,000-meter event, just 200 meters short of the finish, it was even more stunning, as if he had been forced down by sorrow alone. Watching from the gallery, Brother Mike, 24, had just assured a sister: "Dan's made it through the toughest turns. He's fine now." At the 600-meter mark, Jansen was .31 sec. faster than any of the competition. Then his right skate "caught an edge"—hit the ice on the side instead of the bottom of the blade—sending him to his hands and knees and into a wall. For a moment he sat on the ice, unbelieving, until Coach Mike Crowe and Teammate Nick Thometz came over to help him off. Arriving at the bench area, he embraced his fiancée, Canadian Speed Skater Natalie Grenier, and sobbed.

The scene brought to mind heartbreaking falls of American Olympic track stars: Jim Ryun tumbling at Munich, Mary Decker's astonished spill in Los Angeles. Jansen's mother Gerry, who had seen the race on TV, spoke for the millions who watched at home and in Calgary, where a cheering crowd fell into shocked silence: "I think we were all just kind of numb." Jansen's spills brought down much of the U.S. hope for a men's speed-skating medal. The team had gone to Calgary

DOUBLED AGONY
The sprinter in superb form during the 1,000 shortly before fortune's final twist left him and the watching world stunned

125

seeing a chance to replay some of 1980, when Eric Heiden took all five skating golds. But the team arrived feuding bitterly and publicly over starting lineups. When he was not named to race in the 1,000, dissident Captain Erik Henriksen filed two unsuccessful appeals with the U.S. Olympic Committee.

Meanwhile the competition has been reaching dizzying new speeds. In Sunday's race, 27 skaters broke Heiden's old record. After Jansen, the best U.S. hope for a medal had been Sprinter Nick Thometz. But following months of battling a low blood-platelet count and a recent bout of the flu, he finished eighth in the 500 and 18th in the 1,000. That race went to the Soviet Union's Nikolai Guliaev in 1:13:03. The silver went to East Germany's Jens-Uwe Mey, already winner of the 500 with a 36.45 record. Finally on Saturday the U.S. medal drought ended when Eric Flaim, who placed fourth in both the 500 and the 1,000, took second in the 1,500-meter event.

The day before, Jansen had flown home by private jet to attend his sister's funeral. "We hugged and we cried," said Mrs. Jansen. "My daughter's death has now become more of a reality to him." Later that day Jansen visited his sister's husband and her three young children. He gave them his Olympic participant's medal. At home the postman keeps bringing carts of mail full of sympathy and admiration. Jansen may have fallen on the ice, but the world would reach out if it could to lift him up.

By Richard Lacayo.
Reported by Lee Griggs/Calgary and
Georgia Pabst/West Allis

QUESTIONS AND ACTIVITIES

Comprehension Questions

1. When did Dan Jansen fall the first time in the Olympic games in Calgary?

2. What does it mean to "catch an edge"? Why was Jansen's second fall more dramatic and disappointing than his first?

3. What other U.S. athletes have fallen in Olympic competition?

Discussion Questions

1. Have you ever attended the Olympic games or watched them on television? If so, which ones? Which events did you watch? Which events are your favorites?

2. If you were an Olympic athlete, do you think you could have raced under the circumstances that Dan Jansen did? Why or why not?

Group Activities

Some argue that the Olympic games should be discontinued because they have become too political. Others claim that their continuation helps keep international goodwill alive. In groups of approximately six to eight, choose one position or the other to support. Each position must be chosen by at least one group. In your groups, develop arguments in defense of the position chosen. After your discussion, present your arguments to the entire class.

Individual Work

Do you think participating in an Olympic competition is worth all the years of training and sacrifice an athlete must endure? Explain your answer in a written statement (one and a half pages maximum).

Article Two

BACKGROUND NOTES
for **Zapping Back at Children's TV**

Preview

The number of children's television programs is increasing and so is the amount of commercial advertising on each program. Parents and other concerned individuals are criticizing the content of certain shows, as well as their commercialism.

Culture

bubble-gum cards: small cards found in packages of bubble gum, popular among children and some adults for collecting and trading. The cards often contain pictures and information about baseball stars and other sports figures.

cable: cable television; television whose images are transmitted through a cable, not broadcast through air. Cable TV is known as "pay TV" since one must pay a monthly charge to have it.

Clarabell: a clown who appeared on the "Howdy Doody Show" in the 1950s. He frequently squirted water from his seltzer bottle at other characters on the show. The show was one of the earliest TV programs aimed totally at children.

Federal Communications Commission (FCC): the federal agency that regulates television and radio broadcasts

Hasbro ['hæz,bro]: a major toy manufacturer

Mattel [mə'tɛl]: a major toy manufacturer

PBS: Public Broadcasting System. Known as "educational" channels, PBS channels usually carry no commercial advertising and broadcast cultural and educational programs. The programs are supported by grants and donations.

Vocabulary

aegis ['idʒəs]: protection; sponsorship

barrage [bə'rɑʒ]: a concentrated outpouring; a steady attack

deregulatory [,di'rɛgjələ,tori]: characterized by a reduction in the number of rules and regulations

dub: to nickname; to provide another name for

flexing muscles: showing one's strength

gross-out: objectionable; highly offensive (slang)

kidvid: television shows for children

laissez-faire [,leze'fɛr]: characterized by a lack of governmental interference

nemesis ['nɛməsəs]: a rival; an opponent

probe: an investigation; an examination

stricture ['strɪkʃɚ]: a restriction; something that limits

villain ['vɪlən]: a mean person; a wicked person

watershed: a crucial dividing point or activity

Zapping Back at Children's TV

After years of deregulation, kidvid's critics are on the attack

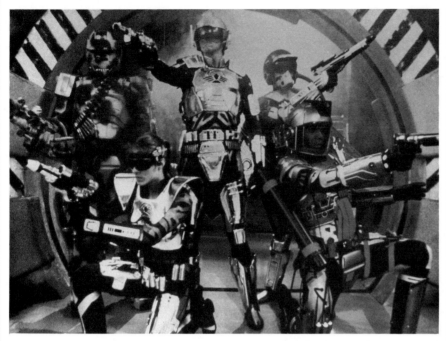

Shows where youngsters pay to play: scene from the "interactive" Captain Power

Ever since the days of Clarabell the clown and his ever ready seltzer bottle, parents have complained about the quality of children's TV programming. But seldom have they had so much to complain about. A typical afternoon of kidvid these days can be a mind-numbing march of cartoon superheroes like He-Man, Brave-Starr and the Defenders of the Earth. Many shows, from *The Transformers* to *Pound Puppies,* are based on hot-selling toys and seem intended to shuffle kids straight from the TV set into the toy store. Worst of all in the critics' view, under the deregulatory aegis of the Reagan Administration, the Federal Communications Commission seemed little inclined to do anything about the situation.

Now the laissez-faire era of children's TV may be coming to an end. One watershed: in June a federal appeals court ordered the FCC to reconsider a 1984 ruling that freed broadcasters from any limits on the amount of commercial time permitted on children's programming. In response, the FCC last month launched a broad inquiry into children's TV. The probe will examine not only whether limits on advertising time ought to be reimposed but also whether restrictions should be placed on the more than 25 shows currently airing that feature toys as their main characters. The inquiry seems to reflect a growing consensus that the FCC's free-market approach has not been enough to protect children from undue commercial influence.

Critics of children's TV programming are flexing muscles in a number of arenas. In September, just three days before its new children's schedule was set to debut, CBS abruptly withdrew *The Garbage Pail Kids,* a cartoon show based on the grossout series of bubble-gum cards by that name. The network denies that it caved in to pressure, but the cancellation came after a barrage of complaints from parents and CBS affiliates.

Legislators too are getting into the act. In the House of Representatives a measure has been introduced that would reimpose formal commercial-time strictures on kids' shows. A Senate bill would require the networks to run at least seven hours a week of educational programming for children. The tone of some lawmakers has grown combative. Says Democratic Representative Edward Markey of Massachusetts: "What was once called a vast wasteland is now more accurately dubbed a vast waste dump."

Children's TV, of course, is not an unredeemed junk pile. PBS and cable offer much quality fare. Most of the networks' Saturday-morning shows are gently inoffensive (*The Smurfs, Jim Henson's Muppet Babies*) and occasionally adventurous (*Pee-wee's Playhouse*). Some of the wit and imagination of pre-TV animation have even resurfaced this season in CBS's *Mighty Mouse: The New Adventures,* from Filmmaker Ralph Bakshi.

More dismal is the picture on independent stations, which typically offer a horde of look-alike syndicated cartoons in the before- and after-school hours on weekdays. Though the networks continue to adhere to pre-1984 limits of twelve ad minutes an hour on weekdays, 9 1/2 minutes on weekends, a recent study of eight big-city independent stations revealed that all but one were exceeding the old limit during weekday children's programming.

The most controversial area, however, is toy-inspired shows, which are criticized by children's TV activists as little more than program-length commercials. "Where is it written that Mattel should control the decision-making in programming for children's TV?" says Peggy Charren, president of Action for Children's Television, the watchdog group based in Cambridge, Mass. "People who want to produce children's programs with something to say instead of something to sell are zapped out of the system."

The activists are especially upset about a new wave of "interactive" shows, like Mattel's *Captain Power and the Soldiers of the Future.* The show, a live-action space adventure, enables children to play along at certain points by shooting at villains on-screen with a special Power Jet weapon (cost: $30 to $40). An electronic signal responds to each "hit" and tots up the player's score. Charren argues that by encouraging children to buy an expensive toy to participate, such shows unfairly divide the young audience into "the haves and the have-nots."

The producers of children's shows reply that the programs are entertaining without the toys and that merchandising tie-ins are hardly new. Walt Disney's *Mickey Mouse Club* was conceived in part to help promote Disneyland, and even critically acclaimed shows like *Sesame Street* have toy spin-offs. Nor, say industry spokesmen, does a hit show necessarily mean a stream of kids lining up at the toy counter. NBC's *The Smurfs,* for example, is one of Saturday morning's top-rated children's shows, but the like-named toys have not been big sellers.

The popularity of toy-inspired shows, however, may be starting to fade because of oversaturation. "We're winding down these programs," says Stephen Schwartz, director of marketing for Hasbro, which has already canceled two toy-linked shows, *Glo Friends* and *Potato Head.* Ironically enough, the marketplace itself is proving to be a nemesis of TV's cartoon characters, just when federal regulators are beginning to think that it is once again time to lay down the law.

By Richard Zoglin.
Reported by Jerome Cramer/Washington and Lawrence Malkin/Boston

QUESTIONS AND ACTIVITIES

Comprehension Questions

1. A federal appeals court has ruled that the FCC must reconsider its 1984 ruling on commercial advertising for children's TV. What did the 1984 ruling do? What limits on advertising for children's shows existed prior to 1984?

2. Why are critics especially concerned about the number of children's shows that are based on toys?

3. What is the purpose of Action for Children's Television?

4. What are "interactive" shows? Why are many people upset about them?

Discussion Questions

1. Do you think there should be TV shows devoted solely to children? Explain your answer.

2. Do you think there should be government regulation of the content of TV shows for children? Why or why not?

3. Do you think there should be government regulation of advertising that occurs during children's TV shows? Why or why not?

Group Activities

In groups of approximately five or six, select one of the statements below to defend. Each statement must be chosen by at least one group.

a. The television industry should regulate itself regarding both content of children's shows and advertising.

b. The government should monitor both advertising and the content of shows for children.

c. Parents should take the responsibility for what children watch on television.

In your discussion, develop arguments in support of the position chosen.

After your discussion, present your position and supporting arguments to the whole class.

Individual Work

1. Select one of the following activities:

a. If you have access to children, poll five of them to learn what their favorite television programs are.

b. Ask five parents what their children's favorite television programs are.

Summarize the results in a brief oral report (10 minutes maximum) to the class. Be sure to include such information as the ages of the children, whether they are boys or girls, and whether any trends are evident in their television habits.

2. Look at the TV listings in your area for a typical weekday. How many shows are aimed specifically at children? What kinds of shows are these (e.g., animated cartoons, puppet shows, etc.)? Have you seen any of these shows? If so, what is your opinion of them? Summarize your findings in a brief oral report to the class (10 minutes maximum).

BACKGROUND NOTES

for **Beyond the Game, a Champion**

Preview

Doug Williams' outstanding performance as a Super Bowl quarterback has inspired countless sports fans, both black and white.

Culture

Disney World: an amusement complex for children and adults located in Orlando, Florida. Disney World and Disneyland in California were created by Walt Disney, the famous producer of cartoons and children's films.

expansion franchise: a team added to those in a professional sports league
[ɛk'spænʃən 'fræn,tʃaɪz]

Grambling State University: a university located in Louisiana. Grambling has an all-black student body.

Super Bowl: a championship football game held annually in January. The two teams that play in the Super Bowl are the winners of the eastern and western conferences of the National Football League.

Vocabulary

drumbeating: publicity; hype

falter: to hesitate; to waver

fidget ['fɪdʒət]: to act nervously; to move restlessly

genial ['dʒi,niəl]: kind; gracious

have the goods: to have the necessary qualifications; to possess the required materials

lionized ['laɪə,naɪzd]: respected; treated as important (often ironic)

lopsided: unbalanced; leaning to one side

painstaking: careful; diligent

paltriest ['pɔl,triəst]: the least; the most trivial

quarterback: a football player who controls the ball and directs the offensive play of the team

racist ['resəst]: a person who believes that one race of people is inherently superior to other races

waffle: to go back and forth; to be indecisive (informal)

wobble ['wabəl]: to move unsteadily; to tremble

Beyond the Game, a Champion

A forgettable Super Bowl yields an unforgettable performance

As a contest, Super Bowl XXII ended by half time. As a lesson, it should last forever. The TV ratings in the late stages were the paltriest in years, but it is pleasing to imagine that this may have only partly been a product of the lopsided score, that a multitude of black children may have already raced outside to raise their arms to the sky. And not just blacks. And not just children.

Climaxing a regular season in which he started and won no games—none in two seasons, for that matter—Washington Quarterback Doug Williams passed for a Super Bowl record of 340 yds. and four touchdowns, as the Redskins massacred the favored Denver Broncos and their lionized leader John Elway, 42-10. By his swagger, the Broncos' young quarterback is known as "the Duke" (though John Wayne never portrayed General Custer). Blond, blue-eyed, Stanford-educated Elway could—in that lemon-squash phrase—do it all. He could hurt you in a lot of ways. He even used his multiple gifts to evade the lowly National Football League team that drafted him No. 1 (the Baltimore Colts) and arranged himself a more genial place in Denver. During the drumbeating for last week's championship game, Elway proclaimed five Super Bowl titles a personal goal.

Meanwhile, brown-haired, brown-eyed, Grambling-educated Williams dutifully reported to the worst expansion franchise in pro football history, the 2-26 Tampa Bay Buccaneers. When two years later he lifted the Bucs to within a game of a Super Bowl, but no nearer, his reward was a rotten watermelon gift-wrapped by a racist fan. For peace as much as money, he eventually jumped to another league. When it folded in 1986, only Washington held out a job. At 32, five years older than Elway, Williams had been standing behind Jay Schroeder for a year and a half when Schroeder faltered in November.

For a while afterward, Washington Coach Joe Gibbs waffled between the two, but by the conference championship game with Minnesota three weeks ago, he knew who his quarterback was. Actually, the players decided. Gibbs could see who moved them, in every way. When a hailstorm of Williams' incompletions fell against Minnesota, Schroeder fidgeted on the sidelines, but the coach never

Williams the role model: instinct , balance, thoughtfulness

blinked. In San Diego, while Elway was envisioning his five titles, Williams was trying to answer the question "How long have you been a black quarterback?" (As far as he could recall, Williams seemed to turn black about the time he left Grambling.) "I'm quite sure the Redskins didn't hire me," he kept saying, "just to be the first black quarterback in the Super Bowl."

The disappointments in Williams' life have not been small. He lost his wife to a brain tumor four years ago, ten days short of their first anniversary. Symbolic little barriers were blocking his way right up to game time. On Super Bowl eve he endured three hours of root-canal dental work. And as the first quarter was closing in a 10-0 Denver rush, Williams' left leg crumpled; Schroeder entered for two plays. Although wobbling like a table, Williams was back for the first snap of the second quarter and

for the remarkable 17 offensive plays that followed. All told, they produced five touchdowns.

Suddenly Williams was on the Wheaties box. His first flash commercial took place right on the sidelines ("Where are you going now, Doug?" "I'm going to Disney World"). Really, the initial stop was the White House, followed shortly by Washington's Howard University. He went there as a way of reaching back to Grambling, to Alcorn State, to South Carolina State, to Texas Southern. He said, "I am a product of all black universities and colleges."

Williams' coach at Grambling, Legendary Eddie Robinson, 68, was present at San Diego. He is the winningest college football coach in history, probably the best of all the black coaches the N.F.L. has never hired. Beginning with the great Green Bay Defensive End Willie Davis, "Coach Rob" has been supplying Super Bowl stars since Game I. But James Harris, a decade ago, and Williams were the first quarterbacks he constructed in such a way that no one could convert them to defensive backs. So painstaking were their preparations back in Louisiana, they had even practiced a few times with a microphone.

Now that Williams is permanently fixed in dreams to come, the practice will help. Being a role model requires more than just good instincts; it takes balance and thoughtfulness. Williams seems to have the goods. He understands the score, but bitterness is not his style. As a boy, his favorite baseball player was Dodger Pitcher Don Drysdale. "Why?" he repeated a question, ignoring the questioner's point. "Because he could really throw. [Drysdale is white.] I can remember going to see the Dodgers play for the first time and being so disappointed that Sandy Koufax was pitching. Why? He's left-handed."

Graceful throwers and speakers are already following Williams, among them Syracuse Quarterback Don McPherson, who told the *Los Angeles Times,* "He's not helping an issue, he's helping people. And the people he is helping are not black, but white." That was the best line of the Super Bowl.

By Tom Callahan

QUESTIONS AND ACTIVITIES

Comprehension Questions

1. Which team was favored to win Super Bowl XXII? Which team won? What was the final score?

2. Who was the winning quarterback? What physical problems was he facing during the game?

3. What two places did Williams visit soon after the Super Bowl game?

4. Who was Williams' coach at Grambling? Why is he called "legendary"?

Discussion Questions

1. Why was so much attention focused on Williams after his team won the Super Bowl? Do you think the attention was appropriate? Why or why not?

2. What did one racist fan in Tampa give to Williams? What did this symbolize? What is your reaction to such a gesture? Do sports fans in your culture ever do things that you think are inappropriate? Give an example.

3. Williams is being called a role model. What is a role model? Do you think Williams is a good role model for children, regardless of whether they are black or white? Explain your answer.

Group Activities

1. In groups of three or four, discuss the questions given below. See if you can reach a consensus on them.
   a. What is prejudice?
   b. What do you think causes prejudice?
   c. What do you think can be done to alleviate prejudice?
   After your discussion, be prepared to summarize your group's ideas for the class.

2. Prejudice against various ethnic, racial, linguistic, and religious groups has existed in nearly every country and culture. Again in groups of three or four, compile a list of examples of prejudicial treatment. Your examples may be historical or contemporary, and they may be taken from your culture or another. Do not discuss the issues involved; merely compile your list to present to the entire class.

Individual Work

1. Listed below are some well-known individuals from the world of sports. Using magazines, books, or cultural informants, find out who they are and write a sentence or two about each one. Also, write a summary sentence or two that describes what they all have in common.
   a. Arthur Ashe
   b. ChiChi Rodriguez
   c. Debi Thomas
   d. Larry Bird
   e. Jackie Robinson

2. Choose one of the topics below to discuss in a short written statement (two pages maximum):
   a. Present your ideas about how prejudicial treatment of particular groups of people can be alleviated. You may incorporate some of the ideas presented in the group work.
   b. Describe an incident in which you felt you were discriminated against, whether because of age, gender, race, religion, or any other reason. Explain how you felt.

Article Four

BACKGROUND NOTES
for **In Praise of the Goddess Pele**

Preview

Nineteenth century missionaries to the Hawaiian Islands once banned the hula. Now after years of disinterest, this traditional dance and its music are enjoying a cultural revival.

Culture

Big Island: Hawaii; the largest island in the Hawaiian Island chain. The other principal islands are Oahu, Maui, and Kauai.

Indiana: a state in the Midwest in which basketball is an extremely popular sport. High school basketball games are important community events in many Indiana towns.

Kilauea [ˌkɪləˈweə]: a volcano on the island of Hawaii. Kilauea has become active again in the past several years.

mainland: the continental United States. The term is used (mainly by Hawaiians) to distinguish between the Hawaiian Islands and the rest of the country.

Vocabulary

beguiled [bəˈgaɪld]: enchanted; bewitched; charmed

caldera [ˌkalˈdɚə]: a volcanic crater. A caldera is formed by the collapse of the walls of the volcano or by explosions.

erotic [əˈradək]: sexually suggestive; arousing sexual feelings

ethnic [ˈɛθnək]: relating to groups of people who share common national origins and customs

impudence [ˈɪmpjədəns]: insolence; boldness; characterized by a lack of concern for others

invoke [ɪnˈvok]: to call forth; to summon

lei [le]: a necklace of flowers

muffled: suppressed; quieted (said of a sound)

percussion [pɚˈkəʃən]: the beating or striking of a musical instrument

prudent [ˈprudənt]: wise; foresighted

rusty: outdated; slow due to lack of practice

sanctified: consecrated; made holy

splaylegged [ˈspleˌlɛgd]: with legs spread apart

swathed [swɑðd]: clothed; wrapped; covered (a rare word)

voluminous [vəˈlumənəs]: full; large; having many folds

The Ka Pa Hula Hawai'i troupe at the American Dance Festival in Durham, N.C.

In Praise of the Goddess Pele

Hula flourishes in a Hawaiian cultural revival

An old woman wearing a crown of green mountain ferns and drapery that looks vaguely Grecian stands alone, arms upraised, and chants in a strong voice to ancient gods. This is polite and also prudent. Kau'i Zuttermeister, 78, is a hula dancer, and she accepts mainland Christianity, first brought to the Hawaiian Islands in 1820 by missionaries. But her uncle Sam Pua Haaheo, an elderly kahuna, or expert practitioner, who taught her the chants, dances and drumming patterns of traditional hula 60 years ago, told her to "pray first to the gods of your forefathers. They were here first."

Some still endure. Most of the ancestor gods are gone now, but on the Big Island, the fire and volcano goddess Pele still lives. She is not worshiped, say modern-day Hawaiians, but she is acknowledged, and in the fiery and overflowing caldera of Kilauea she rules. The first hula, it is said, was chanted and danced in Pele's praise by her younger sister Hi'iaka. Recently Zuttermeister and some 25 other splendid hula performers, the spiritual descendants of Hi'iaka, brought their art to the American Dance Festival in Durham, N.C. It was not modern dance, which is what the festival customarily explores and celebrates. But there were some similarities; the hula is earth seeking, like most of modern dance, not aerial, like classical ballet. It is done with the knees flexed, and, of course, in bare feet. So, often, is modern dance.

When Zuttermeister was young, the ancient, traditional hula—*hula kahiko*—had nearly died out. Islanders with Hawaiian blood took little pride in their ancestry, and cellophane-skirt-and-ukulele imitation hulas were staged mostly for tourists. But her husband Carl, a German immigrant, was proud of Kau'i's Hawaiian blood and convinced her to learn what her uncle had to teach.

A few others of that generation also learned from their elders, and by the early 1970s mainland ethnic-pride movements had strong echoes in the islands. Now there is little danger that the old hula forms will die. Zuttermeister has passed on the chants and dance movements, exactly as she learned them, to her daughter Noenoelani Zuttermeister Lewis, 43, and her granddaughter Hauoliōnalani Lewis, 20. Public schools today teach hula as part of the cultural history of the islands. Teams taught by hula masters compete in hula dance-offs that are approximately as well attended as high school basketball tournaments in Indiana. Such top-ranked groups as the four who traveled to Durham have little chance to grow rusty. This week on the Big Island, for example, the Kanaka'ole sisters will invoke the gods for a space conference and take part in the Kilauea Dance Exhibition.

Noenoelani, kneeling, chants and finger taps the *puniu,* a small coconut-shell drum lashed to the thigh, and thumps the *pahu hula,* a larger sharkskin-covered drum. Hauoli-onalani, leis at wrists and ankles, head erect, chants a formal request—"Let me in, I'm cold"—to be admitted to the *halau,* or dance school. Noenoelani replies as the teacher, "Come in, all I have to offer is my voice . . ." Her daughter begins the rhythmic, liquid swaying of the hula.

It is not hard to see why missionaries in the early 19th century were horrified by the hula. Not only did the dances glorify false gods, but many of them were explicitly and joyously sexual. There were niceties; it is considered vulgar, for instance, to thrust your *opu,* or lower abdomen, forward when you are performing the *ami,* the characteristic revolving hip motion of hula. But even done with good taste, traditional dances celebrating the genital endowment of kings or queens—*Your Oversized Ma'i* is the name of one that compares the *ma'i* of King David Kalakaua with an eel—were too much for the stern mainland men of God.

The preachers succeeded in having the hula banned, and the dances stayed underground until Kalakaua's coronation in 1883. He brought about a public revival, with one concession to puritan sensibilities: male dancers could wear their traditional elaborate loincloths, but women, who had worn skirts of tapa (beaten bark) and no tops, could perform only when covered from neck to knee.

This compromise hardened into tradition. Women are heavily swathed, wearing voluminous outfits or skirts traditionally made of ti plant leaves, sanctified by precautionary over-the-knee bloomers. The result is that male energy and loin-cloth-flipping impudence are expressed powerfully and directly, while the grace and erotic force of the women are somewhat muffled.

Thus it seems that the missionaries' kapu (prohibition) has won. Or has it? The most vivid images a beguiled mainlander takes away from the hula are of Kau'i Zuttermeister, arms raised to the old gods, and the rumbling power of two sisters, Pualani Kanaka'ole Kanahele and Nalani Kanaka'ole, big mountain-shaped women, sitting splaylegged and barefoot on the stage, each beating ancient rhythms on an *ipu* (gourd drum) held between her thighs. A two-volcano percussion section, these Kanaka'oles, and, yes, Pele lives!

By John Skow

Two of the Halau Hula O Hoakalei dancers at Durham

"Pray first to the gods of your forefathers."

QUESTIONS AND ACTIVITIES

Comprehension Questions

1. According to legend, who danced the first hula? What was the reason for the dance?

2. Why did 19th century missionaries to the islands dislike the hula?

3. When the hula was publicly allowed once again in 1883, what changes took place in the dancers' clothing?

4. What has caused the revival of the hula?

Discussion Questions

1. Are there traditional dances associated with your home culture? Are they viewed as something old-fashioned or as an important part of the culture? Do young people typically learn these dances?

2. If you could go anywhere in the world to attend a performance of traditional music and dance, where would you go? Why did you pick the location you did? How did you learn about the place you chose?

Group Activities

In groups of approximately five or six, choose one of the positions listed below to defend. Each position must be selected by at least one group.

  a. It is important to maintain the traditional dances and music of a culture for present and future generations.

  b. Traditional music and dances represent ties to the past and impede progress. People should make no special efforts to maintain them.

After your discussion, present arguments in favor of your group's position to the entire class.

Individual Work

Choose one of the following activities to do:

  a. Decide which of the positions discussed in the Group Activities you support. Write your reasons for holding this position (one page maximum).

  b. Write a brief (one page maximum) description of a traditional dance performance you have attended. Try to describe the music, the dances, and the costumes. Tell about your reaction to the entire performance.

Article Five

BACKGROUND NOTES

for **Heroism, Hugs and Laughter**

Preview

The most recent International Summer Special Olympics attracted 5000 mentally handicapped athletes. All who participated, helped, and watched benefitted from the experience.

Culture

bronze medal: a third-place award. In Olympic sporting events, gold is given for first place, silver for second, and bronze for third.

Pan American Games: an athletic competition held every four years involving athletes from South, Central, and North America and the Caribbean.

second-grade: equivalent to the level of a child in the second year of elementary school. Second graders are generally seven years old.

Vocabulary

blunder: an error; a mistake

bowlathon ['bolə,θɑn]: a bowling competition

choked up: overcome by emotion. A person who is choked up usually is crying and has trouble talking.

collapse [kə'læps]: a state of loss of energy; exhaustion

courageous [kə'redʒəs]: brave; having the strength to survive great difficulty or opposition

derby: a contest open to all

determination: the ability to achieve a goal; the persistence to reach an end

Down's syndrome: a congenital abnormality that results in mental impairment

extraordinary [ɛk'strordənɛri]: remarkable; exceptional

flying rings: two free-swinging rings attached to the ceiling of a gymnasium and used in gymnastics events

hotfoot: to move quickly, as if walking on a hot surface (colloquial)

incandescent [,ɪnkən'dɛsənt]: glowing; shining

medic ['mɛdək]: a person trained to give medical assistance. A medic is not a doctor.

parallel bars: a free-standing apparatus with two parallel bars used in gymnastics events

scrooching: crawling; struggling on one's stomach to get under something

slalom ['slɑləm]: characterized by a zig-zag pattern. Slalom events are often held in skiing.

swirl: to move something with a twisting motion

U.S. Olympic medal winners Mary Lou Retton and Bart Connor with Special Olympians

Heroism, Hugs and Laughter

Special games for courageous spirits and generous hearts

It was hot, the hot kind of hot Indiana hot weather that sends the family dog scrooching under the pickup truck to enjoy the shade. But in South Bend, on the Notre Dame and St. Mary's College campuses, heroic athletes from 70 countries were running and jumping and laughing from the sheer joy of it all. No, these were not the Pan American Games, which were to start a few days later, downstate at Indianapolis. The competitors there, everyone knew, would run faster and jump higher. But not happier; world happiness records were being set here at the Seventh International Summer Special Olympics.

At the Notre Dame gym, lean, well-conditioned gymnasts are performing difficult maneuvers on the flying rings and the parallel bars. Obviously, they are athletes. No first-time observer of this Olympics for the mentally handicapped would wonder why they are competing. At the gym's other end, however, the scene takes the first-timer farther from the familiar, with a floor exercise called "rhythmic ribbons." One by one, young women, most of them shaped by the rough hand of Down's syndrome and all of limited physical ability, walk or run slowly over a patterned course, swirling a long ribbon tied to the end of a stick. Is that all there is to it? Yes. Except that Down's people tend to be short, and short-limbed, and sometimes awkward, the newcomer reflects, and the swirling ribbon is a marvelous way for such teenagers to be graceful, to dance. Any lack of comprehension is swept away as these seven athletes stand on the victory platform to receive their medals and roses. They are so happy, so gloriously pleased to be alive, that passersby watch in astonishment. The rarity they are seeing is momentary, only a flash, but it is beauty.

Out on the not-quite-melted running track, Alice Miller, 67, of South Bend, is hard at work under the hot sun. She is a lean, quick-smiling grandmother with cottony white hair, and what she does is hug. When an athlete here finishes an event, he or she gets a hug—that's a rule, one that might be expanded to the wider world, and Alice is great at it, having practiced on four children and eleven grandchildren.

Some of the athletes are near collapse at the end of long races in the high-90s heat, and medics cool the runners down with towels soaked in ice water. But Eric Tosada, a springy 18-year-old track man from Puerto Rico, doesn't even bother to sit down after clicking off 3,000 meters in 9 min. 38 sec., a new world record for Special Olympians. (The overall world record is 7 min. 32.01 sec.) He bounces around delightedly, and comes to prideful attention when his picture is taken. Another kind of athletic accomplishment is that of George Kelsey of New Jersey, who cannot push with his arms and so maneuvers his wheelchair by reversing it and shoving it along backward, with his left toe, through the 30-meter slalom course. His face is twisted with effort, but he too is laughing with joy as he finishes.

The courage of Juan Alberto Duarte of Paraguay is incandescent. He runs every step of his 300-meter heat with a crooked, skipping swing of his legs, and twice, on nothing but determination, manages to pass the runner ahead of him. But in the end he is last, the ninth of nine. Only eight medals and awards have been prepared. The officials do not know what to do. Eunice Kennedy Shriver does, however. She hotfoots it down from the stands, gives Duarte a second hug and decrees that he get a medal for extraordinary heroism. She is entitled to such expansiveness. She and her husband started a summer camp for the mentally handicapped in the backyard of their Maryland home in 1961, and this was the beginning of the Special Olympics. Eunice Shriver is said to despise public speaking, but her speech was a brief, clear moment in an overlong and somewhat celebrity-clogged opening ceremony. She spoke of the "courageous spirit and the generous heart," and then she told the 5,000 mentally handicapped athletes gathered in Notre Dame Stadium that they had earned the right to live like the rest of us, and with the rest of us.

There was a lot of courage and generosity going around. Almost everything in South Bend was done, and done well, by volunteers, among them some 1,200 members of a service group called Civitan. Community people back in Elizabeth City, N.C., held bass-fishing derbies and bowlathons and the like to help Beverly James compete. She is the tenth of twelve children—"eight of whom have finished college," her mother Penny says with pride—and her father Roscoe has Parkinson's disease. Beverly, 19, who functions at a second-grade level intellectually, is pleasant and mannerly, but she is shy. Townspeople collected enough money to send her mother and two women coaches along for support. Last Tuesday afternoon she hit her start on the button and ran a fast 8.7 50-meter dash, her personal best by 1.9 seconds, good enough for a bronze medal. Her head coach, Sandy Davis, was so choked up he couldn't talk straight.

"You get chill bumps and tears in your eyes," said Cindi McCollough, 31, a swimming coach for the Georgia team who had taken time off from work to make the trip. As she spoke, a slightly confused swimmer began to splash through a third lap of a two-lap, 50-meter freestyle race; a coach, fully clothed, dived in to bring him back. It was a funny moment, and everyone laughed. Good manners tell you, of course, that you do not laugh at a mentally handicapped person's blunder. But this, it was clear, was different. The laughter was friendly, and letting it spill out was just fine; we were all family.

By John Skow

QUESTIONS AND ACTIVITIES

Comprehension Questions

1. Who began the Special Olympics? where? in what year?
2. What are some of the athletic events that are held at the Summer Special Olympics?
3. There are numerous examples of personal courage and determination at a Special Olympics. What are some that were cited in the article?

Discussion Questions

1. What do you think is the main purpose of the Special Olympics? Do you believe it is achieving its goal?
2. Were you familiar with the Special Olympics before reading this article? How did you feel after reading about this event?

Group Activities

In groups of five or six, discuss both of the statements presented below:
  a. Mentally handicapped individuals should be included as much as possible in the daily life of a society.
  b. Mentally handicapped individuals should be kept separate from the general population so that their needs can be better served with specialized programs.

Attempt to reach a consensus in your group regarding these issues. Be prepared to present your conclusion and supporting arguments to the whole class.

Individual Work

Present your own position on the issues discussed in the group session in a written report (two pages maximum).

Article Six

BACKGROUND NOTES

for **So Long on Lonely Street**

Preview

Elvis Presley died more than 10 years ago. His music, as well as Presley-based souvenirs and tourist events, live on.

Culture

Lonely Street: the location of "Heartbreak Hotel," the name of one of Elvis' most successful early songs

Snopesian ['snop,siən]: pertaining to the Snopes family, a fictional family appearing in several novels and stories of William Faulkner. The Snopes clan represents the negative aspects of modern commercial society.

Vegas: Las Vegas, Nevada. The city is a tourist attraction where gambling is legal and where famous performers appear in the numerous nightclubs.

Vocabulary

antic ['æntək]: absurd; ludicrous; extravagant

bedrock: here, basic (Literally, bedrock is a solid layer of rock under the earth.)

bloated: swollen; inflated

brazen ['brezən]: bold; impudent; shameless

compilation: a collection; a composition of items

daunted ['dɔntəd]: intimidated; discouraged

dread [drɛd]: fear; anxiety

estate [ə'stet]: the assets left by a person at death

forge [fordʒ]: to shape; to form

fuss: commotion; unnecessary activity

gospel: a kind of popular religious music. Gospel music is often associated with the southern United States.

hit pay dirt: to succeed (often financially); to discover something of value

leave (someone) in the lurch: to leave someone in a vulnerable or unsupported position (colloquial)

melodrama: dramatic action; an exaggerated story

merchandise [mɚtʃən,daɪs]: goods that are bought and sold

outtake: part of an audio or video recording that is not satisfactory and is deleted from the final product

primacy ['prɑɪmə,si]: the state of being first or most important

purport [pɚ'port]: to intend; to claim

raunch [rɔntʃ]: that which is tasteless or below standard (colloquial)

reassertion: a new declaration; a reaffirmation

saturated ['sætʃɚ,edəd]: filled; soaked

scrupulous ['skrupjələs]: careful; strict

vig: interest paid on a loan (rare)

Elvis in 1957, the year he purchased and moved into Graceland Mansion

So Long on Lonely Street

New records and hype commemorate a decade without Elvis

This is a season of anniversaries. *Sgt. Pepper's Lonely Hearts Club Band* celebrated its second decade in June, being very proper and punctual about the schedule set down in its own song: "It was twenty years ago today/ that Sgt. Pepper taught the band to play." Paul McCartney cut a cake in London and spoke about peace. Two other Beatles failed to show up for the party. One, of course, couldn't.

Next month, on Aug. 16 to be exact, Elvis Presley will have been dead for ten years, an anniversary that will be memorialized on a less moderate scale. This is the sort of occasion that is best honored simply, with fond memories and the playing of some choice sides. But when a record company has product to sell and an es-

tate has merchandise to move, the date suddenly gets writ large. RCA has just released four compilations of Presley material with scrupulous "audio restoration": *The Top Ten Hits, The Number One Hits* and, most crucially, *The Complete Sun Sessions,* recorded at the start of his career, and *The Memphis Record,* recorded in 1969, when all the anger and antic experimentation of rock seemed to have left Elvis in the lurch. The 23 songs on *The Memphis Record* (never released all together until now) were originally conceived as a reassertion of Presley's primacy. In 1987 they sound like a premature last testament. *The Memphis Record,* as it turns out, is one of the great legacies of American music.

For some fans, however, not even the music

is enough. Elvis' Memphis home, Graceland, already a prime tourist attraction, will gear up for everything from candlelight vigils to a 5-km run. Lucy de Barbin, who claims that her daughter Desirée was fathered by Elvis, is pushing the recently published *Are You Lonesome Tonight?,* which purports to dish out the hot sticky behind the entire episode. Meanwhile, the King's official ex-wife, Actress Priscilla Presley, is offering a one-hour video tour of *Elvis Presley's Graceland.* It isn't hard to figure what Elvis would have made of all this fuss: he was used to it. Besides, Colonel Tom Parker, his manager, could always work it out so that he and his boy got a good cut of the action.

There was one thing that was not manageable, though, not even with all Parker's Snopesian smarts. Elvis' reckoning with history was beyond anyone's reach, including, at the last, his very own. He died bloated with his own excess and everyone else's expectations. He did not invent rock 'n' roll, but he forged it and focused it, and he was the first great rock superstar. He haunted his contemporaries, like Jerry Lee Lewis, who once showed up outside Graceland waving a pistol and demanding an audience. John Lennon, Bob Dylan, Bruce Springsteen, John Fogerty—all dreamed of him and were daunted not only by his gift but by his destiny. He was the rocker they yearned to be and feared becoming.

Elvis sold his soul many times over—nightly, in Vegas dates; routinely, in all those musicals filmed in Hollywood as if they were popped out of a microwave—but he never sold out. He probably sang *My Way* in his later years as often as he sang *Heartbreak Hotel,* but it was never clear that Elvis himself thought all the trash amounted to short change. Even during his earliest recording dates at Sun Records, he did a Billy Eckstine favorite as well as an Arthur ("Big Boy") Crudup blues, and he was always a big Dean Martin fan. He could puff and perspire all over a stage on the Vegas strip and show up back home to sing some heavenly gospel. Whatever he did and however he sang, it always seemed as if he were paying the vig on some spiritual debt that kept mounting until, with the aid of a few prescription drugs, it finally crushed him.

It is impossible to know the exact nature of that debt, of course, but its depth can be felt in all his best music. The joy, the brazen melodrama, the low tragedy and the raunch all range free on the two greatest hits packages. *The Sun Sessions,* first released in 1976, is a seminal record. This new version offers alternate takes and outtakes, including an unlikely version of *Harbor Lights,* and makes a fascinating history of one scuffling producer (Sun Founder and Rock Pioneer Sam Phillips) and three good ole boys (Elvis, Lead Guitarist Scotty Moore, Bass Player Bill Black) groping toward greatness. "That's fine," says Sam Phillips after one take on *Blue Moon of Kentucky.* "Hell, that's different. That's a pop song now, nearly 'bout." All the difference, and all the history, hovered around that "nearly." It took a while, but that new territory was finally called rock 'n' roll, and after a time, it looked like it might shut Elvis out.

The material on *The Memphis Record* was meant to catch him up with history, and he hit pay dirt. *In the Ghetto* gave him his first Top Ten hit in four years; the second single from those sessions, *Suspicious Minds,* was his first No. 1 single since 1962. Gregg Geller, the archivist who supervised these four releases, has gathered the songs from those twelve days of studio work into a double album that is a bedrock classic. Elvis never again sang this consistently or this passionately. There are blues and country here, gospel and rock and pop, all sung as if Presley's life depended on each tune. It did, in a sense, and reclaiming himself, just this once, seemed enough. It gave him the strength to get on for another eight years. But listen to *Long Black Limousine,* and it's clear that Elvis knew what was waiting around the corner.

The Memphis Record is full of triumph and dread. It is saturated with Presley's power and baptized with his loneliness. "He tried not to show it," Phillips recalled, "but he felt so *inferior.* Presley probably innately was the most introverted person that [ever] came into that studio. He didn't play with bands. He didn't go to this little club and pick and grin. All he did was set with his guitar on the side of his bed at home. I don't think he even played on the front porch." He sang out and reached out, but, after all, maybe it's just as simple as that. Elvis Presley always sang to himself.

By Jay Cocks

QUESTIONS AND ACTIVITIES

Comprehension Questions

1. What is the name of Elvis' home? Where is it located?
2. How did Elvis die? What special events were planned to commemorate the 10th anniversary of his death?
3. What kind of music did Elvis sing?
4. Why is he regarded as important in the history of modern music?

Discussion Questions

1. Have you ever heard any of Elvis' records? Do you like his music? Do you have any favorite songs? Why or why not? Have you seen any of his movies? If so, which ones? What was your opinion of them?
2. Who are your favorite singers? What is it about them that you like?

Group Activities

It is said that one must pay a heavy price for stardom. In groups of five or six, discuss what you think are the advantages and disadvantages of the kind of fame that Elvis Presley (or any other internationally famous star) had. After your discussion, be prepared to present your ideas to the class.

Individual Work

In a short paper (two pages maximum), explain why you would or would not like to become a world-famous performer.

BACKGROUND NOTES

for **Snowboarders Invade the Slopes**

Preview

A new sport has appeared that combines skiing, surfing, and skateboarding. So far, reactions to the sport are mixed.

Culture

weekend warrior: one who participates in an activity on a part-time basis. The term originally referred (with contempt) to a person serving in the military reserves rather than on active duty.

Vocabulary

adolescent [ˌædəˈlɛsənt]: a person between the ages of puberty and maturity. Teenagers are usually considered adolescents.

bad rap: criticism (slang)

brash: impetuous; rash; done without thought to the consequences

coolest: most popular; most favored by the young and fashionable (slang, generally used by teenagers)

dazzling: impressive; brilliant

flailing: swinging freely; flying about

griper [ˈɡraɪpɚ]: a complainer; one who criticizes (colloquial)

gun (an) engine: to "race" a car engine; to give a car engine a lot of gas

harrowing [ˈhɛrˌoɪŋ]: nerve-wracking; frightening

hotdogging: performing crazy and often dangerous stunts and tricks

outrigger: a floating projection attached to the side of a boat that helps stabilize it

paraphernalia [ˌpɛrəfəˈneljə]: equipment; apparatus (a pretentious word, sometimes used for humorous effect)

proponent [prəˈponənt]: a supporter; one who is in favor of something

shimmy: to vibrate; to tremble

spew [spju]: to send forth in a gush; to exude

squat [skwɑt]: to sit on one's heels

wary [ˈwɛri]: cautious; prudent

Snowboarders Invade the Slopes

Flashy adolescents zigzag through the ranks of skiers

Seconds after pushing off downhill at Breckenridge, Colo., Peter Symms, 23, was out of control. Gaining speed, he torpedoed down a crowded ski slope, squatting sideways on a single plank of laminated wood that resembled a stubby ski. His body shimmied while he extended his arms like outriggers, hands flailing. "I'm going down again!" yelled the weekend warrior. He promptly crashed face down in the white powder. Nearby, a heavyset Texan leaned on his ski poles and watched intently: "Now what in the hell is that?"

Snowboarding. To traditionalists, the breezy fad is a clumsy intrusion on the sleek precision of downhill skiing, but to some 100,000 enthusiasts, many of them adolescent males, it is the coolest snow sport of the season. From Vermont to California, snowboarders are shredding the slopes on a cross between a surfboard and a ski, a 5-ft.-long, 10-in.-wide piece of laminated wood or fiber glass with fixed bindings that can easily strap around any sturdy boot. No poles needed. The newborn sport, like its cousins surfing and skateboarding, requires agility and a keen sense of balance to guide the boards down the slopes at speeds approaching 30 m.p.h.

Five years ago the sport was almost unknown. Today boards cost from $150 to $400, and Burton Snowboards in Manchester Center, Vt., the largest manufacturer, claims its sales have doubled during each of the past four years.

The first attempt at snowboarding can be a humbling experience. Professional skiers and dazzling skateboarders often start at ground zero, and in some cases they stay there. For the novice the only controls are *stop* (sit down) and *go* (very fast). "My butt may be sore, but that's the price you pay for a thrill," says Symms. Fortunately, after a harrowing start, most newcomers master the art as quickly as they fall down. "By your third day you can be skiing slopes that beginning skiers wouldn't touch," says David Alden, a former amateur snowboard champion.

Some proponents maintain that their sport is safer than skiing. Since there is just one board, the legs can never cross, so there are fewer broken ankles and hips. The injuries that do occur are usually bruises to the upper body (thumb, wrist and shoulder) and come from falls and occasional collisions with trees and

An expert swerves with razor grace

"Not about style but raging hormones."

other downhillers. James Lithman, 19, of Los Angeles, says snowboarders get a bad rap because there are so many novices loose on the slopes. "Look at all the crazy skiers," he argues. "The medics carry the bodies down all day long."

Some mountain resorts have been wary of snowboards, fearing that hotdogging teenagers

143

would intimidate regular skiers. Snow Summit, near Los Angeles, Vail in Colorado, and Sugarbush in Vermont are a few places that ban the board, but more than 100 ski areas nationwide allow it. Because rentals are cheaper and paraphernalia not as grand, many resort owners think snow surfing may attract a whole new crowd to try out the slopes. The sport has already achieved the organized trappings of respectability. Next month Breckenridge will play host to the World Snowboard Classic, with more than 200 competitors from ten countries.

Of course, there are holdouts, purists who scorn the brash intruders. Complains veteran Vermont Skier Mary Simons: ''Snowboarding is not about grace and style but about raging hormones. It is adolescent boys with their newest toy.'' Ralph DesLauriers, owner of the Bolton Valley Resort in Vermont, compares the gripers with ''people in the horse-drawn carriages reacting to cars driving by.'' At least skiers can be grateful that snowboarders cannot gun their engines and spew exhaust.

By Martha Smilgis.
Reported by Jon D. Hull/Breckenridge and Gerald Mullany/Stratton, Vt.

QUESTIONS AND ACTIVITIES

Comprehension Questions

1. What is a snowboard?
2. What two skills are mainly needed to snowboard?
3. Some claim that snowboarding is safer than skiing. What reasons do they give for this claim?
4. What evidence is there that snowboarding is becoming accepted as a sport?

Discussion Questions

1. Do you think that snowboarding is a fad or that it will continue to grow as a sport? Explain your answer.
2. Have you ever skied, surfed, or skateboarded? Would you like to try snowboarding? Why or why not?
3. Have you ever tried a sport that is viewed as dangerous? If so, which one? If not, would you like to? Which one?

Group Activities

1. In groups of three or four, make a list of the five sports you consider to be the most dangerous. Present your list to the class. How much consensus among groups is there?
2. In groups of three or four, invent a sport. Your new sport can be a combination of existing sports or a completely new one. Be as imaginative and innovative as possible. Present your new sport to the class.

Individual Work

1. Poll 10 people, asking the following questions:
   a. Have you ever heard of snowboarding? (If not, describe the sport to them.)
   b. Would you like to try it? Why or why not?
   Summarize the findings of your poll in a brief written report (one page maximum).

2. Choose one of the following questions to answer in a written report (two pages maximum):
   a. Why do you think people invent new sports? (Is it due, for example, to boredom, curiosity, competition, creativity, or something else?)
   b. Why do you think people participate in dangerous sports?

Fads & Fashions

Article One

BACKGROUND NOTES

for **One Potato, Two Potato . . .**

Preview

Potato chips have long been a favorite snack for millions of Americans. Today chip lovers can choose among a variety of flavors, colors, and textures.

Culture

Cajun [ˈkedʒən]: characteristic of the Cajun culture. Cajuns are descended from French-speaking Acadians from Canada and primarily live in Louisiana. The word "Cajun" evolved from the word "Acadian." Cajun cuisine is often spicy.

chip: a potato chip; a thinly sliced, fried piece of potato. (In British English, a **chip** refers to an American french fry.)

deli [ˈdɛli]: a delicatessen; a store in which ready-to-eat foods such as meats and salads are sold. New York is famous for its numerous delis.

one potato, two potato . . . : part of a line from a traditional children's saying:
One potato, two potato, three potato, four;
Five potato, six potato, seven potato, more.

Pennsylvania Dutch: characteristic of the Pennsylvania Dutch culture. The Pennsylvania Dutch (from *Deutsch* for German) came to eastern Pennsylvania in the 18th century. They have maintained many rural German customs and even, to some degree, their German language.

Vocabulary

aberration [ˌæbəˈreʃən]: atypical; deviating from the usual

addict [ˈædək(t)]: one who compulsively uses or consumes something

aficionado [əˌfɪʃəˈnɑdo]: a fan; a devotee

burnished: polished; shiny; glossy

cantankerous [ˌkænˈtæŋkɚəs]: grouchy; bad-tempered; ill-natured

cherish [ˈtʃɛrəʃ]: to appreciate; to hold dear

cloying [ˈklɔɪɪŋ]: excessively pleasing

devotee [ˌdɛvəˈte]: a fan; someone who is devoted, usually to a cause

incendiary [ˌɪnˈsɛndiˌɛri]: here, extremely spicy; literally, likely to cause a fire

jalapeño pepper [ˌhɑləˈpenjo]: a type of pepper that is very spicy. Jalapeño peppers are often used in Mexican-American and Southwestern U.S. cooking.

knockoff: an imitation; a copy (slang)

overtone: a suggestion; a secondary taste

parchment: a kind of writing paper made from sheepskin or goatskin.

placate [ˈpleˌket]: to pacify; to soothe by making concessions

preservative: a chemical additive used to preserve food. Some people prefer to eat only foods without preservatives.

quintessentially [ˌkwɪntəˈsɛnʃəli]: characteristic of the most typical example or the best representative

savory [ˈsevɚi]: appetizing; agreeable to the taste

tantalizing [ˈtæn(t)əˌlaɪzɪŋ]: tempting; stimulating

One Potato, Two Potato. . .

No matter how you slice them, chips are in

"**P**lease pass the chips." Time was when that request led to a predictable result: a crackling treat of smooth, fragile, bitingly salty potato chips. No longer. Now staggering possibilities abound: chips sliced from white or sweet potatoes that could be thick or thin, ridged or smooth, and with or without salt and preservatives. They might be natural in flavor or seasoned with Cajun, Italian or barbecue spices, vinegar, jalapeño peppers, cheese alone or with bacon, sour cream (or yogurt) with onion (or chives). There is also a choice of half a dozen or so oils for frying, which can be done in mass-produced, factory-size quantities (approximately 2,500 lbs. an hour) or in the old-fashioned but newly popular kettle batches (500 lbs. an hour), which cook a good deal more slowly and have a harder, crunchier finish.

"The new potato-chip varieties are like the changes made in bread," says Richard Duchesneau, president of Tri-Sum Potato Chip, which has operated in Leominster, Mass., since 1908. "People got tired of standard white, and now when you walk down the supermarket aisle, you'll find wheat, oat berry, cracked wheat and more. It's the same with chips." Though they profess an interest in foods that are low in salt and calories, Americans last year spent an estimated $3.3 billion dollars (an increase of 75% since 1980) on deep-fried chips, generally strewn with salt. The market is dominated by Pepsico's Frito-Lay, Borden's Wise and Procter & Gamble's Pringle's, but around the country the real aficionados prize the local brands.

"Regionality is very important," acknowledges James Green, a vice president of N.S. Khalsa, the Oregon producer of the decent if not distinctive Kettle Chips. "Oregonians like the fact that they are eating chips made from potatoes grown in this state." In Pennsylvania Dutch country, said to be the capital of potato-chip production, Michael Rice, president of Utz Quality Foods, uses cottonseed oil to fry his delicately satisfying line of smooth and ridged chips. But three years ago he introduced a fried-in-lard adaptation of the original potato chip developed by his grandparents in 1921. "Grandma Utz's chips do well in Pennsylvania," Rice reports, "but not in Baltimore or Washington."

Potato-chip fans in Louisiana opt for the fiery seasonings in Zapp's delectable Cajun Craw-Tators, golden brown, crisply curled wafers that are burnished with a savory and peppery spice blend, or the even more tantalizing incendiary jalapeño chips, hot enough to drive the muncher straight to a can of cold

Dixie beer. Judging by the high price of Maui chips (as much as $7.59 for a 7-oz. bag), Hawaiians like heavy grease—as do certain Angelenos. Jurgensen's, a high-toned Southern California grocery, buys all it can get of these dark, oily chips. The steep price does not discourage devotees like Andrea Sharp, a Los Angeles waitress. "I'm not sure what it is, but every time I eat them, I think of Hawaii," she says. Maui has inspired knockoffs, and some of the imitations, such as the parchment-crisp Laura Scudder's, made in California, and the rustic Trader Joe's Haberas Crispus, from Oregon, beat out the original.

To capitalize on the homemade appeal, the major producers have developed spin-off brands. Frito-Lay is doing research on a kettle-cooked chip. Wise now offers New York Deli chips along the Eastern Seaboard and as far west as Dallas, packed in a passionate purple bag that bears no hint of Borden or Wise. With New York Deli, Wise is mining the regional pride and expectations New Yorkers have about deli products being made to order, according to Vice President Chris Abernathy. This is accomplished by using Wise fryers at different temperatures and for different periods of time. The result is a chip with a pleasant potato flavor and nutty overtones.

Similarly, New Englanders who cherish the lingeringly greasy Cape Cod chips, old-fashioned and hand cooked in Hyannis, will find no clue on the package that the company now belongs to Anheuser-Busch. Even Pringle's, the *faux* chips formed of dehydrated potatoes, now comes in a variety of flavors

designed to add character. That goal has not quite been realized, although sales have risen 16% a year since 1981.

Some potato-chip addicts are brand loyal, notably the lovers of the greaseless and quintessentially potatoey Charles Chips, a Pennsylvania Dutch winner that has been going strong for 45 years and that proved best among the 65 varieties tasted for this report. The jalapeño Charles Chips led all other seasoned types. For decades Charles Chips were delivered to homes in 40 states, always packed in the company's trademark mustard-colored cans; now they are sold in supermarkets in typical air-cushioned bags. In Ohio, the loyalty lines are drawn between chips made by two old local outfits: the good, blond wafers of Mike-sell's, produced in Dayton, and the more pallid, "marcelled" Ballreich product, from Tiffin.

A stroll down a supermarket aisle would surely beguile George Crum, the chef at Moon's Lake House in Saratoga Springs, N.Y., who in 1853 is said to have devised "Saratoga chips" to placate a cantankerous customer who complained that the fried potatoes were too thick. But if Crum were to taste chocolate-coated chips, a salt-sweet, cloying aberration priced from $6 to $18 per lb. (the latter from Yuppie Gourmet in Racine, Wis.), he might be sorry he started the whole thing. As a good chef, he would be the first to recognize that even the best idea can be taken too far.

By Mimi Sheraton.
Reported by Janice M. Horowitz/New York and
Liz Kanter/Los Angeles

QUESTIONS AND ACTIVITIES

Comprehension Questions

1. What flavors of chips are now available?
2. What processes are used to produce chips?
3. Why is regionalism an important issue in potato chip sales?
4. Who is thought to be the originator of chips? Why did he develop them? In what year did this occur?

Discussion Questions

1. Do you like potato chips? Do you have a favorite brand?
2. What other snack foods do you enjoy? Do you eat them frequently?
3. Some say that Americans eat too much "junk food" (snacks with low nutritional value). In your opinion, is this true? On what do you base your answer?

Group Activities

In groups of three or four, develop a set of menus for one day's eating with foods that are nutritional, attractive, and interesting. After your discussion, present the menus to the class. Compare the different ones developed. Are there differences in the number of meals, their size, and the types of foods selected?

Individual Work

1. Sit in a student cafeteria or café for half an hour. Observe the snack foods that people are eating. What are the ones most frequently eaten? Report your observations to the class in a five-minute oral summary.
2. Go to a local food store. Make a list of snack items available with a representative brand name for each. Turn in a written summary (one page maximum) of your findings.

Article Two

BACKGROUND NOTES

for **High Life Afloat: Superduper Yachts**

Preview

Yachts were once the domain of the aristocracy.
Today the yacht business is booming for "commoners."

Culture

Johnny Carson: a famous television personality. He has been the host of the "Tonight Show," an evening talk show, for more than 20 years.

Jacuzzi [dʒə'kuzi]: the brand name of a type of whirlpool tub. Jacuzzis are associated with comfortable living.

Jet Ski: a small, motorized water craft used by an individual

Miami Vice: a popular television detective show filmed in Miami, Florida. The show is known for its often fancy settings.

sailboard: a surfboard with a sail, used by an individual

track lighting: a style of electric lighting associated with upscale design

Wall Street: a street in New York City where the New York Stock Exchange and other financial institutions are located. The name is synonymous with wealth.

workaholic [wɚkə'hɔlək]: a person who devotes all his or her energy to work. Workaholics work long hours and rarely take vacations. (slang)

Vocabulary

behemoth [bə'himəθ]: something impressively large

commodious [kə'modiəs]: roomy; spacious

consummate ['kɑnsə,met]: to finish; to complete

deep pocket: a wealthy person. The term refers to pockets where money is kept. (slang)

drydock: a dock located on land, but near water. They are used to build or repair ships.

fast tracker: a person who is rapidly becoming wealthy and influential

flamboyant [,flæm'bɔɪənt]: flashy; showy

grungy ['grəndʒi]: dirty and messy (colloquial)

heyday ['hede]: the period of greatest activity

honcho ['hɑntʃo]: an important person; a person in charge

knot: a measure of a ship's speed. A knot is one nautical mile (1.852 kilometers) per hour.

nudging: nearing; approaching

paparazzi [pɑpə'rɑtsi]: journalistic photographers known for their aggressive behavior and their lack of respect for the privacy of others

renowned [,ri'nɑʊnd]: famous; honored

replete [,ri'plit]: complete; full

tycoon [,taɪ'kun]: a wealthy and powerful businessman

whim: a notion; a fancy

yen: to desire; to yearn

The sleek and sassy *Never Say Never* is a 110-ft. rocket ship that skims the waves at 34 knots full throttle

High Life Afloat: Superduper Yachts

Seeking privacy and luxury, multimillionaires queue up for jumbo boats

When Johnny Carson sought to escape gawkers and paparazzi on his fourth honeymoon, he and his new bride, Alexis Maas, chose to cruise the Mediterranean by chartering the regal *Parts V,* a $6.5 million, 147-ft. world-class motor yacht. When renowned Manhattan Jeweler Harry Winston wanted to lay some choice diamonds before J. Paul Getty Jr. and Henry Ford II down in Palm Beach, Fla., he decided to rent the *Atlantique* as a 131-ft. floating showcase. And when Magazine Mogul Malcolm Forbes wants to mix celebrities like Barbara Walters and Henry Kissinger with advertising tycoons, he lures them with the offer of an evening spin around Manhattan aboard the *Highlander V,* his 150-ft. seagoing palace. "It's worth the cost," maintains Forbes. "It has much more appeal than an evening of dinner and the theater."

No argument there. Besides the lavish ego strokes that luxury vessels bestow, today's yachts satisfy almost every whim imaginable. The sun deck cradles a hot tub that can accommodate eight people, while commodious staterooms boast VCRs and private baths with Jacuzzis. Instead of a grungy galley, the super-yacht has a gleaming kitchen replete with microwaves, commercial-size freezers and stoves, and trash compactors. The bionic boats pack every aquatic toy: water skis, snorkling gear, diving equipment, Jet Skis and sailboards. To help while away foul weather, a free-flowing bar is at the ready, and libraries are stocked with videotapes as well as books, chess and backgammon games. Many decks have saunas, and in one vessel there is a piano with built-in heating elements to guard against warp.

America's yachting heyday was in the early 20th century, when wealthy industrialists competed in creating elaborate waterborne palaces.

Over the years, buying, building and chartering of yachts remained small and select, and in the late '70s, business hit bottom. Today the number of American-owned jumbos, over 100 ft. from stem to stern, is increasing from 80 in 1986 to 129, with the launch of 49 new yachts now under construction. More remarkable is that 33 of these yachts will be products of U.S. yards, rather than foreign competitors. Jumbo yachts sport a hefty price tag, ranging from $6 million to $50 million, depending on size and fittings. Annual maintenance can run up to 10% of the yacht's cost.

Broward Motor Yachts in Fort Lauderdale leads the U.S. in building big boats, with twelve taking shape in the family-owned yards. Its new production plant will add more than 50 architects, skilled fitters and welders to its staff of 250. Broward's most popular boat is an 80-ft. starter, or "yuppie special," that sells for $2 million. The typical buyer is a fast tracker between 35 and 40 who yens for something more than an "off the peg" Hatteras 61-footer. "I just got a personal check in the mail for $1.3 million," says Ken Denison, vice president for new boat sales and construction. "The guy said it would be O.K. We looked into it, and it was. One of the things about this business is that we don't have to talk financing."

Many of his customers return within three years to trade up to a superyacht. "Twenty-five years ago, a 120-footer was for kings and princes," says Denison. "Now the average boat we build is 90 feet." As for size, which matters greatly to yacht owners, King Fahd of Saudi Arabia owns the world's biggest yacht, the 482-ft. *Abdul Aziz,* which includes a mosque and a movie theater that seats 100. Because the King's yacht is currently in drydock, the unquestioned ruler of the waves is Queen Elizabeth's 412-ft. *Britannia.*

One factor that has contributed to the big yacht boom is satellite communications. International Broker George Nicholson, whose British family has been constructing boats for crowned heads and deep pockets since 1782, explains, "Most of the men who own large yachts are workaholics, and they get very nervous if they are out of touch with their offices. They used to plan their cruises around ports with telephones." Now, thanks to satellite linkups, clear communication with the mainland is available from telephones, usually in every stateroom. Telex and facsimile machines transmit contracts and newspapers. "We can consummate a deal anywhere," says Guy Tamboni, a New England real estate developer who enjoys long family cruises on his 108-ft. *Alma.* (The oceans are area coded: Atlantic 871, Pacific 872. Cost to call a yacht: $10 a minute.)

On many new ultracrafts, jet-powered engines have replaced outmoded rudders and propellers, allowing for vibration-free lightweight fiber glass or aluminum hulls and easy entry into shallow-water ports. According to London-based Designer Jon Bannenberg, who has six yachts in the works for Americans, high tech has just about revolutionized the business. "The perception of yachts was big, slow, rather old-fashioned," says Bannenberg. "Now people see something connected to the life they lead ashore. People who step out of their Porsches and Mercedes feel that they are stepping into today's technology."

Designers who favor aluminum hulls maintain they last indefinitely, hold three times as much fuel as fiber glass-hulled boats and are 15% faster. The American buyer wants a boat that looks "like it's going 20 knots when it's sitting at the dock," explains Denison. Perhaps the most stunning example is the Bannenberg-designed, 110-ft. *Never Say Never,* owned by Gary Blonder, a flamboyant entrepreneur who made his fortune in used auto parts. This rocket ship skims the waves at 34 knots full throttle (about 39 m.p.h.) and was used as a setting on *Miami Vice.*

Interiors have also been updated. Instead of the traditional dark teak, many modern designers prefer the pale look of ash and pastel fabrics to lighten below-deck cabins. They often pad walls with Ultrasuede or leather for sound control. Denison's boatyard allows customers to supervise every detail right up to the track lighting. Bannenberg even designs every spoon, every ashtray.

Naturally, behemoth yachts need outsize berths in which to moor. A big-boat marina is in the final planning stages at Manhattan's Battery Park City. The marina expects to sell 21 berths, costing $1 million each—with a $16,000 annual maintenance fee—to high-living investment honchos who want their own pied-à-mere within takeover distance of Wall Street.

If these luxury vessels are used primarily for business and charter, they could bring in tax deductions nudging $1 million a year. More good news for owners: the boats appreciate in value 10% to 20% each year. "I look on it as a piece of floating real estate," says Shipping Executive Joel Rahn of Springfield, Mass., owner of the *Atlantique*.

To offset maintenance costs further, many owners charter out their boats. Missy Harvey, managing director of Yacht Charters Unlimited in Rowayton, Conn., says, "Nothing does more for the ego than to be aboard the biggest, most beautiful yacht as it pulls into the harbor." Rates run $49,000 a week for *Parts V*, $30,000 for the *Atlantique* (which has been chartered by, among others, Sophia Loren, former Secretary of the Treasury William Simon and FORTUNE 500 executives) and $29,000 for *Never Say Never*. The charter party must also pay for fuel ($50 to $75 an hour), food, dockage and tips for the spiffy crew.

But the crowd with whale-size wallets prefers to buy. And if they hurry, there is a bargain on the market, the 282-ft. *Nabila*, complete with disco and swimming pool. Until recently the pride of financially troubled Arms Dealer Adnan Khashoggi, the yacht is up for sale at a mere $35 million.

By Martha Smilgis.
Reported by Bonnie Angelo/New York

Posh main salon of *Never Say Never* is a mix of bright pastels and cushy leather

QUESTIONS AND ACTIVITIES

Comprehension Questions

1. When was the heyday of American yachting?

2. What is the minimum size of a jumbo yacht? What is the price range for yachts of this size?

3. Who is the typical buyer of the "yuppie special"?

4. Who owns the world's biggest yacht? Who owns the second biggest? What size are these ships?

Discussion Questions

1. It is said that satellite communications have aided the yacht business. Explain this statement.

2. Some view the purchase of a yacht as a good investment. What reasons are given for this belief?

Group Activities

In groups of three or four, imagine that you can afford to have a yacht built to your specifications. What would you include in it? Be as imaginative as possible. After your discussion, describe your group's yacht to the class.

Individual Work

Write an explanation (one and a half pages maximum) of why you believe the water (whether a lake, a river, or an ocean) is so appealing to people.

Article Three

BACKGROUND NOTES

for **"Time Bombs on Legs"**

Preview

Pit bullterriers are becoming known for their vicious attacks on humans. Some claim, however, that the owners, not the dogs, are at fault.

Culture

Sherlock Holmes: a fictional detective created by Arthur Conan Doyle. One of the many Sherlock Holmes books written by Doyle is *The Hound of the Baskervilles.*

Humane Society [ˌhju'men sə'saɪədi]: an organization devoted to the compassionate treatment of animals

Our Gang: the fictional name of a group of children who, with their friend Spanky, starred in a series of 1930s movies. The dog in the series was a pit bullterrier that was playful and lovable.

Scarface: the nickname given to Al Capone, a notorious and feared gangster of the 1930s. The name suggests ugliness and violence.

SPCA: the Society for the Prevention of Cruelty to Animals; the Anti-Cruelty Society. The SPCA is concerned with the welfare of both domesticated animals and animals used for medical research.

Vocabulary

aggressiveness [ə'grɛsəvnəs]: assertiveness; forceful behavior

aura ['orə]: an atmosphere; a distinctive surrounding air

bloodletting: bloodshed; slaughter

boob: a simpleton; one who is stupid (colloquial)

brandish: to exhibit in an aggressive way; to show something in a threatening manner

canine ['kenaɪn]: a member of the animal family that includes dogs, wolves, and foxes

crack: smokable cocaine in crystalline form

disfranchised [ˌdɪs'fræntʃaɪzd]: deprived of one's rights. (A more common word is **disenfranchised**.)

felony ['fɛlə,ni]: a serious crime, which carries severe punishment. (The category of less serious crimes is **misdemeanors**.)

ferocious [fə'roʃəs]: fierce; savage

hot sauce: a spicy sauce used in Mexican, Cajun, and certain other types of cooking.

low man on the totem pole: the least important or influential person. Totem poles are tall pillars with faces carved by some native groups in the northwestern United States.

macho ['mɑtʃo]: male; assertively masculine

maladjusted [ˌmælə'dʒəstəd]: badly adjusted; not in harmony with one's surroundings

malevolent [mə'lɛvələnt]: ill-willed; demonstrating hatred

maul [mɔl]: to mangle; to injure by beating

orgy ['ordʒi]: a period of excessive indulgence

switchblade ['swɪtʃ,bled]: a type of pocketknife with a spring-operated blade. Switchblades are often carried by gang members.

verge [vɚdʒ]: the edge; the threshold

All muscle and steel-trap jaws: a three-year-old pit bull in New York City

"Time Bombs on Legs"

Violence-prone owners are turning pit bulls into killers

Fire burst from its open mouth, its eyes glowed with a smouldering glare, its muzzle and hackles and dewlap were outlined in flickering flame. Never in the delirious dream of a disordered brain could anything more savage, more appalling, more hellish, be conceived than that dark form and savage face.

It is as if the vicious hound of the Baskervilles that burst upon Sherlock Holmes out of the fog has returned to haunt the streets of America. The creature last week attacked a 71-year-old woman in Stone Mountain, Ga., dragging her across her driveway and savaging her so badly that she required 100 stitches. It snapped and tore at an unemployed man as he watched the July 4 fireworks in Rochester; last week he died from his multiple injuries, including a 15-in. wound from calf to thigh. And in Atlanta, Houston and Ramsay, Mich., it has seized small children like rag dolls and mauled them to death in a frenzy of bloodletting.

The new canine terror is the American pit bull, a dog with a squat, muscular body and thick, steel-trap jaws that is descended from the fighting bulldogs of 19th century England. In 2½ years it has been responsible for 16 deaths

across the country, six of them in the past year, leading many municipalities to pass laws to restrict ownership. It is estimated that there are now 500,000 unregistered, often poorly bred pit bullterriers in the U.S. So fearsome is the dog's reputation that it has become imbued with much the same malevolent aura as the beast in Arthur Conan Doyle's story. That is exactly the effect sought by some owners, among them dog-fighting enthusiasts, members of street gangs and drug pushers, many of whom use revolting and painful techniques to bring the animals to the verge of bloodlust.

Officials of animal-protection societies tell of pit bulls being given live kittens or small dogs, such as poodles, to tear apart. Often they are fed gunpowder or hot sauce in the mistaken belief that this will increase the animals' pain threshold. Jean Sullivan, director of the Memphis-based Humane Society, charges that some owners have tried to increase their dogs' natural aggressiveness by keeping them tied up with collars of baling wire or running them on treadmills until they are exhausted. The pit bull's jaws—which can exert as much force as 1,800 lbs. per sq. in.—are strengthened by swinging the dog on a rope, its teeth clamped

to a tire. This, she says, makes the animal a "lethal weapon. They hang on until their prey is dead." Such techniques, says Franklin Loew, dean of the Tufts University veterinary school, turn the dogs into "time bombs on legs." Many are used for high-stakes dog fighting, which has a sizable nationwide following, even though it is a felony in 36 states.

Ferocious pit bulls can be seen any day with their drug-dealer owners on the corner of Ninth and Butler streets in North Philadelphia. The dogs, with names like Murder, Hitler and Scarface, wear metal-studded collars concealing crack and cocaine and the day's proceeds. They are equally visible on Chicago's West and South sides, where teenage boys have taken to brandishing their fierce pit bulls just as they would a switchblade or a gun. "It's a macho thing, like carrying a weapon," says Jane Alvaro of the Anti-Cruelty Society.

Why are so many Americans indulging in this orgy of pain and violence? "The dogs are almost like an extension of the owners' egos," says Orville Walls, a Philadelphia veterinarian. "The owners think, 'I may be low man on the economic totem pole, but I have the meanest, toughest dog on the street.'" Owning a pit

Fads & Fashions

"Steady temperament and intense loyalty"

Austin Kear, 4, of Yonkers, N.Y., and pet

bull, says Robert Armstrong, Houston's chief animal controller, ''is a warning to others to stay off the sidewalk.'' Randall Lockwood of the Humane Society notes that the animals have become increasingly popular as dog fighting has moved from rural areas into cities. They appeal ''to the disfranchised and the unemployed. The owners themselves are often violent.'' Tufts' Loew sees the bonding of owner and dog as akin to a ''horror movie,'' with maladjusted owners training their dogs to be an ''extension of themselves.''

As a result of the growing fear of these killer dogs, responsible owners have been put on the defensive. The name pit bull loosely applies to a crossbred strain of the American Staffordshire terrier and the American pit bullterrier as well as to other varieties. The most ferocious dogs, says Pat Owens, director of the Women's S.P.C.A. of Pennsylvania, are crossbred with German shepherds or Doberman pinschers. Richard Laue of the Northern California Pit Bullterrier Association accuses these ''backyard breeders'' of producing unpredictable ''garbage dogs.''

Despite the dogs' bloody reputation, owners such as Laue insist that purebred pit bulls have a ''steady temperament and intense loyalty.'' Indeed, breeders believe that in time the animal will regain its gentler image of the 1930s, when a pit bull played Pete in the Our Gang films. Only 30 years ago, notes Ed Almeida, a dog trainer in El Monte, Calif., the Doberman was the most vicious of dogs. Now, he says, after years of careful breeding, Dobermans are ''big boobs'' compared with the pit bulls.

By David Brand.
Reported by Scott Brown/Los Angeles and D. Blake Hallanan/New York

QUESTIONS AND ACTIVITIES

Comprehension Questions

1. The name *pit bull* is used for a number of varieties of dogs. What is the most prevalent strain? What are the most ferocious mixes? What dogs are they descended from?

2. What are some owners doing to make their dogs more vicious?

3. What have some towns done to counteract this canine menace?

Discussion Questions

1. Do you have or have you ever had a pet? If so, what kind? If not, would you like to? What kind?

2. What do you think is the main problem with pit bulls—the dogs themselves, the owners, or both? Explain your answer.

Group Activities

In groups of six to eight, brainstorm possible solutions to the problem of pit bulls. In your discussion, you may wish to consider the following:
   a. whether the breed should be outlawed
   b. whether the owners of dogs that attack humans should be punished

Individual Work

Take a poll of 10 people to learn the following:
   a. Do you have a pet?
   b. If so, what kind? Why do you enjoy it?
   c. If not, would you like to have one? If so, what kind? If not, why not?

Summarize the findings of your poll in a written report (one page maximum). Be sure to indicate any trends you may have found. Be prepared to report your findings orally to the class, as well.

Article Four

BACKGROUND NOTES

for **Here Come "Malls Without Walls"**

Preview

Already successful in other countries, hypermarkets have begun to appear in the United States. These huge stores offer an amazing variety of goods.

Culture

discount store: a store that offers a wide variety of goods at reduced prices. Smaller, family-owned shops often cannot compete with large discount stores.

hot line: a telephone that provides instant access to someone with important information

supermarket: a store that sells a wide variety of food items. Supermarkets have replaced most shops, such as butcher shops and bakeries, which sold only one kind of food.

Vocabulary

archrival ['ɑrtʃ'rɑɪvəl]: one's main competition; the primary rival

concept ['kɑn,sɛpt]: a thought; a notion; an idea

cranky: grouchy; bad-tempered

disaffection: estrangement; alienation of affection

disorienting: confusing

emporium [,ɛm'pɑriəm]: a commercial center; a store that carries a variety of goods (a pretentious word, often used humorously)

get (someone) rolling: to (make someone) become active; to (make someone) get enthusiastic

haberdasher ['hæbɚ,dæʃɚ]: one who sells men's clothing and supplies

launch: to initiate; to begin

lure: an attraction; an enticement

marathon: an endurance contest; something that tests one's strength

markup: the difference between the price of an item and its cost to the seller

perpetuate [pɚ'pɛtʃu,et]: to cause to continue; to cause to last

The floor space and the discounts are breathtakingly huge at the new Hypermart in Topeka

Here Come "Malls Without Walls"

Hypermarkets sell everything from antifreeze to zoom lenses

Are these prices for real? Ground beef, 87¢ per lb. Oranges, eight for $1. Car batteries, $25. Videocassette recorders, $180. Yes, but that is just the beginning of the surprises. Here comes a clerk—*whooosh!*—on roller skates. And just look at these 20-ft. mountains of merchandise, from catsup to cameras, mustard to mufflers. Disoriented yet? This is the green zone, where groceries are sold. For everything from mouthwash to antifreeze, go to the blue zone. Tired? Here, sit down on one of the convenient wooden benches and sip some free cider or coffee with other weary shoppers.

What is this place? Welcome to Hypermart USA, where the floor space (222,000 sq. ft.) and the discounts are both breathtakingly huge. The suburban Dallas emporium belongs to a booming category of retail store called the hypermarket. "I've never seen so much under one roof," says Martha Mason, a homemaker visiting Hypermart USA. "I could spend days in here." Sam Walton certainly hopes so. The founder and chairman of booming Wal-Mart discount stores opened his first Hypermart USA last December as a joint venture with the Cullum retail chain. Last week he opened a

second in Topeka. "It's a test," says Walton, whose 1,114 Wal-Marts are generally a third the size of the Hypermarts. But as he tells his troops, "I'm more excited about this than anything in the history of our company. This new store could revolutionize the way America shops."

A lot of competitors agree. Suddenly hypermarkets, which can cover five football fields, are springing up across the U.S. in places as diverse as New Orleans and Kalispell, Mont. The oversize stores provide the ultimate in one-stop shopping: customers can get a haircut, buy a refrigerator and stock up on paper towels in one trip. Most "malls without walls," as Walton calls them, draw crowds with an old-fashioned lure: everyday discounts. Prices are reduced as much as 40% below the full retail level. Hypermarkets make money even at such thin profit margins because they sell such an enormous volume of goods. Hypermarket sales average at least $1 million a week, compared with $200,000 for a conventional-size discount store.

While the idea of a store so big seems quintessentially American, the idea for hypermarkets comes from France. A small-town

haberdasher and a grocer, taking advantage of their country's lack of American-style supermarkets, teamed up in 1960 to start the first hypermarket at an intersection just outside Annecy, in the foothills of the Alps. They named their store Carrefour, the French word for crossroads, and it was an instant success. Their prices were so low that shoppers expected them to go out of business, a rumor they gleefully perpetuated by keeping their front windows coated with whitewash. Carrefour launched dozens of outlets, as did copycats. Today France has more than 600 hypermarkets that together account for some 14% of the country's retail trade. Carrefour, which now operates hypermarkets in Spain, Brazil and Argentina, plans to open its first U.S. outlet this week, in suburban Philadelphia. Among the store's innovations: a rubbery floor surface to ease the punishment on shoppers' feet.

While hypermarkets have spread across Canada, which has 22 such stores, they have only now become a hot concept in the U.S. One reason is that America has so many competing discount stores and supermarkets that the Carrefour concept had trouble gaining acceptance. Analysts estimate that Bigg's, a Cincinnati hypermarket opened by Euromarché, a French firm, has lost at least $9 million since it was opened three years ago. But the large U.S. chains believe they can make the idea work by selling namebrand goods at paper-thin markups. K mart announced last September that it will form a joint venture with Bruno's, an Alabama-based grocery-store group, to open a national hypermarket chain. Archrival Wal-Mart, meanwhile, hopes to open 50 Hypermart USA stores during the next eight years.

Even successful hypermarket operators will encounter limits to expansion. The sheer size of the megamarkets will restrict growth, since a city of 500,000 can support only about two stores. Also, hypermarkets may face disaffection from customers who expect assorted brands of any one product; thus well-stocked hardware stores or grocers are unlikely to be run out of business by the invading hypermart. Cases in point: Hypermart USA's sporting-goods department offers fishing poles but no lures or other tackle. The paint department sells only one color: white.

The hypermarkets are doing their best to help shoppers feel comfortable in what is sometimes a disorienting space. Dallas' Hypermart USA installed hot lines in its aisles so shoppers can get information and directions. Its bakery can churn out 20,000 tortillas a day. To make sure cranky toddlers do not prompt their parents to hurry too much, Hypermart offers a Ball Room, where parents can deposit their children to be supervised. But anyone who wants to shop in a 200,000-sq.-ft. store should remember to don jogging shoes. Says Melba Lincoln, a Dallas homemaker: "Shopping here is like running a marathon."

By Barbara Rudolph.
Reported by Mary Cronin/New York and Richard Woodbury/Houston

QUESTIONS AND ACTIVITIES

Comprehension Questions

1. What is a hypermarket? How much larger than a discount store is a hypermarket? What is the difference in volume of sales between the two types of stores?

2. Where did the concept of hypermarkets begin? What countries already have them?

3. Why were hypermarkets slow in coming to the United States?

Discussion Questions

1. What are the advantages of a hypermarket for the consumer?

2. What are the disadvantages for the consumer?

3. Are there discount stores in your hometown? If so, do you shop at them? Why or why not? If not, would you like one to be built? Why or why not?

Group Activities

In groups of four or five, compile a list of ideal features that you'd like a store to have. You may wish to consider the following in your discussion:
   a. range of selection of merchandise
   b. prices
   c. hours and days of service
   d. other amenities
Present your list of features to the class.

Individual Work

Keep a diary for a day of the stores that you go into and what you do or purchase in each one. Do you tend to do all your shopping in a few stores, or do you make many different stops? Write a brief summary (one page maximum) of your activities.

Article Five

BACKGROUND NOTES

for **In Virginia: Homes with Gusto**

Preview

The Jersey Devil is a unique architectural group. Not satisfied with merely designing unusual homes, they build them as well.

Culture

Airstream: the brand name of a kind of travel trailer. Airstreams are recognizable by their sleek appearance and silver color.

cookie cutter [ˈkʊki, kədɚ]: a metal or plastic form used when cutting cookies out of dough.

Erector set [əˈrɛktɚ sɛt]: a popular children's toy consisting of many pieces that can be used to construct miniature houses, bridges, and the like

Grateful Dead: a contemporary rock music group. The group had a large following in its heyday, and is still popular today.

hero or hoagie [ˈhogi]: a sandwich made with an eight-inch to 12-inch piece of Italian bread, several kinds of meats and cheeses, lettuce, tomatoes, mustard, and mayonnaise. There are at least five regional names for the sandwich and none is recognized nationwide. Other names are *submarine, grinder,* and *poor boy.*

Don Quixote [ˌkiˈ(j)odi]: a fictional character in the book *Don Quixote de la Mancha* written by Miguel de Cervantes. Don Quixote was an idealist and a romantic.

Frank Lloyd Wright: an early 20th century American architect. Wright's homes are noted for their uncluttered geometric lines—a direct contrast to the Victorian architecture popular at the time.

Vocabulary

cholesterol [kəˈlɛstəˌrɔl]: a waxy substance present in the tissue of humans and other animals. High cholesterol levels in the blood are thought to contribute to heart disease.

exhibitionism: behavior designed to attract attention

get (one's) juices flowing: to make one feel creative or enthusiastic

gusto: enthusiasm; great enjoyment

improvisation [ˌɪmprɑvəˈzeʃən]: something done in an offhand manner; something done in an unplanned way

irreverence: a lack of respect

itinerant [ˌaɪˈtɪnɚənt]: traveling from place to place

jukebox [ˈʤukˌbɑks]: a cabinet that contains a record player. Jukeboxes are coin-operated.

makeshift: temporary; expedient

pioneer [ˌpaɪəˈnɪr]: characteristic of the early settlers in the American West. Pioneers were known for their hardiness.

renegade [ˈrɛnəged]: traitorous; acting against the establishment

rousing [ˈraʊzɪŋ]: exciting; stirring

tackiness: shabbiness; something characterized by poor taste (colloquial)

trademark: a word or name that legally belongs to the maker or seller of a product. Egg McMuffin℠, for example, is a trademark of McDonald's.

transvestite [ˌtrænsˈvɛstaɪt]: one who adopts the dress and behavior of the opposite sex

The Devil's "Helmet House"

In Virginia: Homes with Gusto

Y ou don't see many trailers like Steve
Badanes' 1956 silver Airstream anymore. Round and compact, it is one of those
sleek design achievements of the 1950s that
can make people nostalgic for tackiness.
Badanes even travels with a plastic pink
flamingo that he props outside the door
wherever he parks. Most recently, the trailer—
and flamingo—was parked in a wooded lot of
a wealthy northern Virginia suburb while serving as home for Badanes, his itinerant opera-
singing girlfriend Donna Walter, and their dog
Floyd Bite (after Frank Lloyd Wright). But if a
tacky trailer in an expensive Colonial suburb
seems a little out of place to you, consider what
Badanes and his three colleagues, architect-
builders who call themselves the Jersey Devil,
were constructing on the same lot: a multimillion-dollar house that's shaped like an over-
grown hero sandwich.

"We didn't set out to make it look like a
hoagie," says Badanes, appearing only slightly guilty about it all. "It just sort of turned out
that way. But I have to admit it's kind of ironic.
The guy's a heart surgeon, and we go and build
him a house that looks like a cholesterol
lunch."

Badanes clearly enjoys the joke. In fact,
such irreverence is his group's trademark.
Born at Princeton University during the
counterculture days of the 1960s, the Jersey
Devil is a traveling band of renegade architects
who rejected standard careers to design the
really far out and then, in an even more radical
break with modern architectural practice, get
out the saws, hammers and nails and build
these unusual structures themselves.

Since their first project, a child's play structure built to resemble an enormous cockroach,

they've painstakingly assembled twelve
houses, from San Francisco to New
Hampshire, parking tents, trailers or makeshift
cardboard homes on site so they could live
there as they worked, encouraging clients to
pick up hammers on weekends, and throwing
parties in partly built houses to celebrate the
completion of a foundation or their topping off
of a roof. No, the Jersey Devil, which takes its
name from a mythical creature said to threaten
people in New Jersey's Pine Barrens, is no ordinary architectural firm. But don't get them
wrong. Badanes, Jim Adamson, Greg Torchio
and John Ringel are serious about what they
do, and say it is in the best tradition of the
American pioneer spirit.

"When all of us went to architecture
school, we thought being an architect had
something to do with building," says Badanes,
43, sitting in the Jersey Devil office trailer

parked beside his Airstream. "But most architects these days sit in their offices, design
their places down to the last details and then
hand the plans over to be built by someone else.
Now I ask you, which approach do you think
would make for better results? Do you sit in
your office and look up stock answers in your
books? Or do you move to the guy's property,
immerse yourself in that piece of land, take
your time, and do a one-off piece of art? In the
early days, that's how buildings were made.
Where did we go wrong?"

The atmosphere inside the office trailer is a
bit like that inside a college dorm room. On one
wall is an autographed picture of the transvestite movie star Devine; on another, a 1950s
vintage ad for the Mysto Erector Set ("Hello
boys, what are you building?" says a
stereotypical father to his stereotypical sons.
"Come, Dad, come look!"). Everywhere
there are pictures of some of the group's other
projects: the "Football House," built a quarter
of a mile from California's San Andreas Fault
and shaped like a football, they say, so that if
a quake comes, the house will simply roll down
the hill end over end. And the "Helmet
House," built for a New Hampshire man
whom Badanes describes as having a "kind of
Don Quixote personality." That house won the
1978 *Enquirer* Weird Home award.

"As we understand it, the change happened
sometime around the end of the last century,"
says Ringel, a dark-bearded character who
looks a trifle like the Grateful Dead's Jerry Gar-
cia. "Up until then, architects built their own
stuff, and they traveled around just like we do.
But with the Industrial Revolution, the demand
grew to build more buildings faster. Most architects gave up building and stuck to design."

"Hell," says Badanes, "the American Institute of Architects decided in 1909 to ban architects from building. Now that tells you
where their heads were at. But we found an
easy way around that one: we just never applied
for a license."

"The fact is," says Adamson, "that
whatever the A.I.A. or the Industrial Revolution did, it stifled the creativity of American
home design. Just look at the standard
American suburb. All the houses look like they

Arthitect Steve Badanes and the Jersey Devil

were cut out of a cookie cutter. That may be cost efficient, but it has no relation to the way we live today.''

''What's worse,'' says Badanes, as he props his feet on a drafting table, ''is that as Americans we've shown no interest in creating and supporting an architecture of our own. Sure, that Colonial stuff was great, but it was all built off European ideas. Now if I had a dollar for every architecture lecture where they show pictures of Rome, I'd be a rich man. And then they show you a crappy picture of an American cityscape with the message, of course, being 'Why can't we be more like Europe?' But I think we should ask, 'Why can't we be more like America?' ''

Jersey Devil clients are a special breed. For one, they have to accept the notion that their dream house will be built with more than a little improvisation. ''Hell, sometimes we don't even use any plans,'' says Ringel. Noting that practice, one client took out life insurance on Badanes, aware that most of the design for the house was in the architect's head. Then, too, hiring the Jersey Devil takes a bit of exhibitionism. ''To our clients, a house is more

than just another box on a street,'' says Torchio. ''It is a means of self-expression.''

Today the group is putting the finishing touches on the Hoagie, built for a family out to express itself in a big way. Besides the twelve-room, 10,000-sq.-ft. house, the complex includes a separate guesthouse and separate caretaker's house (both shaped like smaller hoagies), maid's quarters and a swimming pool. There's even a gift-wrapping room. ''Hey, don't look at me,'' says Badanes. ''The guy's got a lot of kids and a lot of birthday parties.'' But right now, the dilemma is over what car grille to order for the fireplace in the living room. ''I'm looking for a '60s Chrysler,'' says Badanes, ''but I could live with a '51 Buick if I could hinge all that stuff.'' He points to a picture of the Buick's metalwork front. ''Remember,'' sayd Adamson, ''the guy wants headlights that work!''

The car-grille fireplace isn't the house's only unusual feature: the ''media room'' has been modeled after an old Wurlitzer jukebox, and until the client vetoed it, the pool was planned to resemble an anatomical heart. ''I guess it was just too close to the real thing,''

sayd Badanes. ''If you look at hearts all day, maybe the last thing you want to do is come home and go swimming in one.''

With the Hoagie in order, the Jersey Devil is already dreaming of new challenges. Adamson is eager to build a lobster farm in South Carolina, and a college in Seattle wants them to build a floating guesthouse in Puget Sound. But it is Cleveland's proposed new Rock and Roll Hall of Fame that really gets the Jersey Devil's juices flowing. ''If I have a dream commission, it is to design the Rock and Roll Hall of Fame,'' says Badanes, mocking the manner of a politician at a press conference. His colleagues give him a rousing round of applause. ''I mean, could you imagine a better job? We could do the walls in black pressed vinyl. And there's be a lot of black-light posters around everywhere. Of course, we'd have to listen to records for months before tackling it. Research, gentlemen, research. And then, who knows? Maybe we'd even make the thing in the shape of a pair of blue jeans.''

By Todd Brewster

QUESTIONS AND ACTIVITIES

Comprehension Questions
1. When did the Jersey Devil begin to work together?
2. What makes this group of architects unique?
3. When did American architects stop constructing the buildings they designed? How did the Jersey Devil avoid the problem that architects are not supposed to build what they design?

Discussion Questions
1. What style of architecture is characteristic of homes in your town? Describe a typical home to the class.
2. Would you like to live in one of the homes described in the article? Why or why not?

Group Activities
In groups of three or four, collectively ''design'' an ideal home. Be as imaginative as possible. In your discussion, you may wish to consider the following:
   a. size
   b. number of rooms
   c. location
   d. amenities
Be prepared to describe your group's dream home to the class.

Individual Work
Select a picture from a book, magazine, or newspaper (or use a photograph you have taken) of a building you find unusual or interesting. Write a brief description of the building (one page maximum) and indicate why you find it unusual or interesting. Don't forget to include the picture with your written statement.

Article Six

BACKGROUND NOTES

for **The Whole World Goes Pandas**

Preview

Pandas are one of the most popular species of animals in the world. Their numbers, however, are dwindling rapidly.

Culture

get-well card: a greeting card sent to someone who is ill. The card wishes the person a speedy recovery.

Lower 48: the 48 states in the continental United States. Alaska and Hawaii are the other two, for a total of 50 states.

valentine: a greeting card sent to a friend or sweetheart as a token of affection to celebrate Valentine's Day. Valentine's Day falls on Februray 14.

Vocabulary

ample: plentiful; abundant

bleak: not likely to end positively; lacking hope

blessed event ['blɛsəd,i'vɛnt]: a birth (a cliché, often used humorously)·

chaos ['ke,as]: a state of great confusion

comely ['kəmli]: attractive; handsome

conjunction: connection, association

cuddly: inviting hugging or caressing

demise [də'maɪz]: death; a ceasing of activity

denizen ['dɛnəzən]: an inhabitant; one who lives in or frequents a place

extant ['ɛkstənt]: currently existing; still in existence

famine ['fæmən]: extreme scarcity of food

glimpse: a brief view; a short look

incurable [,ɪn'kjɚ·əbəl]: having no cure; having no solution

innate: inborn; native; inherent

nibble: to chew in small bites; to bite gently

posterior: the buttocks; the part of the body used for sitting (a polite euphemism)

reverence ['rɛvrəns]: respect; honor

stir: a state of excitement or activity

waddle ['wadəl]: to walk awkwardly and clumsily; to walk swaying from side to side

Yong Yong testing the furniture in her expensive New York digs

The Whole World Goes Pandas

Two Chinese ambassadors receive cheers in the Bronx

He had good news for New Yorkers, Mayor Edward Koch said last week: taxes were being reduced, and the police department was being enlarged. "But the single thing people will care about," he added, "is that the pandas have come to town." How right he was. Last Thursday morning, as a gong was sounded and a comely female named Yong Yong waddled into her enclosure at the Bronx Zoo, New York City was gripped with that well-known but incurable fever: pandamania.

WELCOME TO NEW YORK, PANDAS, said a handmade sign held up by one of several dozen waiting schoolchildren, HELLO, LING LING AND YONG YONG, said another. And even more to the point: NEW YORK IS THE PANDAS! Before Ling Ling (Ringing Bell), the male half of the team, and Yong Yong (Forever and Ever) go home at the end of October—they are on loan from the Peking Zoo for only six months—an estimated 2 million people (2,000 an hour) will have seen and no doubt fallen in love with them. "There's something special about pandas," says Koch. "They bring people back to their childhood."

Even the meanest people, those who kick dogs, throw bottles at cats and step on robins' eggs, get teary-eyed and putty-legged when they see a panda rolling around on its ample posterior, twisting its puffy body into a seemingly impossible position, or eating an apple—nothing more exotic than an apple!—with its handlike paw. "I can't think of any animal that

compares," says William Conway, director of the New York Zoological Society. "People love penguins, but the interest in pandas is extraordinary. There appears to be an innate response of, 'Oh, isn't it cute?' "

At the seven zoos outside China in which they have taken up permanent residence, pandas are always the top act. If the adults cause a stir, their babies cause chaos. When Tokyo's Ueno Zoo had a blessed event last year, 270,000 people suggested names for the little cub. Tong Tong (Child) was the eventual choice, and 13,000 stood in line for the first glimpse of that particular child. Another 200,000 a day called the "Dial-a-Panda" hot line to hear him squealing.

In Washington, the only U.S. city that has pandas on permanent exhibit, schoolchildren send them yearly valentines. When the female (also named Ling Ling) fell ill in 1982, she received thousands of get-well cards; some admirers tearfully called for the latest word on her condition. China lent a pair to the Los Angeles Zoo in conjunction with the 1984 Olympics; attendance more than doubled, and pandamaniacs endured three-hour waits. San Francisco's zoo, where the couple went next, saw attendance jump 50%.

But Ling Ling, Yong Yong and the other actors in what might be called China's Traveling Panda Act—two more will be lent to the Netherlands' Beekse Bergen Park this month—are meant to do more than entertain.

Pandas also carry a message: they are an endangered species with a bleak future. Only a few, 700 or so, still roam the mountains of central China, and there are not enough in zoos to ensure their survival.

Like most other endangered species, the pandas are a victim of what Conway terms the "inexorable increase in human beings." Chinese farmers have chopped down many of the bamboo stands that once fed them, and the pandas have been forced to ever higher ground and smaller spaces. But bamboo is not very nutritious (90% is water), and pandas must eat as much as 40 lbs. a day to maintain their cuddly look. Actually, they love meat, but nature has made them too slow to catch anything worth nibbling on. So they are left with bamboo, which moves only with the wind.

The hapless animals are also bedeviled by what many other species—rabbits, for instance—would consider an unhappy sex life. Solitary by nature, they rarely enjoy one another's company. During their stay in New York, for instance, Ling Ling, who at $1\frac{1}{2}$ is too young for mating anyway, will never be allowed out at the same time as the six-year-old, heavier (187 lbs., vs. 119 lbs.) and presumably more aggressive Yong Yong.

One answer to the pandas' plight is obvious: the Chinese should give them more space and more bamboo. In recent years the Chinese, with considerable financial help from panda lovers worldwide, have tried to do that. They have set aside twelve reserves that have different varieties of bamboo; if one kind dies out, the pandas will not starve to death, as at least 138 did during a major bamboo famine in the mid-'70s. Indeed, Conway, whose zoo has taken a lead in preserving endangered species, gives the Chinese high marks. "They're spending more effort on pandas than the U.S. is on grizzly bears, which are even rarer in the Lower 48 states," he says. "They're an example to us."

But high marks may not be good enough. Unless reserves are made larger, he says, and connected so that their denizens can move from one to another, "the demise of the panda is predictable." He adds, "There are probably fewer pandas extant than there are Rembrandts. We ought to give them at least as much reverence as we give the works of man." The crowds cheering them on at the Bronx Zoo last week seemed to be doing just that.

By Gerald Clarke

Schoolchildren greeting the furry visitors

QUESTIONS AND ACTIVITIES

Comprehension Questions

1. What is the native habitat of pandas? What is their primary food?
2. What has caused the number of pandas to diminish?
3. What have the Chinese done to aid the pandas?
4. In how many zoos outside of China do pandas live permanently?

Discussion Questions

1. Why do you think people are so fond of pandas? Have you ever seen any in real life? If so, where? Did you find them enjoyable to watch? If not, would you like to see one?
2. What efforts, if any, do you think should be made to save the panda population?

Group Activities

In groups of five or six, discuss the following statements:
   a. It is the responsibility of the country where the animals are indigenous to save endangered species.
   b. It is the responsibility of the world community to work together to save endangered species.
   c. Man should not intervene at all to save endangered species. Nature should be allowed to take its course.

Try to reach consensus in your group about these issues. Present your group's conclusions to the class.

Individual Work

Interview 10 people. Ask what their two favorite zoo animals are. Then ask them to identify two endangered species. Did anyone mention pandas for either category? Is there any consistency among the answers? Summarize your findings in a written report (one page maximum). Be prepared to report orally to the class, as well.

Index of Vocabulary and Culture Terms

The following articles have been abridged from the original:

- "The Child-Care Dilemma"
- "The New Whiz Kids"
- "Shrinking Shores"
- "Spiffing Up the Urban Heritage"

The following articles contain minor editorial changes:

- "Dreaming the Impossible at M.I.T."
- "High Life Afloat: Superduper Yachts"
- "Shrinking Shores"
- "Trapped Behind the Wheel"
- "Zapping Back at Children's TV"

Photographs, Illustrations, and Maps
Cover Illustration by Richard Hess

Carl Iwasaki/*Time Magazine*, iii (top), 3; Ted Thai/*Time Magazine*, iii (upper middle), 39, 41; Used with permission of Holton–Photo Researchers, iii (lower middle), 73; Used with permission of M.I.T. Media Laboratory, iii (bottom), 87 (top), 88; Matthew Naythons/*Time Magazine*, iv (top), 112; Antonio Suarez/*Time Magazine*, iv (bottom), 121, 162, 163; Leo Mason/*Time Magazine*, iv (middle), 125; Steve Liss/*Time Magazine*, 7, 35, 49, 70, 81, 87 (bottom); Used with permission of Adam Bartos, 9; Alan Levenson/*Time Magazine*, 13; Frank Micelotta/*Time Magazine*, 17, 96, 150, 151; Used with permission of Gerry Grapp, 18; Bill Foley/*Time Magazine*, 22; Copyright 1987 Time Inc. All rights reserved.

Reprinted by permission from *TIME*, 23, 24, 29 (map), 68 (map); Used with permission of Richards—Picture Group, 28; Used with permission of Horan—Picture Group, 29; Used with permission of Peter Sis, 31; Drawing by W. Miller; © 1986 *The New Yorker Magazine*, Inc., 45; Slick Lawson/*Time Magazine*, 52; Used with permission of James A. Finley—Wide World Photos, 55; Used with permission of Lustbader—Photo Researchers, 59; David Falconer/*Time Magazine*, 62; David Cross/*Time Magazine*, 65; Kenneth Parker/*Time Magazine*, 68; David Muench/*Time Magazine*, 76; Steve Northup/*Time Magazine*, 84; Used with permission of

Matt—Gamma/Liaison, 90; Karl Schumacher/*Time Magazine*, 93; Used with permission of Popper—Picture Group, 99; Used with permission of Rob Brown, 103; Illustration by Sandra D. Burton, 106; Used with permission of Ian Ross, 109; Used with permission of Hemsey—Gamma/Liaison, 115, 153, 154; Used with permission of Arnold Roth, 118; *Time Magazine*, 128; William Hart/*Time Magazine*, 131; © 1987 Jay Anderson, 134, 135; Used with permission of Ken Regan—Camera 5, 137; Photo used by permission, Estate of Elvis Presley, 140; Team Russell, 143; Used with permission of Peter de Seve, 147; Eli Reichman/*Time Magazine*, 156; Bill Ballenberg/*Time Magazine*, 159.